KU-113-601

THE ART OF READING

ESSAYS IN MEMORY OF
DOROTHY GABE COLEMAN

edited by

Philip Ford and Gillian Jondorf

CAMBRIDGE FRENCH COLLOQUIA
CAMBRIDGE · 1998

Copyright © Cambridge French Colloquia

First published 1998

Cambridge French Colloquia
Clare College
Cambridge CB2 1TL

*All rights reserved. No part of this publication may be
reproduced, stored in a retrieval system, or transmitted, in any
form or by any means, electronic, mechanical, photocopying,
recording, or otherwise, without prior permission.*

Printed and bound in Foxton, Cambs., by The Burlington Press

ISBN 0 9511645 5 4

PQ36.C65
ART

QMW Library

23 1165223 9

THE ART OF READING

DATE DUE FOR RETURN

NEW ACCESSION

CANCELLED

Contents

CONTENTS

Illustrations

Dorothy Gabe Coleman
(26 March 1935 –16 September 1992)

Foreword

The format chosen for the essays in this memorial volume in honour of Dorothy Gabe Coleman, a short text followed by a close reading, is intended to highlight that aspect of her own literary approach which pupils and colleagues found particularly stimulating. Dorothy was a great respecter of texts, and brought to them enormous sensitivity and enthusiasm, as well as a wide-ranging and profound erudition based on her knowledge of Latin and Italian as well as French literature. Her engagement with French literature was always passionate, and by no means limited to the sixteenth century where her international reputation was made. Thus, when in 1981 she was appointed to a Readership, she chose to hold it under the title Reader in French Literature. This commitment to reading could often make her intolerant of critical approaches which she felt ignored the text, leading her to write in her introduction to the first volume in the Cambridge French Colloquia series, *Ronsard in Cambridge*: 'What is particularly impressive about the papers is...the absence of theoretical and abstract propositions: the guests were not avid disciples of psycho-analysers, ideologers, metalinguists, semiologists, intertextualisers, or graphologists. They were concerned with Ronsard.' Ironically, Dorothy herself was an intertextualiser by instinct, writing in 1979 in *The Gallo-Roman Muse*: 'Images, allusions, parallels from Ancient literature or mythology play their part in awakening the *right* body of associations needed to understand the piece of communication', and putting this notion into practice in her own textual analyses, nowhere more so than in her highly perceptive readings of Montaigne.

The essays in *The Art of Reading*, written by pupils and colleagues, all offer the kind of approach of which Dorothy would have approved. Moreover, their range, from medieval Occitan to twentieth-century fiction, is also something which she would have appreciated. The reader of this volume will find original research on major writers of French literature as well as a series of models for critical readings which it is hoped will prove to be stimulating and enjoyable. Many of the texts chosen for commentary are ones that Dorothy worked or lectured on herself, and virtually all are marked by that poetic use of language, whether in poetry, prose poem, or narrative fiction, to which she herself was so sensitive.

Dorothy's own commitment to literature began at Ystalyfera Grammar School in Swansea, where she was introduced by a Leavisite school-master to the poetry of John Donne, and found in him some of the qualities of intellect and feeling she was later to expound so vigorously in the poetry of Maurice Scève. Going up to Girton College, Cambridge, in 1953 as a Scholar, she read French, Latin, and Italian, and after obtaining a starred First she began a doctoral study on Scève. Interest in Scève as an emblem poet led her to the riches of the Stirling Maxwell collection at the University of Glasgow, where in 1958 she took up her first teaching job under Alan Boase, who had done much to put Scève and other French 'metaphysical' poets on the academic map. In 1962 she and her classicist husband Bob Coleman returned from Scotland to university posts in Cambridge, where Dorothy became a Fellow of New Hall.

Dorothy was interested in prose as well as poetry, and her first published full-length study was on Rabelais (*Rabelais: A Critical Study in Prose Fiction*); Montaigne held perhaps the highest place of all in her esteem (*Montaigne's 'Essais'*, 1987) and she chose to have a passage of Montaigne, along with Donne and Dylan Thomas, read at her funeral. Nor did she ever forgot her early reading of Latin poetry, and this emerged most clearly in her study of du Bellay, *The Chaste Muse*, and in *The Gallo-Roman Muse,* a study of sixteenth-century French poetry and prose in which she argued that French writers and readers of the Renaissance were virtually bilingual in French and Latin.

But it was Scève to whom she returned again and again (with two major books in 1975 and 1981), obliged to do so perhaps more than she would have wished because her reputation as a critic of Scève was so well established that she was constantly asked to contribute papers on him to conferences and colloquia. Indeed, after her death, in 1994, her absence from the collection of papers edited by Jerry C. Nash, *A Scève Celebration: 'Délie' 1544-1994* (Saratoga, Anma Libri), was movingly lamented, concluding with the words: 'She was at the forefront of Scève studies, and will be greatly missed.'

A stroke fractured Dorothy's life in 1965. She felt that her use of language was permanently impeded by the stroke, even when she had recovered from the aphasia which it caused. It is true that her writing was inelegant. But her scholarship was sound, her perceptions acute, and her convictions strong, and whether writing in English or French she punched and thumped the language into submission, excelling at communicating the excitements of reading, the sensuous qualities of language, its suggestiveness and allusiveness. In an essay on Rabelais and Queneau which she wrote for a collection in honour of Alison Fairlie who, with Odette de Mourgues, had taught her French literature at Girton, Dorothy mentions Rabelais's and Queneau's 'treatment of words as living things' and gives a definition of poetic prose as exhibiting 'imagination, judgement, sensitivity, word-consciousness and the inter-locking of rhythm and imagery' (in *Words of Power*). These were the qualities she most enjoyed in literature and taught her pupils to enjoy, while also impressing on them by precept and example the need for erudition and exact scholarship.

PJF

GJ

Acknowledgements

The editors of this volume would like to express their gratitude to the three Cambridge institutions with which Dorothy Gabe was associated, Girton College, New Hall, and the Department of French, for their gen-erosity in making the publication of these essays possible.

A List of Major Publications by Dorothy Gabe Coleman

Critical Books

Rabelais: A Critical Study in Prose Fiction (Cambridge: CUP, 1971)

Maurice Scève, Poet of Love: Tradition and Originality (Cambridge: CUP, 1975)

The Gallo-Roman Muse: Aspects of Roman Literary Tradition in Sixteenth-Century France (Cambridge: CUP, 1979)

The Chaste Muse: A Study of Joachim du Bellay's Poetry (Leiden: Brill, 1980)

An Illustrated Love 'Canzoniere': The 'Délie' of Maurice Scève (Geneva: Slatkine, 1981)

Montaigne's 'Essais' (London: Allen & Unwin, 1987)

Edited Books

The Equilibrium of Wit: Essays for Odette de Mourgues, edited by Peter Bayley and Dorothy Gabe Coleman (Lexington, KY: French Forum, 1982)

Words of Power, edited by Dorothy Gabe Coleman and Gillian Jondorf (Glasgow: Glasgow University Printing Department, 1987)

Articles

'Some Notes on Scève and Petrarch', *French Studies*, XIV (1960), 293–303

'Dizain 104 in Maurice Scève's *Délie*', *Modern Language Review*, LVIII (1963), 215–17

'Scève's Choice of the Name *Délie*', *French Studies*, XVIII (1964), 1–16

'Les Emblesmes dans la *Délie* de Maurice Scève', *Studi francesi*, XXII (1964), 1–15

'Images in Scève's *Délie*', *Modern Language Review*, LIX (1964), 375–86

'Propertius, Petrarch and Scève', *Kentucky Romance Quarterly*, XVIII (1971), 77–89

'Rabelais and *The Water-Babies*', *Modern Language Review*, LXVI (1971), 511–21

'"Hearing" Scève: Sound-Play and Verbal Delight in Scève's *Délie*', *French Studies*, XXX (1976), 257–63

'Montaigne's "Sur des vers de Virgile": Taboo Subject, Taboo Author', in R. R. Bolgar, ed., *Classical Influences on European Culture, AD 1500–1700* (Cambridge: Cambridge University Press, 1976), 135–40

'Notes sur l'édition grecque de Diogène Laerce que possédait Montaigne', *Bulletin de la Société des Amis de Montaigne*, 27–8 (1978), 93–5

'Allusiveness in the *Antiquitez de Rome*', *L'Esprit Créateur*, XIX (1979), 3–11

'Catullus in Montaigne's 1580 Version of *De la tristesse* (I. 2), *Bibliothèque d'Humanisme et Renaissance*, XLII (1980), 139–44

'L'Exemplaire de Virgile daté de 1539 que possédait Montaigne', *Bulletin de la Société des Amis de Montaigne*, n° 1–2, janvier–juin 1980, 61–5

'Figurative Language in Maurice Scève's *Délie*', *New Zealand Journal of French Studies*, I (1980), 5–20

'Scève: A Virile Intellect Aerated by Sensibility', in *The Equilibrium of Wit: Essays for Odette de Mourgues*, edited by Peter Bayley and Dorothy Gabe Coleman (Lexington, KY: French Forum, 1982), 17–27

'L'Exemplaire d'Horace daté de 1543 que possédait Montaigne', in *Mélanges d'histoire et de critique littéraires offerts à Henri Weber par ses collègues et ses amis*, edited by Marguerite Soulié (Geneva: Slatkine, 1984), 345–55

'Language in the *Tiers Livre*', in *Rabelais in Glasgow: Proceedings of the Colloquium Held at the University of Glasgow in December 1983*, edited by James A. Coleman and Christine M. Scollen-Jimack (Glasgow, 1984), 39–53

'Montaigne and Longinus', *Bibliothèque d'Humanisme et Renaissance*, XLVII (1985), 405–13

'The Poetic Sensibility of Scève', in *Pre-Pléiade Poetry*, edited by Jerry C. Nash (Lexington, KY: French Forum, 1985), 125–35

'A Commentary on Variants in Two Late Sonnets', in *Ronsard in Cambridge: Proceedings of the Cambridge Ronsard Colloquium, 10–12 April 1985*, edited by Philip Ford and Gillian Jondorf, with an introduction by Dorothy Gabe Coleman (Cambridge: Cambridge French Colloquia, 1986), 139–45

'Du Bellay, Turnèbe and Montaigne', in *Acta Conventus Neo-Latini Sanctandreani: Proceedings of the Fifth International Congress of Neo-Latin Studies, St Andrews, 24 August to 1 September 1982*, edited by I. D. McFarlane (Binghamton, NY: MRTS, 1986), 299–308

'Montaigne: The Living Text', *French Studies*, XL (1986), 393–400

'Some Echoes of Virgil in France', in *Virgil in a Cultural Tradition: Essays to Celebrate the Bimillenium*, edited by Richard A. Cardwell and Janet Hamilton (Nottingham: University of Nottingham, 1986), 86–105

'Lire Scève et entendre Scève', *Cahiers textuel 34/44*, III (1987), 9–14

'Polyphonic Poets: Rabelais and Queneau', in *Words of Power*, edited by Dorothy Gabe Coleman and Giilian Jondorf (Glasgow: Glasgow University Printing Department, 1987), 43–68

'"De l'exercitation" (II, 6): La Fonction des ajouts', *Revue d'Histoire Littéraire de la France*, LXXXVIII (1988), 949–55

'Densité et intelligence créatrice dans les dizains de Scève', in *Il Rinascimento a Lione: Atti del Congresso Internazionale* (Macerata, 6–11 maggio 1985), a cura di Antonio Possenti e Giulia Mastrangelo (Rome: Edizioni dell'Ateneo, 1988), 335–45

'L'Évolution de l'art de Rabelais d'après les variantes du "Tiers Livre"', in *Rabelais en son demi-millénaire: Actes du Colloque international de Tours (24–29 septembre 1984)*, publiés par Jean Céard et Jean-Claude Margolin (Geneva: Droz, 1988), 59–65

'Montaigne's Text: "Neglegentia Diligens"', in *Montaigne in Cambridge: Proceedings of the Cambridge Montaigne Colloquium, 7–9 April 1988*, edited by Philip Ford and Gillian Jondorf (Cambridge: Cambridge French Colloquia, 1989), 103–13

'"La Fortune opulentement grasse" dans un dizain de Maurice Scève', in *Il tema della fortuna nella letteratura francese e italiana del Rinascimento* (Florence: Leo S. Olschki, 1990), 473–80

'Minerve et *L'Olive*', in *Du Bellay: Actes du Colloque International d'Angers du 26 au 29 mai 1989* (Angers: Presses de l'Université d'Angers, 1990), 161–9

'Denys Lambin's Own Copy of Longinus' "Peri hupsous"', *Bibliothèque d'Humanisme et Renaissance*, LIII (1991), 743–8

'L'Histoire et la psychologie: interprétation de l'*Essai* I, 38', in *Montaigne et l'histoire: Actes du colloque international, Bordeaux, 29 septembre–1er octobre 1988*, Textes réunis par Claude-Gilbert Dubois (Paris: Klincksieck, 1991), 267–73

'Maurice Scève: A Person Honoured by Lyon', in *Intellectual Life in Renaissance Lyon: Proceedings of the Cambridge Lyon Colloquium, 14–16 April 1991*, edited by Philip Ford and Gillian Jondorf (Cambridge: Cambridge French Colloquia, 1993), 193–203

Text(s) and Meaning(s) in the *alba* of Giraut de Bornelh

Sarah Kay

I   Reis glorios, verais lums e clartatz,
    Deus poderos, Senher, si a vos platz,
    Al meu companh siatz fizels aiuda;
    Qu'eu no lo vi pos la nochs fo venguda,
5   Et ades sera l'alba!

Glorious king, true light and brightness,
powerful God, Lord, please
be a faithful help to my companion,
for I have not seen him since nightfall
and soon it will be dawn.

II Bel companho, si dormetz o velhatz,
    Non dormatz plus, suau vos ressidatz;
    Qu'en orien vey l'estela creguda
    Q'amena.l iorn, qu'eu l'ai be conoguda,
10   Et ades sera l'alba!

Fair companion, whether you sleep or
wake, sleep no more, gently rise;
for in the East I see the star has grown
which brings the day – I have recognised
it indeed – and soon it will be dawn.

III Bel companho, en chantan vos apel;
    Non dormatz plus, qu'ieu auch chantar
                     l'auzel]
    Que vai queren lo jorn per lo boschatge,
    Et ai paor que.l gilos vos assatge,
15   Et ades sera l'alba!

Fair companion, I appeal to you in song:
sleep no more, for I hear the bird sing

as it goes seeking the daylight in the grove,
and I am afraid the jealous one may assail
you, and soon it will be dawn.

IV Bel companho, issetz al fenestrel
    Et regardatz las estelas del cel;
    Conoisseretz s'ie.us sui fizels messatge.
    Se non o faitz, vostres n'er lo dampnatge,
20   Et ades sera l'alba!

Fair companion, go out to the window
and look at the stars in the sky;
you will know if I am a faithful messenger.
If you do not go, you will suffer for it,
and soon it will be dawn.

V Bel companho, pos me parti de vos
    Eu no.m dormi ni.m moc de genolhos,
    Ans preiei Deu, lo filh Santa Maria,
    Que.us me rendes per leial companhia,
25   Et ades sera l'alba!

Fair companion, since I left you
I have not slept nor risen from my knees,
instead I prayed to God, holy Mary's son,
to give you back to me for loyal
companionship, and soon it will be dawn.

VI Bel companho, la foras als peiros   Fair companion, out there at the block
  Me preiavatz qu'ieu no fos dormilhos,   you begged me not to sleep, but rather
  Enans velhes tota noch tro al dia;   stay awake all night till daybreak;
  Ara no.us platz mos chans ni ma paria,   now neither my song nor my friendship
30   Et ades sera l'alba!   please you, and soon it will be dawn.

This is the text of an *alba* (or dawn song, from *alba*, 'dawn') by the troubadour Giraut de Bornelh (*c.* 1140–1200) as edited by Adolf Kolsen from MS *C*; it is also transmitted in six other manuscripts (*EMüPRSgT*).[1] Probably the oldest extant *alba* in Occitan (there is an earlier exemplar in a combination of Latin and Romance), its identification as an *alba* hinges on the use of a refrain invoking the dawn, which is a characteristic both of the early macaronic text and of the later Occitan examples.[2] The six stanzas make up a monologue spoken — or rather sung — by a friend apparently stationed outdoors to keep watch (ll. 27–8), and who issues increasingly anxious warnings to the *companho* within about the danger he faces at daybreak from the *gilos* — a word which usually denotes a jealous husband. This scenario is commonly taken to be that of the subsequent erotic *alba*, where a watchman calls on lovers to separate at dawn and so avoid discovery by the woman's husband.

Although Giraut is one of the most virtuoso poets of the Occitan tradition, this particular poem is remarkably low key, drawing on the so-called 'popularising register' of lyric composition which is also characteristic of some of the other *albas*.[3] It has a very simple poetic form: the

---

[1]   Adolf Kolsen, *Sämtliche Lieder des Trobadors Giraut de Bornelh*, 2 vols (Halle, 1910–35), I. 342. See also *The Cansos and Sirventes of the Troubadour Giraut de Borneil: A Critical Edition*, edited by Ruth Sharman (Cambridge, 1989), p. 365, but Sharman does not include the variants of MS *Mü*.

[2]   For the text of the tenth-century macaronic *alba* from Fleury-sur-Loire, see Philipp-August Becker, *Zur Romanischen Literaturgeschichte: Ausgewählte Studien und Aufsätze* (Munich, 1967), p. 161. For Occitan *albas*, see Martín de Riquer, *Las albas provenzales: Introducción, textos y versión castellana* (Barcelona, 1944) (19 exemplars), and the section 'Old Provençal and Old French' by Brian Woledge in *Eos: An Inquiry into the Theme of Lovers' Meetings and Partings at Dawn in Poetry*, ed. A. T. Hatto (The Hague, 1965), (nine poems, all but one of which have a refrain featuring the word *alba*). Several of the *albas* are anonymous, making dating difficult. Giraut's is usually taken to be the oldest, but see discussion in Maria Picchio Simonelli, *Lirica moralistica nell'Occitania del XII secolo: Bernart de Venzac* (Modena, 1974), pp. 181 sqq.

[3]   See Pierre Bec, *La Lyrique française au moyen âge (XIIᵉ–XIIIᵉ siècles): Contribution à une typologie des genres poétiques médiévaux*, 2 vols (Paris, 1977–

stanzas, grouped in pairs by the rhyme, are each composed of four deca-syllabic lines arranged in couplets and with cesuras at the fourth syllable, with the six-syllable feminine refrain echoing the second hemistichs (also six-syllable and feminine) of the second couplet of each stanza. This form is only slightly more complex than the most ballad-like of the anonymous *albas*, which has monorhymed decasyllabic tercets and a decasyllabic refrain.[4] The presence of the refrain is another 'popularising' trait, and contributes to the extensive use of repetition in Giraut's poem. The address 'bel companho' occupies the opening hemistich of all the stanzas except the first, forming with the refrain a nexus of repeated material across the stanza boundary. 'Companh' further figures at the cesura (l. 3) and 'companhia' at the rhyme (l. 24), both points of emphasis in the stanza. Forms of *dormir*, all negated, also keep recurring, with the hemistich 'non dormatz plus' following 'bel companho' in stanzas II and III, and being followed in turn by causal structures construed with *que*. The watcher sings like the bird at dawn ('chantan', 'chantar', ll. 11, 12), but his song ('chans', l. 29) is ignored. The strongly formulaic cast to this language makes it appear to stem from a popular, oral tradition, reminiscent of that of other songs — such as *chansons de mal-mariée* and May songs — which invoke a kind of carnivalesque *vox populi* to license the cuckolding of husbands and laugh at their shame.

At the same time, however, Giraut's *alba* owes a widely recognised debt to Latin liturgical texts: notably morning prayers and dawn hymns.[5] The solemn melody, which survives in *R*, is later used as the setting for a lament on the death of St Agnes in a fourteenth-century Occitan play.[6] The imagery of light in the poem's opening line recalls devotional texts such as this Ambrosian hymn:

---

8), I. 33 sqq., for the distinction between the *registre popularisant* and the *registre aristocratisant* (the latter being characteristic of the *grand chant courtois*). A 'register' is an ensemble of textual practices — rhetorical, lexical, metrical, and thematic — that can be analysed formally; it is neutral with respect to authorship or ultimate origin; although the *alba* was seen in the nineteenth century as having folk origins, identifying a text as *popularisant* in Bec's typology carries no implication to this effect.

4 *En un vergier*, no. 1 in both de Riquer and Woledge.

5 On the significance of dawn hymns for the *alba*, see Becker, chapter 5; for the relations between the *alba* and liturgies of morning prayer, see J. M. Scudieri Ruggieri, 'Per le origini dell'alba', in *Cultura Neolatina* III (1943), 191–202, especially pp. 198–9.

6 Woledge, p. 383.

Splendor paternae gloriae,	Oh radiance of fatherly glory
de luce lucem proferens,	bringing forth light from light,
lux lucis et fons luminis,	oh light of light and fount of brightness,
diem dies illuminans.[7]	day illuminating day.

The successive images of the dawn in stanzas II and III (the morning star and the first bird calls) can be paralleled from other well-known hymns by Prudentius and Ambrose, as well as from a host of others. For example, stanza III of St Ambrose's *Ad galli cantum* opens:

Hoc excitatus lucifer	The morning star arisen
Solvit polum caligine[8]	frees the sky of darkness

and a Lauds hymn by Peter Abelard begins:

Auroram lucifer	The morning star precedes
Praeit, sol sequitur.[9]	the dawn, the sun follows.

The first line of Prudentius' famous 'Ales diei nuntius / lucem propinquam praecinit' ('the bird, messenger of daybreak, sings to herald the approaching light') is taken up by numerous other hymns;[10] and compare this Lauds hymn:

Aurorae lux dum rutilat	While the light of dawn glistens
et ales cantus intonat...[11]	and the bird takes up its song...

The meaning of the phrase 'estelas del cel' (l. 17) is less clear. Why does the watcher ask his companion to 'look at the stars'? Perhaps because they are decreasingly visible? The fading of the stars as daylight grows is referred to in a number of dawn hymns.[12] The reading 'estelas' is not, however, found in all the manuscripts, but only in *CPSgT*; whereas *ER* have 'ensenhas' (cf. *Mü*, 'esenge'). If 'ensenhas' is taken to mean 'signs', then other common indications of approaching dawn

---

[7] Parallel adduced by Picchio Simonelli, p. 202.

[8] *Analecta hymnica medii aevi*, ed. Clemens Blume and Guido Maria Dreves, 55 vols (Leipzig, 1886–1922), [vol.] 50: [no.] 4. Unless otherwise indicated, quotations are from opening stanzas.

[9] 48. 121.

[10] 50. 22, cited 4. 163, 22. 364, and 23. 186.

[11] 19. 387.

[12] e.g. 51. 5, stanza II: 'Aurora stellas jam tegit' (also cited by Becker, p. 166); 51. 7, 22. 210.

include the brightening of the sky and the return of colour to the world.[13] However, the commonest meaning of *ensenhas* is 'banners', and this would introduce a far more vivid metaphor into this stanza: the band of sky immediately above the skyline, tinged with colour and light by the rising sun, would be likened to the standards of an advancing army. Such martial imagery also finds analogues in dawn hymns. The famous lines of Venantius Fortunatus:

Vexilla regis prodeunt	The royal banners forward go
Fulget crucis mysterium	shines forth the cross with mystic glow

for example, are cited in a number of hymns directed to be sung at Lauds.[14]

There is thus a series of elements in this *alba*, starting with the music and devotional opening lines, and continuing with reminiscences of dawn hymns through stanzas II, III, and IV, which link it with the liturgy of morning worship. When, in stanza V, the singer says that he has prayed to God (l. 23), his words wrap back over the preceding text and redesig-nate it as the morning prayer which all these elements suggest that it might be: a call to God to watch over the Christian in peril (l. 3), and a call to the Christian in peril to rise up and greet the true light (ll. 7 sqq.). Giraut's *alba*, in other words, begins to look like the so-called religious *alba* of which there are six Occitan examples; the earliest one, by Bernart de Venzac, is probably only slightly later in date than Giraut's.[15]

Reis glorios thus has the disturbing quality of combining the ecclesiastical-liturgical with the popular and secular. Is this a prayer for salvation? or just a warning to make a quick get-away before the irate husband arrives? Some readers have denied that there is a problematic tension here. Simonelli, for example, claims that the threatening *gilos* of l. 14 is to be read as the devil. The text, ceasing to contain an erotic narra-tive, becomes a religious *alba* in which a figure of vigilance calls on his fellow to avoid the snares of the devil and embrace the true light.[16] Becker, on the other hand, maintains that the liturgical reminiscences arise by association (born of long familiarity with dawn hymns) between their call for alertness, and the situation of danger in which the poet

---

[13] e.g. the lauds hymn by Prudentius, 50. 23.

[14] 51. 67; 16. 53; 23. 425.

[15] Picchio Simonelli no. 6; de Riquer no. 15, who also prints the other 'religious *albas*'.

[16] pp. 210–17.

visualises the lovers. He sees the text as the earliest erotic *alba*, drawing on appropriate phraseology and imagery. [17] Other critics, however, allow that there are two discourses at work in this poem, and attempt to interpret the gap between them. It may be labelled parodic (Giraut is parodying or profaning hymns), [18] or paradoxical, playing on the contrast between religious values (God's light) and natural impulses (lovers' fear of the light of daylight). [19] Such readings seem to me to be the most fruitful, and it is in this area that my own belongs.

Previous interpretations, however, seem to me to risk hypostatising a contradiction which the text's efforts are bent more towards dissolving. Rather than presenting itself as a hermeneutic conundrum, or a challenge to the *bien pensant*, the poem bends its discourses in such a way as to blur the lines of separation between them. Its imagery, for example, serves to tie together, rather than force apart, different possibilities of meaning. God is light and so is the dawn which seems to bring a threat of danger. If the 'verais' which qualifies the light of God (l. 1) is sup-posed to contrast it with the light of nature, then the contrast is remark-ably easy to overlook. The bird in stanza III recalls dawn hymns, but also the *exordia* of love songs, and serves as a proleptic image of the depart-ing lover, especially if 'queren' is understood as 'lamenting' rather than 'seeking'. The reading 'ensenhas' in stanza IV, if it is taken to mean 'banners', would continue to blur the distinction between ecclesiastical and secular registers: it combines reminiscence of the *militia Christi* with a reminder of the physical risk to the *companho*, threatened with assault by a jealous husband (l. 14). Once past the Latinate opening line, the liturgical imagery — if such it is — bends itself towards vernacular ex-pression and secular concerns. The poem's relatively artless metre, formulaic diction, and solo male first-person invocation, all are features which link liturgical and popular song far more than they divorce them. Several of the instances of repetition, especially, conspire to conflate what the reader might seek to distinguish. God's faithful assistance ('fizels aiuda', l. 3) becomes the singer's role as faithful messenger ('fizels messatge', l. 18); the singer's prayer to God ('preiei', l. 23) is echoed by

---

[17] pp. 166–7.

[18] Hermann Janssen CssR, 'Quelques remarques sur les rapports entre l'ancienne poésie provençale et les hymnes de l'église', *Neophilologus*, XVIII (1933), 262–71, esp. p. 266.

[19] See Jonathan Saville, *The Medieval Erotic Alba: Structure as Meaning* (New York and London, 1972), pp. 88–95, and Sarah Spence, *Rhetoric of Reason and Desire: Vergil, Augustine, and the Troubadours* (Ithaca, NY, 1988), p. 124 and note.

the companion's prayer to his friend to keep watch for him ('preiavatz', l. 27). The first hemistichs of the opening two lines present an internal rhyme (-*os*) which assonates with the -*o* of 'bel companho', the phrase which comes to assume both the position in the stanza of 'reis glorios', and the role of addressee. In line 7, MSS *EPRSg* repeat 'senher, si a vos platz' from the equivalent position in stanza I as though to emphasise this easy transference from God to the companion; although editors agree to print 'suau vos ressidatz' at this point, this reading is found in *C* alone.

This central role accorded to the relationship between singer and *companho* is the *alba*'s strongest device for smoothing together the edges of its potentially discordant discourses. In the later secular, erotic *albas*, the watchman is a servant, or a professional nightwatchman, and forms no part of the world of the lovers which constitutes the emotional centre of these poems. In *Reis glorios*, however, the constant address 'companho' suggests a relative equality, and it is this relationship of *companhonnatge* which is the emotional centre of the text. Just as repetitions blur religious invocation with appeals to the 'friend', so these same appeals are confused with the topoi of secular love poetry. Indeed, this *alba*, like contemporary troubadour love songs, consists of a sustained emotional appeal, the recipient of which remains unmoved despite the range of psychological and emotional strategies deployed to sway him. The singer, like the lover in a *canso*, exploits successively entreaty (l. 11), threats (l. 19), complaints (l. 29), and invocations of divine aid. Like a lover also he suffers, unregarded, in the service of his relationship. A lover is sleepless with love, and the singer here is sleepless in the service of his friend (l. 22); he sings to express his love, but goes ignored.

The *alba* thus makes explicit what is usually implicit in the troubadour love song: that the lover's relationship to his lady is in fact subordinate to, and a vehicle of, his relations with other men. The companion urges his friend to respond lest the lure of the lady undermine the priority that should be accorded to inter-male friendship. His appeals to God may clash with the scenario of adultery but they reinforce the watchman's belief that daylight should bring a return to the public, masculine world of order. Rather than calling attention to a gulf between religious and sensual domains, this *alba* prioritises a masculine symbolic over the heterosexual love affair. The love which it celebrates is that of one man for another. It is less about the separating of lovers than the separation of companions.

Or at least, that is true of the text as printed above. Unfortunately, however, it is not found in any of the manuscripts. Giraut may well have composed a poem very like Kolsen's; but all the evidence we have shows that it was not available in this form to medieval readers.

Although Kolsen follows the graphies of *C*, his text (like that of other major editors of this poem) offers a compromise between *EPSg*, which present six stanzas but intervert IV and V, and *CMüT*, which have the order IV – V, but which all contain one or more additional stanzas; *R*, an intermediate manuscript, has the order of *EPSg* but the same additional stanza as *T*. Here is a summary table (stanza numbers refer to Kolsen's text; the stanza designated as VII has been considered authentic by some scholars, and hence is accorded its own number[20]):

EPSg	I	II	III	V	IV		VI			
R	I	II	III	V	IV		VI			VII
T	I	II	III	IV	V		VI	VIa	VIb	VII
C	I	II	III	IV	V	Va	VI			
Mü	I	III	IV	V	II	IIa				

In Kolsen's text Giraut appears, as Dante was later to represent him, as a poet of rectitude; religious and secular discourses are pulled into alignment in the interests of masculine order. But textual variation tends to prise them apart, widening the gap between them, the dimensions and constitution of which vary from manuscript to manuscript. The 'poem' has to be conceived as fluid and dynamic, not just in the way the various discourses within it bend and flex, but also as they develop different trajectories from text to text.

It is also markedly less orderly in its various manuscript attestations than in Kolsen's edition. It is striking that the pattern of neatly paired stanzas is absent from *all* versions, whether because of interversion (*EMüPRSg*) or inserted material (*CT*). By interverting stanzas IV and V, *EPSg* and *R* not only dislocate the rhyme scheme, they also interrupt the series of dawn images (morning star — bird — dawn sky) and distance stanza V from stanza VI. The prayer to Jesus (l. 23), instead of coming near the end of the poem, resonating with 'preiavatz' (l. 27), and thereby strengthening a Christian frame around the notion of companionship, is pushed earlier. As a result, the singer's complaint that his efforts are un-appreciated (l. 29) is made to appear more bitter, cause for vindictiveness even, since it now follows on much more closely from the threat 'vostres n'er lo damnatge' (l. 19). The harmony of male friendship, sustained by God over the lure of women, as Kolsen's text would have it, is made to seem precarious. Are these men going to fall out, and the woman claim

---

[20] See Sharman's textual notes for summary of opinions, and references.

success? Certainly that is the conclusion of the poem in *R*, whose final stanza reads:

Bel dos companh, tan soy en ric soiorn	Fair gentle companion, I am so richly
Qu'ieu no volgra mays fos alba ni iorn,	lodged that I never wish to see dawn or
Car la gensor qu'anc nasques de mayre	day again, for I hold in my arms the fairest
Tenc et abras, per qu'eu non prezi gayre	lady ever born, so that I care little for
Lo fol gilos ni l'alba![21]	the foolish jealous one, nor the dawn.

Quite a put-down for someone who has been waiting outside all night to issue the very warnings which are here received so dismissively. Stanza IIa in *Mü* is another rejoinder by the lover to the watchman expressing dismay at being roused[22] and thereby counterposing to the claim of the companion the greater attraction of the lady. Although it does not go so far in undermining the bond between the companions, MS *C* inserts an additional stanza after V which also has the effect of sharpening antagonism between them:

Bel companho, quar es trop enueyos,	Fair companion, you cause me excessive
Que quant intrem pel portal ambedos,	torment, for when we both entered through
Esgardetz sus, vis la genser que sia;	the gate you looked up and saw the fairest
De mi.us partiz, lai tenguetz vostra via,	in the world, left me, and made your way
Et ades sera l'alba.[23]	there; and soon it will be dawn.

The dignified singer of Kolsen's text, his voice sustained by the authority of liturgy, seems in danger of turning into a camp cleric whose whingeing needs to be rebutted by a decisive vote for heterosexuality.

This shift in perception of the problem posed by the *alba* is maintained in *T*, which contains not only stanza VII, but also VIb. Here the companion complains at the lover's disregard, and conjures him to listen for love of his lady, whom he (the lover) loves as much as the companion does him. Friendship is pulled into the same discursive orbit as erotic love, and the conflict between them heightened. And in *T* VIa, religious

---

[21] Sharman, p. 366.

[22] Text from Kolsen:

> Bel dolz compan, ben auzi vostre cant,
> Molt me pesa ke tu m trabalhas tant,
> Car tu me trais del fon del paradis.
> Mon leit ai fah, combra me flor de lis,
> Et ades sera l'alba.

[23] Text from Kolsen.

discourse makes a come-back, an address to the Virgin returning us to the interpretive difficulty with which we started:[24]

Gloriosa ce tut lo mon capdella,	Glorious Lady who rules the world, I beg
Merce te clam c'en preant t'en apella:	your mercy, calling on you here in prayer
Cel mieu conpagn prendas e gidagie,	that you should take and guide my
O si ce vos li trametas messagie	companion, and also that you give him this
Per c'ill conosca l'alba.	message, so he will recognise the dawn.

T thus alternates religious appeal (stanzas V, VIa) with the companion's complaint to his friend (VI, VIb–VII). The three affective discourses of *eros* (heterosexual love), *philia* (male intimacy), and *agape* (religious love) are drawn into the same textual web only to pull against each other. *Mü*, like *T* a corrupt and difficult manuscript that no-one would take as the base for an edition, goes further when the lover protests that he cannot respond to his companion 'del fon del paradis' ('from the depths of paradise'). The gap between the worlds of adultery and religion, so care-fully concealed in Kolsen's text, is provocatively flaunted.

Our only knowledge of the poetry of the twelfth century comes via copies made in the thirteenth century or later, copies affected (as *a fortiori* we are too) by hindsight. All the manuscripts containing additional stanzas seek to make *Reis glorios* closer to the erotic *alba*, as it later came to be constituted.[25] Modern readings of it cannot but be influenced by awareness of this tradition, and of that of the religious *alba*. Our recognition of 'discourses' at work in *Reis glorios* is predicated on inter-textual awareness, embracing these later *albas* as well as earlier, liturgical texts (and indeed going back to the Song of Songs). The diffusion of the medieval poem in seven different manuscript copies is only a first, relatively containable, stage in the dispersal of intertextual connections that whirl away indefinitely. It is impossible to reify even the strands in this complex web as discrete entities or states; the song is a multiplicity of discursive practices, fluid and ever changing. Reading it is like being asked to look at the bird as it flies into the woodland, the 'estelas del cel' as they vanish away, or the mysterious 'ensenhas' that beckon and threaten on the horizon.

---

24 Diplomatic text from Sharman (who does not volunteer a critical edition, perhaps because of the obscurity of the fourth line), my punctuation.

25 See Picchio Simonelli, pp. 197–8.

2

Image and Argument in a *Dizain* of Scève

Michael Moriarty

Encores vit ce peu de l'esperance,
Que me laissa si grand longueur de temps,
Se nourrissant de ma vaine souffrance
Toute confuse du bien, que ie pretens.   4
Et a me veoir les Astres mal contentz
Inspirent force au languissant plaisir
Pour non acoup de vueil me dessaisir,
Qui, persistant a ses fins pretendues,   8
A mon trauail augmente le desir,
Strigile vain a mes sueurs perdues.

I

Scève's poem (*Délie* 174) articulates a peculiar sense of purpose and purposelessness operating in combination. A complex emotional dialectic achieves no conceptual resolution: it culminates in, or is disguised by, an image that brings together the contradictions and ambiguities of the preceding lines, and lays bare some new ones of its own.[1]

The poem is dominated, until the final line, by abstract nouns. The construction of relationships between them is largely entrusted to the preposition *à*, which occurs in five of the last six lines: a slight enough

---

[1] The poem is discussed by Dorothy Gabe Coleman herself in *Maurice Scève, Poet of Love: Tradition and Originality* (Cambridge: Cambridge University Press, 1975), pp. 173–4. She argues that the powerful last line does not really bring the preceding abstract argument alive. In a sense, this is very true, and my concern here is with the image as a pseudo-resolution to the problems examined inconclusively in the preceding lines. In 'Scève: A Virile Intellect Aerated by Sensibility' in *The Equilibrium of Wit: Essays for Odette de Mourgues*, edited by Peter Bayley and Dorothy Gabe Coleman (Lexington, KY: French Forum, 1982), 17–27, p. 27, n. 21, she draws attention to the importance of sensation in Scève, and cites this poem as an example.

11

support for so weighty an argument. In line 6, it simply marks the indirect object; in line 8 a goal or destination. In lines 9 and 10, its function is harder to gauge. In line 9, it seems to express a relationship of combination, as if it were *avec*, but with the possible additional overtones of matching or complementarity; in 10 it connects a noun with its complement, introducing, into the relationship of complementarity, a possible idea of purpose. The attempt to find purpose in the succession or combination of feelings is indeed central to the poem; for most of the abstract nouns denote psychological states: 'esperance', 'longueur de temps', 'souffrance', 'bien', 'force', 'plaisir', 'vueil', 'fins', 'trauail', 'desir'. They too pose problems for interpretation, for several are near-synonyms ('vueil' and 'desir', 'souffrance' and 'trauail') and the question is then whether they can be treated in context as synonyms or as differentiated by fine shades of meaning. But before embarking on the task of interpretation, we should note that these nouns largely determine the feel of the poem. Abstraction is of course characteristic of Scève's style, and one can find other *dizains* that display it to no less an extent (D 195, to name but one). Yet if we read D 174 (leaving out for the moment the final line) against the other poems in the cluster of nine to which it belongs (D 168–176), it does stand out as relatively more abstract. The other poems are situated with reference to the world of sense-experience, which furnishes not only metaphors but concrete objects, incidents, and locations. D 169 works out the image of the glove and the hand, 'gantz' being the second word of the poem. In D 170 the poet and his lady are in a meadow: he rushes to take shelter from the rain, and finds that she has not followed him. Weather returns in the next poem, D 171. D 172 begins with the glorious image of the alabaster, and is centred on the blue girdle actually worn by the lady, which reappears in D 173; D 175 evokes the image of nightfall, and D 176 that of the moon.

These images are, admittedly, laden with symbolic associations: they belong to a poetic tradition which helps to ensure a fairly ready passage between the image and the concept, between the everyday incident or object and the symbolic realm. D 168 is more abstract, but it derives a certain concreteness from the preceding emblem, that of Actaeon, the motto of which is echoed in line 9. And here too there is a movement from the concrete and the immediate, the recollection of Délie's name, to an intense spiritual experience, a mystical loss of self.

D 174, on the contrary, is not thus rooted in the world of daily experience. It begins in the abstract register and ends with a concrete image; and this particular movement makes it more difficult to think of the poem, as one may think of the others, as enacting the transfiguration of the concrete everyday into a spiritual reality. (The 'Astres', by the way, of D 174, line 5, do not contradict this: they are not seen in the way the autumn weather is seen in D 171, or the evening sky in D 175: their operation is inferred from the poet's experience.)

In D 174, there is no orientation of feeling towards an object: the lady, so vividly present in most of these surrounding poems, is absent. (If, after all, she is the subject of 'laissa' in line 2, a point discussed below, the tense banishes her to a definite past: it certainly cannot vouch for her presence.) Experience is a pure succession of emotional states, one might even say, a rhythm of abstract nouns. Until the last line, and the strigil.

II

In his edition of the *Délie* McFarlane mentions the word *strigile* twice, in his Introduction, and in his note on D 174, l. 10, as either a Latinism or an Italianism. [2] On the latter occasion he notes that it is also 'perhaps a neologism'. The *Dictionnaire historique de la langue française* credits Scève with the first use of the word, and Wartburg (s.v. *strigilis*) concurs. Huguet mentions this poem, but also Jean de Coras's translation of the *Altercatio* between the emperor Hadrian and the philosopher Epictetus. But this appeared in 1558, fourteen years after *Délie*. It does look, then, as if Scève's is the first use of the word in French not constrained by the needs of translation. But Scève's neologisms are 'not over-numerous', says McFarlane (p. 49), and 'with the exception perhaps of some of the technical words employed as images [they] do not seem intended to make their impact by sudden surprise, as if they came from a completely different world' (p. 50). 'Strigile', in D 174, though, appears to work precisely like that. So Scève is employing a word by definition unusual, because in all probability new — which is in itself relatively unusual for him — and employing it in what is again, for him, an unusual way. So the word stands out: and all the more so because, as has been already suggested, the poem it occurs in has hitherto been notably abstract, more so than its immediate neighbours.

So what is a *strigile*? Basically, the answer is simple: a kind of skin-scraper employed by the Romans as part of their bathing ritual, prior to their being anointed with oil. This is certainly the sense in which Scève uses it here. But a look at the *Dictionarium seu Latinae linguae thesaurus* of Robert Estienne (Robertus Stephanus) makes the term appear

---

2 *The 'Délie' of Maurice Scève*, ed. I. D. McFarlane (Cambridge: Cambridge University Press, 1966), pp. 49 and 214.

more problematic. For a start it is insecure morphologically: Estienne's first edition (1531) lists the headword *strigil*; by the second edition (1543, the year before *Délie*) it has become *strigilis*. Estienne gives several senses for it: that of an instrument for rubbing down horses (*étrille*, a 'currycomb'); the sense that concerns us here ('strigile vtebantur veteres ad radendas corporis sordes, sudoremque tergendum praecipue in balneis, antequam comederent'); a kind of vessel (to name but three). In the second edition, however, he notes that the passages where *strigilis* has been read as denoting a type of vessel can also be read as referring to the 'strigilis balneatoria', 'quae cum ampulla vnguentaria ferebatur, vt post frictionem & sudoris abstersionem, quae strigili fiebat, vngerentur'.

Estienne's article, therefore, shows that the learned could be unclear as to the sense of *strigilis* in various passages. Scève, however, is unmistakably precise: 'sueurs' makes clear that his 'strigile' is the 'strigilis balneatoria'. The precision of his poetic image is enhanced by contrast with a certain vagueness in contemporary philological and archaeological knowledge. As if to compensate for the preceding abstraction, the poem climaxes on a highly concrete and specific term; but this too might be misunderstood, so the context must disambiguate it. Amid the haze of sentiment, there is, it seems, at least one thing to get hold of: something hard, metallic, abrasive.

The passages quoted by Estienne tell us something more about Scève's use of the term. McFarlane observes (p. 48) that 'many of [Scève's] Latinisms...appear to come from Ciceronian or Virgilian sources'. *Strigile* is less well-connected. Estienne does, indeed, quote one use of it by Cicero (*De finibus* IV. 12. 30). Cicero is alluding to the Stoics' contempt for bodily goods, which they illustrate by saying that a wise man would prefer to have 'ampulla aut strigilis', an oil-flask or a scraper, rather than not to have them; but that they contribute nothing to his happiness, properly speaking. For Cicero, the example trivialises the issue. And indeed the other occurrences of the term quoted by Estienne are mostly in comic or satirical contexts. A couple of Plautus's parasites mention the *ampulla* (oil-flask) and the *strigilis* among their few possessions.[3] (The fact that *ampulla* and *strigilis* come together in these last three examples suggests that Scève's equipment is deficient: he is undergoing only part of the bathing experience, missing out on the anointing with oil to which the scraping of the skin is a preliminary.) In Horace, *Satires* II. 7, a slave swaps a stolen strigil for grapes; in Persius' *Satire* 5 a slave is ordered to take some strigils to the baths. If the Roman bath for

---

3 Plautus, *Stichus* I. 3. 320; *Persa* I. 3. 124.

us evokes images of luxury and hedonism, the strigil's associations are also mundane and servile. Pascal Quignard's remark that 'le latinisme, chez Scève, tomberait aussi bien sous la détermination de l'argot', whether valid in general or not, seems apposite here. [4]

III

In contrast to the inanimate implement, the poem begins by dealing with organic processes. Hope is a living thing (l. 1): as such it requires nourishment, and the nourishment is provided by my 'vaine souffrance' (l. 3). (There is another possible reading of lines 2 and 3, which I shall come to shortly.) But is the suffering really vain, if it nourishes hope? To get a grip on this question, we have to consider the way in which the poem deals with ideas of purpose and goal.

Within the Aristotelian world view that still prevails in Scève's day, these ideas are not confined to the human sphere. [5] The poem does indeed mention one, possibly two, human agents, acting with a purpose in view. But it also mentions non-human agents, the 'Astres' of line 5: they are personified, credited with feelings and intentions, and, in a Renaissance poem, there is no need to read this purely as a poetic figure. Thirdly, feelings and passions can themselves be credited with a function, rather than being taken purely as effects; Aristotle says that 'anger must be defined as a movement of a body...in a particular state roused by such a cause, with such an end in view [*heneka toude*]'. [6] Yet the function of the passion might not necessarily correspond with the goals consciously pursued by the subject of the passion; and this is the problem raised by Scève's poem.

Suppose my suffering keeps hope alive: then, perhaps, it has a purpose. But equally from another viewpoint, another conception of my best interests, I might pronounce it vain. At the same time, I cannot subscribe entirely to that condemnation. I cannot stand aside from and judge my feelings as if they were alien to me; they are only my feelings insofar as I

4 Pascal Quignard, *La Parole de la Délie: essai sur Maurice Scève* (Paris: Mercure de France, 1974), p. 176.

5 This is not to suggest that Scève is endorsing an Aristotelian philosophy: his interests are more in neo-Platonic thought (see, for instance, D 444, which begins 'Nature au Ciel, non Peripatetique'). The suggestion is simply that the Aristotelian concern with teleology forms a background to this poem.

6 Aristotle, *De anima* I. 1 (403a) in Aristotle, *On the Soul, Parva Animalia, On Breath*, tr. W. S. Hett, Loeb Classical Library (Cambridge, Mass.: Harvard University Press, 1936).

am subject to them. I cannot say 'Hope is still alive', without saying 'I still hope', and this undermines my will to judge, and in some sense thereby purge, my passions. The subject is split between a position of identification with emotional states, and one of distance and denial.

IV

Where does the hope come from? Its source is unclear, because line 2 is unclear. McFarlane glosses it as 'qu'elle me laissa si longtemps'. This certainly makes sense. In that case, Délie might also be the subject of 'se nourrissant'. 'For a long time she left me with some hope — and even now it is not quite dead — as she battened on my useless suffering.' This agrees with D 199, where she is also represented as feeding on his passion. But it is striking that Délie's presence as subject should be thus merely implied and, simultaneously, effaced; as if for fear of endorsing the suspicion this reading evokes: of being used, devoured by a parasite.

Doubtless, we should keep this reading in play. But the elision of the subject 'elle' opens up a less embittered reading, where the subject is 'si grand longueur de temps'. The poet's state is then ascribed not to Délie's behaviour, but to the nature of human existence in time. But time's work-ings are ambiguous. The antecedent of 'que' could be 'l'esperance' or 'le peu de l'esperance'. In the first reading 'le peu de' merely conveys some additional information of secondary importance, and the sense is 'Length of time brought me hope, the promise of waiting's fulfilment'. In the second, the sense is rather: 'The length of time that has elapsed with no fulfilment has left me with but little hope.' Even on the first, more san-guine, reading, the hope is scarcely endorsed: length of time bequeathed hope, but in a definite past ('laissa'). The hope survives but time has brought no further validation.

It survives, then, but only because it feeds on suffering (as perhaps Délie does too; and if so, the lover's feelings are in complicity with his lady, each acting against an alternative view of his best interests).

What is intractable about the hope is that the suffering on which it feeds is bound up ('confuse') with 'le bien, que ie pretens'; that is, with the aspiration towards good. Inasmuch as the poet can affirm this 'bien', he cannot simultaneously endorse the condemnation of the suffering as futile. 'Pretens' and 'vaine' thus come into conflict, and they renew their encounter at the end of the poem, reappearing in lines 8 and 10 (they are the only words to be so marked out by repetition).

V

At this point, the stars intervene. This may be just a figure of speech, de-noting blind misfortune. But there is the emphasis on the stars' *seeing* him; and that they are 'mal contentz' implies that their action serves a purpose. But is it punishment or remedy? It may be that they are dis-pleased, in the sense of sorry to see him in such a hopeless plight, and therefore inject new strength into his pleasure, to enable him joyfully to affirm his situation: to confirm him in possession of his desire (l. 7). But it may be that their reaction casts new light on the first quatrain, suggest-ing that, amid all the complexities and ambiguities of the situation, what has been taking shape is a loss of desire and hope, supported by a judgement that the suffering involved has been futile: and it is this back-sliding that has incurred their displeasure. They have confirmed him, in-deed, in possession of his desire: but then they were 'mal contentz', and what he wants at some level is to be free of it. Their purposes are not his: or rather, their purpose is to hold him to a purpose in which he was weakening, as a negative judgement on his position began to take shape.

The syntax of what follows is far from clear. Renaissance syntax is of course freer than the norms imposed by Vaugelas and his successors permit. But although loose syntax can lead to lack of clarity, it need not. So if we find uncertainty of meaning resulting from syntactic ambiguity in Renaissance writing, there is no need to assume that the problem is purely of our own creation, the effect of an anachronistic imposition of classical standards of coherence, and that a more relaxed attitude to syn-tax on our part would allow a single meaning to emerge. Here lack of clarity seems to be part of the essence of the poem: there is a sense of connections being made, but being unable to impose themselves: of stories taking shape, but always imperilled by the possibility of rival stories. The poet and lover's self-scrutiny is unable to grasp more than shifting configurations, like an inexpert sky-watcher who sees alternative patterns of stars that fail to correspond with the clear outlines of the constellations as they are mapped out in books. It makes sense to take the antecedent of 'qui' (l. 8) to be 'vueil' (l. 7). In that case '[le] vueil... augmente le desir'. So the syntax prompts us to seek some means of distinguishing these two quasi-synonyms. McFarlane observes (p. 33) that 'vueil' designates free will. In that case, we could read 'vueil' in the sense of 'choice', conscious acceptance of the situation in virtue of an end one has in view. 'Desir' of line 9 would then be more in the nature of appetite, blind longing, a passive state contrasted with 'vueil' as active disposition. The stars, then, revive my pleasure in the situation, so that my will to accept it does not fade, and so my passion mounts along with my suffering (l. 9). Yet it is not inconceivable that we should read line 7 as a parenthesis, and it is simply pleasure, the urge towards gratification, that boosts desire for that gratification.

The distinction matters, because it affects how we read the parenthesis 'persistant a ses fins pretendues' in line 8, which seems important because it offers a gloss on the situation. The expression harks back to 'le bien que ie pretens' (l. 4), so we could take the second phrase as a simple reprise of the first: the celestial influences keep the poet faithful to what is after all a spiritual quest.

Having said which, there seems no reason why Scève should not have written 'mes fins pretendues' if that is what he wanted to say. '*Ses* fins', contrasted with 'mon trauail', 'mes sueurs', implies, yet again, a splitting of the subject, but one that is reduplicated by the ambiguity of the syntax discussed above. Take 'plaisir' as the implied subject of 'persistant', and the goals, 'ses fins pretendues', will be those of a sensual appetite of which I am the victim, not those of conscious choice. But if 'ses fins' refers back to 'vueil', then it is the aspiration towards the good, which is in a sense me, and even the best part of me, that pursues goals subtly and tragically distinct from those I would recognise as my own. That 'vueil' is mine in a sense appears from line 7: the stars act so as not to dispossess ('dessaisir') me of it. But its ends are its own, and for their sake, not for my good, it boosts desire to match suffering ('trauail'). (The idea of 'matching' seems implicit in the 'A' of line 9; unless that preposition denotes adverbially an effect (compare 'à mes dépens'): 'it increases desire, thus producing suffering.') Desire, moreover, is not my desire: it is the impersonal 'le desir'. My suffering regenerates desire and hope, the resultant frustration renewing my suffering. So elegant is this cyclical motion that it seems to bespeak design. Some purpose is being fulfilled, and being consistently fulfilled ('persiste'), but it is not mine: my purposes, those in the name of which I pronounced my suffering 'vaine', are being frustrated. What is definitely left to me is 'trauail' (l. 9), and 'sueurs' (l. 10).

But even here my own experience cannot tell me its own significance. We may compare this poem, which begins with hope, and ends with 'trauail', with the last line of D 69: 'I'espere, apres long trauail, une fin.' D 69 is preceded by the image of the woman with the distaff and spindle (VIII), and the motto 'Apres long trauail vne fin'. This simply implies the idea of a final rest from labour. But in the poem (D 69, that is) it is hard to exclude the further sense of 'fulfilment': 'Because I have suffered

18

so long, I hope that my suffering will receive its natural reward, that it will not be in vain.'

One may say, indeed, that the ambiguity of 'trauail' runs right through the *Délie*. It can usually be read as equivalent to 'suffering' or 'ordeal'. Release from that would depend on the arbitrary: either the fact of death, or the goodwill of the lady. But occasionally the sense of 'labour' appears. In D 69, this idea arguably carries over from the preceding picture to the poem; and the same could apply to D 312, where the last line, 'Je fuis la peine, & le trauail me suyt', echoes the image (XXXV) of the ass toiling in a mill, and D 249, where the poet's work is implicitly compared to that of the armourer in the preceding picture (XXVIII). 'Trauail' also seems to have the sense of 'labour' in D 437, line 6; and in D 438, where the word 'trauail' does not appear, the poet describes his condition in terms of work: 'exercice' (l. 1), 'seruice' (l. 3), 'labeur' (l. 9). Most of these passages stress the painful side of labour, but the very notion of labour implies a purpose in view, and the use of 'trauail' in D 174, hovering between 'suffering' (visited upon me) and 'labour' (undertaken by me, with an end in view) prolongs this existential question raised by the poem: how far am I responsible for my own suffering, how far is it the result of the purposes I have pursued?

VI

The strigil that offers relief is desire itself. Paradoxically, desire, and not its gratification. Desire in fact is its own gratification. And this offers a hope of salvation, for in that sense gratification is no longer precarious, dependent on the desire of another. Suffering, dirty and sweaty, is compensated for by the rituals of the bath, themselves evoked in the ritualistic symmetry of the verse: the strigil is a harsh experience, but it leaves the body sleek, fresh, ready for gratification ('antequam comederent', Estienne says the Romans used it). Desire purifies and intensifies existence; and, what is more, without suffering it would be meaningless, as the strigil presupposes the bath that produces sweat. The stars are to be blessed, after all, for thus preserving it.

But the enigmatic strigil — emerging from nowhere, and wielded by what slave? — is 'vain'. The adjective grates against the noun. How can an instrument be 'futile' when, *qua* instrument, it accomplishes a function? How can a kind of blade be 'empty'?

Desire relieves suffering, and compensates for it. But it cannot redeem it. The bath is a preparation, but the lover here is prepared for nothing except more of the same. That the sweat has been removed by the strigil, and that there is some pleasure and relief in this, does not mean that it was expended in a good cause. This is why the 'strigile' is 'vain', and the sweat 'perdues'.

VII

All that is left is a metal instrument of uncertain value ('of gold, silver, or iron', says Estienne, though in fact other materials were used). Perhaps, then, a beautiful well-crafted luxury object; perhaps the rusty metal article of the comic parasite who otherwise has nothing but the clothes he stands up in.

Strigile: it is impossible not to hear the scrape of metal against flesh in the fricative consonants, and the rhythmical movement in the symmetry of the repeated vowel. But that the strigil brings no harmonious resolution to the situation is emphasised not only by its own harsh sound but by its phonetic isolation: *i* disappears from the line after the first word, displaced by *a* sounds ('vain', 'a') and a combination of *e* and *u*. In the first case, there is an exceptionally harsh quasi-hiatus ('vain a'). In the second, instead of the subtle and euphonious modulation of vowel sounds in which Scève excels when he wishes (see for instance the last line of D 367) we have an awkward alternation between *e* and *u* sounds: 'mes s*ueu*rs p*erdues*'. The result of moving from one to the other is grimace: at the end, the mouth broadens on the first syllable of 'perdues', the lips purse on the second, as if the mouth had filled with the sour saliva of disappointment.

VIII

The instrument, emerging, as we said, from nowhere, has the force of a revelation. The 'tortuous investigation of an experience' in Dorothy Gabe's own account of the poem (p. 174) is interrupted by a metaphorical term so obscure, so concrete, that it is instantly authoritative, imposing itself as absolutely precise, absolutely adequate to the situation. But this only intensifies the problem raised by the poem: can the triumph of the image as image, within the poem, carry over into the world outside the poem? The strigil works in the poem, yet it is *vain* in terms of what it represents: desire, claiming, yet not imposing its claim, to be its own justification. As such the image of the strigil brings together the paradox of which the poem is composed: it bears witness to the existence in the world of purpose, yet at the same time to my failure to realise my purposes within it, to the obscure awareness that the purposes I serve are other than mine.

3

Allegories and Secrets:
Cymbalum Mundi, Dialogue 2

John O'Brien

Quis enim mysteriorum peritior quam Mercurius...?
(Erasmus, *Adages*, II.10.10)

RHETULUS. Or, messieurs, il ne vous desplaira point si je prens
congé de vous, car voyla monsieur le Senateur Venulus, avec lequel j'ay
promis d'aller souper, qui m'envoye querir par son serviteur.
MERCURE. A Dieu, donc, monsieur!
TRIGABUS. Voyla de mes gens; il sera assis au hault bout de la table,   5
on luy trenchera du meilleur, il aura l'audivit et le cacquet par-dessus
tous, et Dieu sçait s'il leur en comptera de belles.
MERCURE. Et le tout par le moyen de ma pierre philosophale!
TRIGABUS. Et quoy donc? Quand ce ne seroit jà que les repues
franches qu'ilz en ont, ilz sont grandement tenuz à toy, Mercure.   10
MERCURE. Tu voy de quoy sert mon art. Or il me fault aller faire
encor quelque message secret, de par Jupiter mon pere, à une dame,
laquelle demeure au près du temple d'Apollo; et puis il me fault aussi
ung petit veoir ma mye, devant que je retorne. A Dieu!
TRIGABUS. Tu ne me veulx donc pas tenir promesse?   15
MERCURE. De quoy?
TRIGABUS. De m'enseigner les motz qu'il fault dire pour changer ma
trongne et mon visage en telle forme que je vouldray.
MERCURE. Ouy dea, c'est bien dict; escoute en l'oreille.
TRIGABUS. Comment? Je ne t'oy pas, je ne sçay que tu dis; parle   20
plus hault.
MERCURE. Voyla toute la recepte; ne l'oblie pas.
TRIGABUS. Qu'a-il dict? Par le sambieu! je ne l'ay point entendu et
croy qu'il ne m'a rien dict, car je n'ay rien ouy. S'il m'eust voulu
enseigner cela, j'eusse faict mille gentillesses, je n'eusse jamais eu   25
paour d'avoir faulte de rien, car quant j'eusse eu affaire d'argent, je
n'eusse faict que transmuer mon visage en celluy de quelcun à qui ses
tresoriers en doyvent, et m'en feusse allé le recevoir pour luy. Et pour
bien jouyr de mes amours et entrer sans danger chez ma mye, j'eusse

pris souvent la forme et la face de l'une de ses voisines, à celle fin que 30
l'on ne m'eust cogneu, et plusieurs autres bons tours que j'eusse faict.
O la bonne façon de masques que c'eust esté, s'il m'eust voulu dire les
motz et qu'il ne m'eust point abusé! Or je reviens à moy-mesmes et
cognois que l'homme est bien fol, lequel s'attend avoir quelque cas de
cela qui n'est point, et plus malheureux celuy qui espere chose 35
impossible.[1]

Cymbalum Mundi is a text which has had a particularly controversial interpretative history, and its second dialogue has been the source of special contention. Its basic narrative data are clear: three *philosophes*, Rhetulus, Drarig, and Cubercus, scrabble around looking for fragments of the 'pierre philosophale' in the sand of an 'arene'. This early detail is not insignificant, since Cotgrave, one notes, defines 'arene' not only as 'a Theatre for Fencers', but also as 'a place to jest in, strowed with gravel': the definition encodes the response which the reader will be invited to make, and embodies at least one of the interpretative dilemmas he or she will encounter. The information about the *philosophes* is provided by an onlooker, Trigabus, in conversation with the god Mercure; it is Trigabus who supplies data or offers interpretations not available to the *philosophes*. The exclusion of the *philosophes* and the implicit inclusion of the reader establishes an irony of situation, turning the *philosophes* into objects of derision and amusement, and allowing the reader access to particular information not shared by all the characters. It is through this shuttling between the outer frame of the observers Trigabus and Mercure and the inner frame of the observed, the *philosophes*, that the dialogue establishes a primary sense of privilege. It suggests a pact, of sorts, with the reader, honouring the age-old contract which makes of literature a source of knowledge, enlightenment, and special insight.

The reader's privileges and certainties are fully in evidence at the beginning of the passage above where Mercure, recognised by the reader and Trigabus, remains unrecognised by the *philosophes* who supposedly act under his aegis. The opening exchange between Rhetulus and Mercure — 'Mercure n'est pas tousjours favorable à tous' 'Je le pense!' — places the reader firmly on the side of the ironists Mercure and Trigabus. Rhetulus declares that he must leave for a dinner party.

[1] Bonaventure des Périers (?), *Cymbalum Mundi*. Texte établi et présenté par Peter Hampshire Nurse. Préface de Michael A. Screech (Geneva: Droz, 1983), pp. 21–2. A new edition of this work has recently been published by Yves Delègue (Paris: Champion, 1995).

Mercure's response, 'A Dieu, donc, Monsieur', is a dismissal as well as a farewell, effectively closes the inner frame in which the *philosophes* have been the object of ironical scrutiny, and gives rise to the moral glosses which Trigabus then makes. From Trigabus' comments, Rhetulus emerges as a self-important windbag, stuffed full of prime meat ('on luy trenchera du meilleur') and his own rhetoric ('caquet', 'il leur en comptera de belles'): he is a particular and satirical combination of *mets* and *mots*. In this moment of brief but shrewd characterisation, Rhetulus is shown to be little more than an after-dinner *raconteur*, inventing stories which he takes as his truth and peddles to others as wisdom.

The very name 'Rhetulus' points moreover to a further level of debate which has stimulated critical speculation.[2] The disparity between the immediately comprehensible name Mercure and the less comprehensible forms Rhetulus and Trigabus is a feature which has triggered the search for allegory; this search has focused on the anagrams supposedly hidden under the names of the *philosophes*. That the text does appear to invite the reader to anagrammatise is part of the larger problematics of Dialogue 2, a problem of extrapolating meaning by viewing the whole episode as an allegory. In that respect, the second dialogue is commonly regarded as continuing the allegories of the first. However, there is no unanimous agreement among critics about exactly how to decipher these allegories to complete satisfaction. It has been usual to take the initial dialogues as a sequence concerned with the failings of the Established Church (Dialogue 1) and the Reformed Religion (Dialogue 2).[3] In this context, it is tempting to follow the trail of anagrammatisation and interpret Rhetulus as Luther, Cubercus as Bucer, and Drarig as Erasmus or Girard Roussel.[4] Such a strategy would be entirely in keeping with Renaissance belief in the power of anagrams.[5] It would also hold decided interpretative advantages. For if the anagram can be successfully deciphered, the implicit pact with the reader is preserved: the anagram has kept its

---

2 See, for example, Max Gauna, *Upwellings: First Expressions of Unbelief in the Printed Literature of the French Renaissance* (London and Toronto: Associated University Presses, 1992), p. 113.

3 So, for example, Nurse, p. xxxix and Gauna, *Upwellings*, p. 190.

4 Screech, pp. 11–14, opts for Roussel rather than Erasmus. The whole effect is to emphasise the allegorical decipherability of the text and turn it into a sort of *roman à clé*.

5 Cf. François Rigolot, *Poétique et onomastique: l'exemple de la Renaissance* (Geneva: Droz, 1977), pp. 222–7 and Geneviève Demerson, *Dorat en son temps: culture classique et présence au monde* (Clermont-Ferrand: Adosa, 1983), pp. 214–24.

promise to provide a key to the text's secrets, to yield or help yield the text's meaning. Hence anagrams and, by extension, the larger schemes of allegory could be counted on to act as a secure set of referents, anchoring the text into a transcendental system of meaning, a stable set of signs constituting a decipherable semiosis.

The allegorical reading implied by the anagrams finds apparent support in the 'pierre philosophale' which the *philosophes* are seeking. This alchemical allusion has been interpreted as truth, especially religious truth, which each *philosophe* believes is his. What is at stake therefore is the Stone as a source of validating authority, bestowing power and pres-tige on the *philosophes*, even if the resulting prestige is — bathetically — no more than that of the after-dinner speaker. Trigabus tells us at the opening of the dialogue that Mercure has smashed the Stone and scattered fragments of it amidst the sand of the theatre. Consequently, Mercure's comment about Rhetulus and implicitly the other *philosophes* — 'Et tout par le moyen de ma pierre philosophale' — compounds the irony that the authority so ardently sought by the *philosophes* is based on a famous non-entity, but one which for the sixteenth century had lost none of its power of attraction. The historicity of the allusion to the Philosopher's Stone is crucial to the functioning of the text, in that this episode in *Cymbalum Mundi* can be read as a moment in the history of fakes, so fascinatingly studied by Anthony Grafton.[6] The Philosopher's Stone is thus an especially manifest instance of the textual secret, and yet it turns out to be a fake, a myth, a fiction.

If the Philosopher's Stone is a fiction, then the creator of that fiction himself holds an equivocal position. Several classical models were avail-able for the character of Mercure in *Cymbalum Mundi*: the Hermes Logos of Plato's *Cratylus* and, by extension, the god of eloquence; Hermes the neo-Platonic *mystagogus* and *psychopompos*; Hermes the educator of humanity; and — in another vein — the Egyptian Hermes,

---

[6] Anthony Grafton, *Forgers and Critics: Creativity and Duplicity in Western Scholarship* (Princeton: Princeton University Press, 1990); *Defenders of the Text: The Traditions of Scholarship in an Age of Science, 1450–1800* (Cambridge, Mass.: Harvard University Press, 1991), esp. pp. 76–103. For *philosophe* as a Renaissance equivalent of *alchimiste*, see Delègue, p. 18, n. 2; and for the alchemical title 'Hermes père des philosophes', see the alchemical treatise studied by Didier Kahn, 'Alchimie et littérature à Paris en des temps de trouble: le *Discours d'autheur incertain sur la pierre des philosophes* (1590)', *Réforme Humanisme Renaissance*, XLI (1995), p. 95.

Hermes Trismegistus. [7] These particular models are characterised by a moral seriousness which implicitly guarantees their worth and sanctions their potential redeployment within Renaissance literature. Yet other traditions, less elevated and stately, but no less widespread, also made use of Mercury: Hermes the thief; Hermes the god of merchants; Hermes the god of lies. [8] It is common to argue that by transforming Mercure from the august Hermes of various Ancient Theologies into the errand boy of Jupiter (not unlike the Mercure of the prologue to Rabelais's *Quart Livre*), the text gives priority to a further model, the Lucianic, [9] and that, in consequence, the dignity and the integrity of the other classical models are compromised by the parody to which the figure of Mercure is subjected. This tends to conceal a further characteristic of *Cymbalum Mundi*, namely that it keeps a number of traditions in play simultaneously; selectivity and priority do not operate quite as uniformly as one might ideally wish or suppose. Thus Mercure is not only the messenger of the gods, as the present scene emphasises; he is also the psychopomp (pp. 5, 10), and yet is linked to theft (pp. 9–11) and deception (p. 18). Some of the most intractable problems of *Cymbalum Mundi* arise precisely because of its

---

[7] For these various traditions, cf. Erasmus, *Adages*, II. 10. 10 ('Mercurius enim eloquentiae disciplinarumque parens est'); Guy de Tervarent, *Attributs et symboles de l'art profane, 1450–1600: Dictionnaire d'un langage perdu*, 2 vols (Geneva: Droz, 1958), I. cols 268–70, citing Horace and Giraldi; Frances Yates, *Giordano Bruno and the Hermetic Tradition* (London: Routledge and Kegan Paul, 1964), esp. pp. 1–19; Ludwig Schrader, 'Hermes im Humanismus: Mythologische Anmerkungen zu Guillaume Budé, Alfonso de Valdés und Bonavanture des Périers', in *Italien und die Romania in Humanismus und Renaissance*, Mélanges E. Loos (Wiesbaden: Steiner, 1983), pp. 229–45; Garth Fowden, *The Egyptian Hermes: A Historical Approach to the Late Pagan Mind* (Cambridge: Cambridge University Press, 1986); Ingrid Merkel and A. G. Debus (eds), *Hermeticism and the Renaissance: Intellectual History and the Occult in Early Modern Europe* (Washington, DC: Folger Shakespeare Library, 1988); and especially the collective volume *Mercure à la Renaissance*, ed. Marie-Madeleine de la Garanderie (Paris: Champion, 1988).

[8] Cf. Norman O. Brown, *Hermes the Thief: The Evolution of a Myth* ([Madison]: University of Wisconsin Press, 1947).

[9] See Christopher Robinson, *Lucian and His Influence in Europe* (London: Duckworth, 1979), pp. 116–21; François Berriot, *Athéismes et athéistes au XVIe siècle en France* (Lille: Cerf, [1984]), pp. 669–79; C. A. Mayer, 'The Lucianism of Des Périers', *Bibliothèque d'Humanisme et Renaissance*, XII (1950), 190–207 and *Lucien de Samosate et la Renaissance française* (Geneva: Slatkine, 1984), pp. 165–90; Christiane Lauvergnat-Gagnière, *Lucien de Samosate et le lucianisme en France au XVIe siècle: athéisme et polémique* (Geneva: Droz, 1988), pp. 262–74; Gauna, *Upwellings*, pp. 130–2, 180–2.

polyvalent use of the myth of Mercury: 'la figure de Mercure se compose librement de plusieurs segments'[10] which are not infrequently incompatible and offer conflicting readings of the god's position and status. In *Cymbalum Mundi*, the various traditions sometimes stand alone, sometimes are combined and sometimes are played off against each other. The overall effect is that of a *contaminatio*, a babble of voices rather than a harmonious blend or a calm dialogue between this Renaissance text and its classical predecessors. In this light, the epistemology of the intertext can become unusually difficult to decipher and evaluate, since in common with the rest of the book, Dialogue 2 uses intertext not as a clarifying feature of its hermeneutics, but as a further source of obfuscation, parody, and satire.

This technique is nowhere clearer than in the specific case of Hermes Trismegistus, a model whose precise relevance is suggested by the use of the 'pierre philosophale' theme and the alchemical associations of Hermetic lore.[11] As interpreted in the Renaissance, of course, Hermes Trismegistus exemplified the tradition of the *prisca theologia*, a tradition of arcane secrets *par excellence*.[12] Dialogue 2 is coloured by these traditions and allusions when Trigabus, in the extract before us, asks Mercure to keep his earlier promise and divulge the secret of transformation. It could have been a moment of special intensity in Renaissance literature: an incarnate symbol of the classical past stands ready to impart the deep secret of the gods. It is a potential *transmissio studii* in highly visual form, realising a Renaissance dream of direct dialogue with a resurrected classical past. Indeed, such a scenario would directly echo analogous situations in the *Hermetica*, where the display and transmission of knowledge are frequently dramatised by a dialogue between a god and an

---

10 Wolfgang Boerner, 'La Mythologie antique dans l'œuvre de Bonaventure des Périers', in *Mercure à la Renaissance*, p. 115.

11 Cf. A.-J. Festugière, *La Révélation d'Hermès Trismégiste*, 4 vols (Paris: Gabalda, 1944–54), I. 217–82; Fowden, *The Egyptian Hermes*, pp. 87–91; Jean-François Maillard, 'Mercure alchimiste dans la tradition mytho-hermétique', in *Mercure à la Renaissance*, pp. 117–30; Brian P. Copenhaver, *Hermetica: The Greek Corpus Hermeticum and the Latin Asculapius in a New English Translation, with Notes and Introduction* (Cambridge: Cambridge University Press, 1994), pp. xxxiv–xxxvi.

12 Cf. D. P. Walker, *The Ancient Theology: Studies in Christian Platonism from the Fifteenth to the Eighteenth Century* (London: Duckworth, 1972), *passim* for Hermes Trismegistus and the Ancient Theology. On the Renaissance debunking of Hermes Trismegistus, see Grafton, *Defenders of the Text*, chapter 5, 'Protestant versus Prophet: Isaac Casaubon on Hermes Trismegistus', pp. 145–61, and chapter 6, 'The Strange Death of Hermes and the Sibyls', pp. 162–77.

acolyte; direct communication with the god is the source of revelation.[13] The scene at this point in Dialogue 2 is moreover phrased in precisely the vocabulary of desired enlightenment associated with such moments in classical literature (note 'enseigner' repeated twice in close succession), which Trigabus seeks to enforce by reminding Mercure of his promise ('Tu ne me veulx donc pas tenir promesse?'). Intellectually and ethically, the text presses for a contract between its characters to be honoured, and, collaterally, the desire of its readers to be satisfied by the transmission of hidden knowledge. Yet is the contract honoured? Is there *transmissio studii* here or just comic nonsense? Does Mercure whisper a secret or merely babble? If there was a secret, Trigabus cannot understand it ('je ne sçay que tu dis') and his subsequent reactions point to the fact that the moment of desired contact was, like the Philosopher's Stone itself, perhaps only a fantasy, a 'songe' which is also a 'mensonge'. In the event the only 'message secret' with which Mercure is certainly entrusted is a *billet-doux* from Jupiter to an *innamorata*; and Mercure adds that he will also take the opportunity to see 'ma mye, devant que je retorne'. The reader's desire likewise remains frustrated or at least deferred, as the high poignancy of supreme cultural exchange falls into bathos; indeed it is undermined even before it happens, since these comments by Mercure precede the whispering of the 'secret'.

As Mercure disappears from the scene (only to reappear, like some Renaissance magus, in the following dialogue), the focus shifts to Trigabus, whose soliloquy closes the dialogue. Previously Trigabus had stood alongside Mercure, in what has been termed the outer frame, caustically commenting on the absurd activities of the *philosophes*. It is now clear in retrospect that he moves from the outer to the inner frame, drawn in by the lure of a secret, a privileged message that the text might hold for a favoured reader. Yet Trigabus wanted Mercure's secret for no high or noble purpose. He freely admits that he sought the god's magic powers of transformation simply to gain money and to promote his love affairs.[14] He openly interprets his encounter with Mercure as a failed opportunity for trickery and deception: 'O la bonne façon de masques que c'eust esté, s'il m'eust voulu dire les motz et qu'il ne m'eust point

---

13 Cf. Festugière, *La Révélation d'Hermès Trismégiste*, I. 317–19 ('Révélation reçue au cours d'un entretien avec un dieu').

14 On the association of Hermes Trismegistus with magic, see Festugière, *La Révélation d'Hermès Trismégiste*, I. 283–308; Yates, *Giordano Bruno*, pp. 44–61; Fowden, *The Egyptian Hermes*, pp. 79–87; Brian P. Copenhaver, 'Hermes Trismegistus, Proclus and the Question of a Philosophy of Magic in the Renaissance', in *Hermeticism and the Renaissance*, pp. 79–110.

abusé!' And his closing words then revert to expressly moral criteria by which to evaluate the preceding narrative events:

> Or je reviens à moy-mesmes et cognois que l'homme est bien fol, lequel s'attend avoir quelque cas de cela qui n'est point, et plus malheureux celuy qui espere chose impossible.

The terminology is of blindness followed by insight, ignorance enlightened by knowledge, taking leave of one's senses and returning to one's senses. The sentence is an unremarkable example of extrapolating from the particular to the universal, while its form and content recall *sententiae* and aphorisms. In intertextual terms, this sentence reverses a topos of the Hermetic Corpus, according to which the acolyte receives insight in a trance or an ecstasy: here, 'je reviens à moy-mesmes' is in implicit contrast with 'le fait d'être "sorti de soi"'[15] found in the Hermetica, and Trigabus' 'insight' comes only when he has returned to his senses, not when he has left them. Taking all these features together, it is tempting to treat this sentence as a metatextual gloss encapsulating the point of the dialogue. This final sentence would in that case have the status and the function of an authoritative *exemplum*, a court of final instance which delivers the verdict on the narrative events, imparts a message, and draws the episode to a close on a firm if negative note.

Nonetheless, we should be suspicious of the idea that the entire meaning of this episode reduces exclusively to the terms contained in Trigabus' *retour sur soi*. Three reasons might persuade us to exercise caution. For one thing, we can grant special status to Trigabus' words only by allowing that there *was* a revelation after all — not the revelation of Mercure's secret, but Trigabus' self-revelation, his awareness of his own folly. In a text which seems so ambiguous about revelations and secrets, it would be paradoxical to grant special status to one character among others, especially as that character has no further part to play in the work as a whole. Secondly, in allowing Trigabus' utterance to act as a commentary, we stay — paradoxically — within the realm of Hermetic influence. Marie-Madeleine de la Garanderie highlights the fact that in Budé's *De studio* Mercury dominates 'tous les aspects de la "science des lettres" (philologie, commentaire, herméneutique, etc.)', and she concludes: 'Et [Mercure] est forcément le patron de la Renaissance, puisque l'herméneutique et le commentaire sont alors la forme d'expression

---

15 Festugière, *La Révélation d'Hermès Trismégiste*, I. 313 (cf. pp. 312–17 for 'révélation au cours d'un songe ou d'une extase').

privilégiée.'[16] In glossing his situation, Trigabus remains under the influence of the very god he feels has deceived him. Finally, and not least, in looking for a message or secret readily extractable from this dialogue, the reader runs the risk of being likewise drawn into the ironical frame, of being the dupe of the textual snares and devices which have beguiled first the *philosophes* and then Trigabus.

The reader's task in Dialogue 2 is accordingly far from straightforward. Indeed, the difficulties in establishing the reliability and authority of Trigabus' final remarks betoken thornier problems in establishing their full hermeneutic implications. For if *Cymbalum Mundi* is indeed an allegory, then the reader might expect to be able to decode textual details with some reasonable degree of confidence; moreover, the very notion of a revelation, as exemplified in the present extract, would reinforce the Renaissance topos that 'la lecture est une opération de dévoilement'.[17] Yet this work presents no such easy decipherability; it simultaneously stimulates and blocks the exegetical process. The difficulty therefore lies in knowing precisely how far to allegorise or whether indeed allegorisation is the correct response. A case in point is Trigabus' comment on Mercure: 'qu'il ne m'eust point abusé.' The verb *abuser* echoes the term 'abuseur' in the very opening line of Dialogue 2, likewise applied to Mercure by Trigabus. Mercure is a trickster, a characteristic confirmed by the joke he plays on the *philosophes*. Should we allegorise this remark — in line with Lucien Febvre and others — as a satire of Christ, the divine messenger?[18] That interpretation remains uneasily on the horizon of the

---

16 Marie-Madeleine de la Garanderie, 'Le Nom de Mercure, signe du discours humaniste', in *Mercure à la Renaissance*, pp. 16 and 160 respectively. In *De studio literarum recte et commode instituendo*, Mercury is defined as 'Mercurius, id est priscarum literarum peritia' (ed. Marie-Madeleine de la Garanderie (Paris: Les Belles Lettres, 1988), p. 53).

17 Michel Jeanneret, *Le Défi des signes: Rabelais et la crise de l'interprétation à la Renaissance* (Orléans: Paradigme, 1994), p. 23.

18 See Lucien Febvre, 'Origène et Des Périers ou l'énigme du *Cymbalum Mundi*', *Bibliothèque d'Humanisme et Renaissance*, II (1942), 8–131, and Mayer, *Lucien de Samosate*, pp. 165–90, *passim*. For discussions of this identification, see V.-L. Saulnier, 'Le Sens du *Cymbalum Mundi* de Bonaventure des Périers', *Bibliothèque d'Humanisme et Renaissance*, XIII (1951), 137–71, esp. p. 145; Wolfgang Spitzer, 'The Meaning of Bonaventure des Périers' *Cymbalum Mundi*', *Publications of the Modern Languages Association of America*, LXVI (1951), 795–819, esp. pp. 795–801; Ian R. Morrison, 'The *Cymbalum Mundi* Revisited', *Bibliothèque d'Humanisme et Renaissance*, XXXIX (1977), 263–80, esp. 265–6; Wolfgang Boerner, *Das* Cymbalum Mundi *des Bonaventure des Périers: eine Satire auf die Redepraxis im Zeitalter der Glaubenspieler* (Munich: Wilhelm

text, a consequence of the inexorable logic of allegoresis which, once unleashed, can easily expand to engulf all characters and textual phenomena. In a similar way, Trigabus' words 'l'homme est bien fol, lequel s'attend avoir quelque cas de cela qui n'est point', might be taken to suggest a disbelief in any transcendental system, as symbolised by the Stone and Mercure's secret. But if the text seems to adumbrate that possibility, it does not sanction it as the unique reading, and such an interpretation remains one among others. The text teases and tricks; perhaps Mercure is not the only 'abuseur' in *Cymbalum Mundi*.

This in turn raises the whole issue of how to describe a work of this kind. Its interpretative difficulties are endemic to an apparently allegorical text which resists or evades the kind of *décryptage* it seemingly invites, and in which satire and irony play the principal rhetorical roles.[19] Various possibilities of interpretation appear either fleetingly amid the interstices of the text or as the logical outcome of the allegorical tendency. On a grave view, *Cymbalum Mundi* is a grimly ironic piece which progressively erodes any trust that the reader might place in interpretative activity (finding the Stone, learning the secret) or in a transcendent narrative standpoint (Mercure; Trigabus' moment of self-awareness). Yet this reading necessarily privileges one set of interpretative criteria over others and effectively dispenses with the comic perspective. The reader of Dialogue 2 and of *Cymbalum Mundi* as a whole is in fact uncomfortably caught in a double bind: if he or she treats the work as an allegorical satire, then he or she may fall foul of that desire for 'deeper meanings' which the text lampoons; on the other hand, to treat the text only as a comic polyphony without further implications would be to disregard those moments when it does gesture towards some totalising interpretation, with its accompanying vocabulary of moral instruction, enlightenment and self-awareness. If we opt for *prodesse*, we lose *delectare*; if we prefer *plaire*, we neglect *instruire*.

We should not infer from this, however, that frustration alone is the likeliest outcome of any attempt at interpretation of Dialogue 2; it does not follow that the search for epistemology will inevitably end in aporetics. On the contrary, such movement between multiple hermeneutic op-

---

Fink Verlag, 1980), pp. 192–6; Berriot, *Athéismes*, p. 674; Lauvergnat-Gagnière, *Lucien de Samosate*, pp. 269–72; Gauna, *Upwellings*, pp. 184–8. The parallel between Christ and Mercury occurs in Budé's *De asse* and in his *De transitu Hellenismus*.

[19] On the increasingly ambiguous status of allegory and its place in the exegetical process, see Jeanneret, *Le Défi des signes*, 'L'Exégèse à la Renaissance', pp. 21–31.

tions in this dialogue is fundamental to its *zététique*, allowing the dis-placement and re-inscription of demarcation lines between seriousness and comedy, instruction and pleasure, the offering and the withdrawal of meaning.[20] The implications of this activity are far-reaching, affecting how we derive epistemologies from a text, how we classify the data a text presents and how we follow the exegetical leads offered by rhetorical schemes such as allegory. Thus, if one concludes, in view of the rhetori-cal self-consciousness of *Cymbalum Mundi*, that Dialogue 2 lays bare, to satirical effect, the mechanisms by which texts lure their readers and interpreters into the hunt for a secret message, one must add that such mechanisms seem nevertheless crucial to the operation of texts: they can be demythologised, but they cannot be dispensed with. What is queried at the hermeneutic level remains central at the narrative level as an impetus to the very activity of reading.[21] It may be that this dialogue contains no ultimate message, nothing beyond the play of rhetorical devices and ploys — the text will not make that decision for us. Yet, as the remainder of *Cymbalum Mundi* amply demonstrates, the desire for such a message, for privileged access to a hidden core, for a new secret, often a curiosity or a novelty, remains undiminished, bearing witness to Montaigne's observation that 'il n'est desir plus naturel que le desir de connoissance. Nous essayons tous les moyens qui nous y peuvent mener.'[22] And per-haps this is only to be expected from a piece which takes place, according to one's interpretation, in either a theatre of conflict or a theatre of enter-tainment and which stands so manifestly under the sign of Hermes, god of secrets, of eloquence, and of lies.

---

[20] For a similar re-inscription of boundary lines, see Terence Cave, 'Imagining Scepticism in the Sixteenth Century', *Journal of the Institute of Romance Studies*, I (1992), 193–205.

[21] Cf. Jeanneret, *Le Défi des signes*, p. 16, where after speaking of 'l'ambiguïté des consignes de lecture et l'indétermination des signes', he is careful to concede: 'Patente ou latente, la volonté d'orienter la lecture jalonne les récits, en concurrence avec les stratégies de retrait.'

[22] Michel de Montaigne, *Essais*, ed. Pierre Villey et V.-L. Saulnier (Paris: PUF, 1965), III. 13, p. 1065.

4

Ronsard's Integrated Worlds:
Readings of *Amours* (1552–3), 37

Margaret McGowan

Les petitz corps, culbutans de travers,
  Parmi leur cheute en byaiz vagabonde
  Hurtez ensemble, ont composé le monde,
  S'entracrochans d'acrochementz divers.   4
L'ennuy, le soing, & les pensers ouvers,
  Chocquans le vain de mon amour profonde,
  Ont façonné d'une attache féconde,
  Dedans mon cuœur l'amoureux univers.   8
Mais s'il avient, que ces tresses orines,
  Ces doigtz rosins, & ces mains ivoyrines
  Froyssent ma vie, en quoy retournera   11
Ce petit tout? En eau, air, terre, ou flamme?
  Non, mais en voix qui tousjours de ma dame
  Par le grand Tout les honneurs sonnera.[1]   14

This sonnet is an early work which Ronsard included in his cycle of poems dedicated to Cassandre: *Les Amours* (1552–3). Written in decasyllables, the poem seems — at first sight — to offer a simple structure whose images and sound patterns are well harmonised and in which the argument flows in straightforward fashion through two paralleling quatrains; it is interrupted by a question at line nine which threatens to break the equilibrium that has been established, but which is abruptly and ingeniously resolved in the concentrated final two lines. The simplicity of the patterning, however, hides a wealth of reading, erudite reference, and linguistic renewal which — to judge from the commentaries of Muret and

---

[1] The poem is cited from the edition of H. & C. Weber, *Les Amours*, Classiques Garnier (Paris, 1963), p. 25, which also provides variants from all editions 1567–1587.

Belleau on Ronsard's early works [2] — contemporary writers (and possibly court audiences too) appreciated.

In this sonnet, a Renaissance view of the world and of man's place within it is reflected in order to put the reader in touch with the poet's feelings and especially to satisfy Ronsard's poetic ambitions of extending the evocation of individual experience beyond its temporal life back into a pre-time expanded sphere where creativity itself is caught in the process of shaping the universe.[3] The reader is asked to contemplate Epicurus' view of how the world was created out of its original chaos, and that world is evoked — in the first quatrain of Ronsard's poem — as it hustled into being: the tiny atoms in their pre-determined slanting trajectories tumble together, seemingly wayward yet cohering — 's'entracrochans d'acrochementz divers'. They created the world, however precarious and haphazard their wandering flight had seemed.[4]

There is no immediate explanation of this direct cosmic intrusion into a cycle of love poems. A sixteenth-century reader — accepting a theory of the universe in which the little world of man (the microcosm) faithfully reflected, and corresponded with, the larger world (the macrocosm) — would have anticipated the next moves in the poem.[5] Within the context of such a view of the world, the shift from the universe at large to creat-

---

2 These commentaries have been published in *Les Œuvres de Pierre de Ronsard: Texte de 1587*, Introduction and notes by Isidore Silver (University of Chicago Press, 1966), 2 volumes; volume I reproduces the commentaries of Antoine de Muret (pp. 115–16 for the sonnet under discussion), and volume II provides the annotations of Remy Belleau to Book II of the *Amours*.

3 The sense of divine mission, apparent throughout Ronsard's work, has been explored by many critics. See (for example) Isidore Silver in *The Intellectual Evolution of Ronsard*, 2 volumes (St Louis, 1973); the second volume, *Ronsard's General Theory of Poetry*, chapter xii, 'The Poet's Divine Mission' (pp. 402–45) is relevant; and Malcolm Quainton, *Ronsard's Ordered Chaos* (Manchester: Manchester University Press, 1980), particularly chapter 7, pp. 173–218.

4 The opening of the sonnet reproduces fairly faithfully the random falls of the atoms as described by Lucretius in the opening sections of Book II of *De rerum natura* (ll. 62–332) where he evokes atoms simply falling through the void like hail, now and then bumping into each other and sticking together, colliding with larger structures, dissolving and forming again. The intellectual context of Lucretius' work has recently been examined in James Miller's comprehensive book, *Measures of Wisdom: The Cosmic Dance in Classical and Christian Antiquity* (Toronto: University of Toronto Press, 1986), pp. 153 sqq.

5 Muret paraphrases Ronsard's poem and the opinion of Epicurus and his followers, buttressing his comments with multiple learned references to Empedocles, Epicurus, Lucretius, and Cicero.

ing an individual, inner sphere of love is a natural and perhaps inevitable one; yet, the pace of this new, second creation is quite different. In Ronsard's version of creation, the atoms which created Epicurus' universe sped fast, touched and stuck in a rush as they fell upon each other. The speed of contact and the immediacy of their action is caught in the poem through verbs like 'culbutans' and 'hurtez', and through a succession of sounds which repeat and echo each other and culminate in line four cited above.

In contrast (yet in parallel structure) the ingredients which make up the poet's world of love are introduced with a heavier beat, and the rhythm builds up more slowly over the quatrain to the words 'l'amoureux univers' which are kept to the last. The weighty tread of 'L'ennuy, le soing, & les pensers...' suggests a more deliberate and more painful creation. The deep emptiness which waits to be filled is gradually shaped and given being; and, once created, its existence seems firmly rooted, more permanent perhaps than the randomly created larger universe fashioned precariously by the atoms. The relationship between these two creations is clearly drawn not only by the echoing sounds and images with 'Chocquans' (line 6) recalling the sounds of line 4; 'attache féconde' (line 7) reminding us of 'acrochementz divers' (line 4); but also because each set of quatrains aims unambiguously towards creation: 'ont composé le monde' (line 3); 'Ont façonné...l'amoureux univers' (lines 7–8).[6] There are links in the making, though the wider cosmos here has no sentient character while the inner world has only feeling. Feelings are the stuff of *Les Amours* and thus, in the poem, 'l'amoureux univers' seems the more significant, and it derives some of its power too from the apparent reversal of the hierarchy which (conventionally) set man inside and subordinate to the universe.

Then comes the question which interrupts the creative powers which the poet's feelings have engendered and which threatens the very existence of the seemingly solid world they had created. What if the beguiling fingers of his mistress should unravel that which had so painfully been made? The tercets explore this possibility while, at the same time, carrying through to the end of the sonnet the idea of the two worlds — the small and the great — in competition with each other.

---

[6] For some discussion of the interrelation between sound patterns and content in Ronsard's poems, see Tom Conley's book *The Graphic Unconscious in Early Modern French Writing* (Cambridge: Cambridge University Press, 1992), especially chapter iv, pp. 91–115, 'The Turn of the Letter: from Cassandra to Hélène'.

The hypothesis is given a hesitant, searching, and almost reluctant formulation: 'Mais s'il avient, que...', suggesting perhaps that the threatened collapse and dissolution is not likely. Yet the busy, meddling fingers and the vibrant tresses of his mistress have enormous destructive power. Simply named, and characterised only by their colour whose sound is insistently repeated in 'orines', 'rosins', and 'ivoyrines',[7] they crush the life out of the poet, 'Froyssent ma vie' (line 11) — the strength of the verbs becoming further underscored by the *enjambement* and its positioning at the beginning of the line. The little world ('Ce petit tout') which seemed so substantial a moment ago is to dissolve (as the Great Universe might do were it to collapse) into the constituent elements on which life depends 'En eau, air, terre, ou flamme' (line 12). Although only the inner world is threatened, mention of the four elements keeps the larger universe in mind. Whilst the world of Epicurus could dissolve back into its natural parts (and, in Lucretius' account, it frequently did so in the process of creation), if the poet's world is to break, it will explode into a voice that will reverberate around 'le grand Tout', thus fusing and integrating both. At the end of the sonnet, the poet's voice fills the cosmos. His song preserves the world of love that feeling had created, its resonance will continue to ring through the wider universe which is also miraculously preserved by that same voice on which the poem ends, 'voix qui tousjours...sonnera' (lines 13–14).[8]

Ronsard's own readings of this poem over twenty years, between 1567 and the posthumous edition of the *Œuvres* in 1587, raise interesting questions of interpretation and taste.[9] The work of revision was continuous. Ronsard re-read his poems regularly and sought to render their rhythms smoother, more elegant and flowing. Thus, from 1578, the first line of the poem became 'Ces petits corps qui tombent de travers',

---

[7] Ronsard's use of these conventional terms is discussed by Louis Terreaux, *Ronsard, correcteur de ses œuvres* (Geneva: Droz, 1968), pp. 287, 346, and 376.

[8] The lasting power of the poet's voice became a major theme in the *Sonets pour Helene*. In his commentary on the poem, Muret shows how Ronsard deviates from the position of the ancient philosophers, who had argued that complex structures, when they decompose, revert to their original elements, by adding a new dimension: the poet's metamorphosis, after death, into a voice that continues to resonate around the world. This resonance implies that Love's power (and that of poetry) is greater than the movement of natural forces when they disintegrate.

[9] *Œuvres* 1567, 1578, 1584, and 1587 contain the most extensive variants; for their character, see H. & C. Weber's discussion (ed. cit., pp. xliv–lxxiv), Louis Terreaux's work, and the comments of Fernand Desonay, *Ronsard poète de l'amour*, 3 volumes (Brussels, 1969).

eliminating the picturesque 'culbutans', which had sharply visualised the movement of the atoms, and introducing the demonstrative adjective which assumed and drew on the reader's knowledge of Epicurus' system.[10] The same search for greater harmony reduced the number of echoing sound patterns; in this way, the second 'acrochementz' in line four is removed and replaced in all editions from 1567 by the more anodyne 's'entr'acrochans de liens tous divers'.[11] Some changes clarify, such as the late insertion of 'les pensers *couvers*' for 'ouvers', whose meaning was obscure; but other adjustments are more technical and, it can be argued, less happy in their effect. Systematically in his readings and revisions, Ronsard sought to suppress *enjambements*, to remove adjectives used as substantives,[12] and to replace concrete terms that implied precise images by more abstract words that let the rhythms flow free. In this poem, the striking line six — 'Chocquans le vain de mon amour profonde' — which conjured up the vast space of the poet's longing filled to bursting with the torment and weight of his feelings, is transformed into: 'Tombez espais en mon amour profonde', thus reducing the space and the pain.[13] Similarly, the powerful words 'froyssent ma vie' (line 11) disappear in favour of a more conventional rendering which (in place of the strong physical thrust of the first version) offers the traditional abstractions associated with love and pining: 'mort' and 'beauté', and which — more seriously — suppresses 'le petit tout' which had brought the original poem round full circle to mirror microcosm with the macrocosm. The conventional is even more marked in the final reading (1584/1587) where the words 'Rompent ma trame' are introduced underlining the fictional and more removed effect which the poem has now acquired. That same aesthetic process of simplification and rendering more abstract is emphasised yet further by the changes Ronsard made to the last line of the poem: first, in 1578, 'Par le grand Tout les honneurs sonnera' becomes 'Par l'univers crira la cruauté'; and then, in 1584, is changed to 'Accusera l'ingrate cruauté'. It will be apparent that the resonance of the poem has been significantly reduced; the poet's voice, which rang through the cosmos preserving images of man and the power of love, is transformed into the carping tones of the unhappy lover which shriek out his mistress's cruelty and ingratitude — those abstract

---

10 Terreaux (pp. 114 and 445) discusses these early changes to the poem.

11 Terreaux (pp. 345 and 579) supports the changes as avoiding repetition, but he does not comment on the aesthetic consequences.

12 See Terreaux, pp. 361–371.

13 H. & C. Weber also regret the modification, ed. cit., p. lii.

terms which were always given in the petrarchan tradition to the resistant lady by a rejected lover. A poem of general import, through the demands of ironing out rhythms and chastening the vocabulary, has acquired a more individual but less vibrant focus. Ronsard's final reading has been to produce a love poem which fits neatly into the frame he had created in his cycle of poems to Cassandre.

It was, of course, intended that we read the poem in the wider context of *Les Amours* and that we should pick up parallel structures and themes, variations on the same or similar topics. On this broader canvas, many aspects of interpretation are strengthened and clarified. The same thematic patterning, for example, can be found in 53[14] where, through the agency of Love, the ordering out of chaos which was 'Sans art, sans forme', in a comparison that is made explicit — 'Ainsi', is likened to the fashioning of the poet's self 'Sans art, sans forme, & sans figure entiere' (line 7). The tercets elaborate the shaping process through which the dance ('branle') of Love, which repeats the figures of the heavenly spheres,[15] determines the form of the poet's soul: 'Les pas suyviz du globe de mon ame.' The world 'globe', just like 'le tout' in sonnet 37, draws together in a single image and culminating moment the principal work and import of the poem. Part of the potency of both images is provided by the preparation which leads in each instance to the notions of a world either readily projected as a globe that can be turned by the hand or as a vast abstract entity waiting to be filled.

The theme of the tresses[16] which entice, flow around, and finally en-trap the poet's soul, and which Ronsard emphasises in his rewritings, is introduced early on in the Cassandre cycle. In Sonnet 3, for instance, Ronsard describes two parallel movements: first, the fiery impact of Love's shafts; and then, more expansively, the alluring dance of Cassandre's hair that tempts, entwines, and captures. Under this double attack, submission is accepted as inevitable and uncomplaining, summed up in a final, evenly-balanced line: 'Le feu me brusle, & l'or crespe me lie' (line 14).

---

[14] H. & C. Weber, ed. cit., pp. 34–5.

[15] For an examination of sixteenth-century beliefs in these correspondences, see my work *Le Ballet de cour en France, 1581–1643* (Paris, 1963).

[16] On the thematic approaches, see H. & C. Weber's introduction to the *Amours*, and in Henri Weber's discussion of the themes in 'La Poésie amoureuse de la Pléiade', chapter V of *La Création poétique au XVIe siècle* (Paris, 1956), pp. 231–398. The theme of the hair is specifically discussed pp. 262–73, 304–6.

In later poems of the collection, the trapping power of his mistress's hair is no longer a source of complaint. In sonnet 47, the tresses, perfumed and soft to the touch, are praised for their charm and for their capacity to enthral such that the poet willingly offers his neck to be caught and encircled as his soul melts into submission. The revised versions of the sonnet to Cassandre (37) had stressed the cruelty; yet the variation on this recurrent theme in *Amours diverses* (47) emphasises the poet's complete acquiescence in tones that are almost reverent:

> Et de voz nœuds crespez tout le col m'enserrer,
> Afin que prisonnier je vous puisse asseurer
> Que les liens du col sont les liens de l'ame.[17]
>
> (lines 12–14)

In the first versions of *Les Amours*, Ronsard exploited conventional sonnet structures to inflate the power of the feelings he was projecting; and so the reader participates, anticipating rhythms that build up to a crisis usually expressed through a verb with strong meaning such as 'froisser' or 'piller', for example. In 'Les petitz corps, culbutans de travers' (37), the rhythm of the tercets quickly led up to 'Froyssent ma vie'; in later sonnets in this same cycle to Cassandre, the verb *piller* is often kept to the last line. In 'L'homme est vraiment ou de plomb ou de bois' (205), a sequence of clauses introduced by *quand* leads inexorably to the final unequivocal statement that Cassandre's presence has the effect of 'Piller les cœurs de mile hommes qui passent', while in the previous poem, 'L'or crespelu, que d'autant plus j'honore', the rhythm, after an uninterrupted sweep to line 11, having halted, restarts and accelerates as the parts of the poet's body affected by the movement of the hair — 'mes sens, mes poumons, & ma voix' — are listed, and terminates on 'ils me pillerent'.[18]

In sonnet 37, Ronsard had taken a step beyond the articulation of the poet's distress and of the extent of his mistress's dominion over him. He had been concerned to exhibit the nature of the feelings aroused and to record the all-embracing power that had stirred them into life, first by catching in words the uncontrolled impulses of atoms in the universe and paralleling these with the elements of alarm that were moulded together to create a world of love deep within his soul. But then, he had introduced

---

[17] The first line of the poem (p. 479) gives the gentle, quiescent tone: 'Doux cheveux, doux present de ma douce Maistresse.'

[18] Ed. cit., pp. 127–8.

the voice of the poet and its reverberating power. It seems that, although the paralleling and the integration of 'le petit tout' into the larger globe of the universe ('le grand tout') provided the initial idea, it is the power of song that ensures preservation and renewal. In poems dedicated to Hélène de Surgères, Ronsard took a further step.[19] Book II, sonnet 20, 'Yeux, qui versez en l'ame, ainsi que deux Planettes', assumes the same correspondences between the two worlds of man and of the universe, but the powers of the latter are transferred. Hélène usurps the beneficial effects that belong to the harmony of the spheres, and by becoming a second sun, she performs magical effects, 'des miracles en moy' (as Ronsard puts it, line 6), which so transform the poet's being that he is blinded to all feeling and perception. The final line of the poem sums up the metamorphosis: 'Ayant en moy l'effect qu'a le Soleil au monde' (line 14).[20]

If one reads across the collection of *Les Amours*, then the nature and the extent of the challenge which Ronsard had set himself emerge very clearly and have an impact on the way an individual poem in the sequence may be viewed. The twin themes of microcosm/macrocosm, the capturing potential of the poet's mistress, and the reverberating power of poetry as an expression of love (which provided the material for sonnet 37) recur many times. On most occasions, the search is for renewal and variation and for extending the image which occasionally is so ingenious that the poem is stretched beyond its capacity to persuade.[21]

Ronsard sought as much the admiration of his reader as he did of his mistresses, and in displaying his astonishing range, he patently tried to balance variety and ingenuity with density and rhythmic innovation. That he was aware of the difficulty of the challenge may be seen from a comment he made in a *Chanson* dedicated to Olivier de Magny where of love

---

[19] The triumph of poetry and of the poet's voice is the main theme of Jean M. Fallon's persuasive book, *Voice and Vision: Ronsard's Sonnets pour Hélène* (New York, 1993). The argument is built on a phrase taken from book II, 73, 'croyez ceste escriture', and although the poet as writer emerges supreme, traces of his love are for ever embedded in the very nature and process of poetry.

[20] Ed. cit., p. 429. The fusion of a woman and cosmic force is a frequent theme in Ronsard's love poems.

[21] See, for example, sonnet 67, 'Ciel, air & vents, plains & montz descouvers', where the images unrelentingly evoked through lists of things that might speak on the poet's behalf are all repeated in the final tercet and are thus drained of effect:

Je vous supply, Ciel, air, ventz, montz & plaines,
   Tailliz, forestz, rivages & fontaines,
   Antres, prez, fleurs, dictes le luy pour moy.

and its character, Ronsard observed: 'C'est peindre en l'eau, c'est vouloir encore / Tenir le vent....' The danger of his song disappearing or of the effects of love left unarticulated seems remote as, four centuries after his death, readers are still drawn to read, analyse, and interpret the *Amours*. Yet Ronsard's fears clearly lingered (perhaps only to be refuted by us), as the sentiments addressed to Magny are repeated almost without varia-tion in the *Elégie* to Hélène added to the collection in 1584:

> Et que mettre son cœur aux Dames si avant,
> C'est vouloir peindre en l'onde, & arrester le vent.[22]

(lines 63–4)

---

[22] Ed. cit., p. 485.

5

Invitation to Love, Invitation to Poetry: Ronsard's Multi-Layered Text

George Hugo Tucker

Quand vous serez bien vieille, au soir à la chandelle,
Assise aupres du feu, devidant & filant,
Direz, chantant mes vers, en vous esmerveillant,
Ronsard me celebroit du temps que j'estois belle.   4
    Lors vous n'aurez servante oyant telle nouvelle,
Desja sous le labeur à demy sommeillant,
Qui au bruit de Ronsard [de mon nom *1584/87*] ne s'aille resveillant,
Benissant vostre nom de louange immortelle.   8
    Je seray sous la terre, & fantaume sans os
Par les ombres Myrtheux je prendray mon repos:
Vous serez au fouyer une vieille accroupie,   11
    Regrettant mon amour, & vostre fier desdain.
Vivez, si m'en croyez, n'attendez à demain:
Cueillez dés aujourdhuy les roses de la vie.   14

       (Ronsard, *Le Second Livre des Sonets pour Helene*, XXIV (1578))

Sexuality and Textuality: Layers of Illusion and Delusion

'S'abuser en amour n'est pas mauvaise chose.' These are the words that immediately preceded the above sonnet in all three of the original editions of Ronsard's *Sonnets pour Helene* appearing in 1578, 1584, and 1587.[1]

---

[1] The sonnet was numbered XXIV in the *Second Livre* of the first edition of the *Sonnets pour Helene* appearing in 1578 (in the fifth collective edition of Ronsard's *Œuvres*) — as later, in Ronsard, *Œuvres complètes*, ed. P. Laumonier, rev. and completed by I. Silver and R. Lebègue, STFM, 20 vols (Paris: Hachette/Droz/Didier, 1914–75), XVII[2] (1959), 265–6, and in *Les Amours*, ed. H. and C. Weber, Classiques Garnier (Paris: Garnier Frères, 1963), pp. 431–2. It was re-numbered (with a variant in l. 8) in the second and third editions of the collection, becoming sonnet XLIII in Ronsard's *Œuvres* of 1584 (sixth collective edition) — as in *Œuvres complètes*, ed. J. Céard, D. Ménager, and M. Simonin, Bibliothèque de la Pléiade, 2 vols (Paris: Gallimard, 1993–4), I (1993), 400–1 — and then sonnet XLII in the posthumous *Œuvres* of 1587 (seventh collective edition), whose

In that late amatory collection — or compilation[2] — they constituted the closing verse of the previous poem ('Ces longues nuicts d'hyver, où la Lune ocieuse'), functioning there as a lucid, ironic comment by the poet upon a recurring dream vividly recalled: over long winter nights his vision of his mistress during his sleep had repeatedly afforded him complete fulfilment of his erotic desire for her ('Rien ne m'est refusé') despite its illusory nature. Indeed, Ronsard's paradoxical, oneiric possession of his beloved is even deemed preferable by him in that sonnet to his customary experience of her in waking reality ('Vraye tu es farouche, & fiere en cruauté'). The poet's closing acknowledgement of the complexity of his relation to the object of his desire, consciously celebrated as a phantasm of his (male) erotic, and then poetic, imagination — as a fictional creation outweighing any real, tangible experience of the (female) other — also serves as a pertinent epigraph for our sonnet, which it introduces. The ironies and complexities of this poem have likewise been recognised by critics.[3]

Ostensibly 'Quand vous serez bien vieille' functions as an invitation to love, as an urgent attempt by the poet-lover to overcome his mistress's haughty 'cruauté' and persuade her instead to consummate their love in the living present. Indeed, the concrete opportunities of this present seem now to take precedence over the sorts of consolation hitherto available in dreams. The literary suitor's chosen method of persuasion is a commonplace of Renaissance love poetry inherited from classical models: an intimidating evocation of future regret in old age for lost opportunities for

---

ordering and text is followed in Ronsard, *Sonnets pour Helene*, ed. R. Sorg, Collection des Chefs-d'œuvre méconnus (Paris: Bossard, 1921) and in *Sonnets pour Helene*, ed. M. C. Smith, TLF (Geneva: Droz, 1970).

[2] See Smith (ed.), Ronsard, *Sonnets pour Helene*, p. 19 (n. 5) on the 'caractère factice du recueil' — a view supported by M. Dassonville, 'Avatars des *Sonnets pour Hélène*', *Œuvres & Critiques* VI, 2 (Hiver, 1981–2) — *Le poète et ses lecteurs: le cas Ronsard*, 95–9 (p. 96).

[3] Notably, D. Stone, *Ronsard's Sonnet Cycles: A Study in Tone and Vision* (New Haven and London: Yale University Press, 1966), pp. 8–12. More generally, on the ironies and complexities of the Hélène cycle, viewed as an anti-Petrarchist collection, see G. Castor, 'Petrarchism and the Quest for Beauty in the *Amours* of Cassandre and the *Sonets pour Helene*', in *Ronsard the Poet*, ed. T. Cave (London: Methuen & Co, 1973), 79–120, pp. 99–120; Castor observes (p. 99) that 'With the *Sonets pour Helene*...the use which Ronsard makes of the petrarchan conventions and the attitudes which his poetry evinces seem to have shifted quite markedly and to have become altogether more complex and more ambivalent than they were in the *Amours*'. The more complex, anti-Petrarchist thesis is supported by Dassonville, 'Avatars', pp. 97–8.

love-making in youth.[4] Such *terre à terre* argument may be in keeping with the consistent anti-Neoplatonic stance of Ronsard's erotic aesthetic in this collection as elsewhere.[5] However, its manipulative presentation of the future is complicated in this poem by the insertion (in the first tercet) of a competing vision — equally traditional and equally classical — of the poet-lover's future, incorporeal after-life in Elysium.[6]

Moreover, the blessed state of poetic immortality that Ronsard thus briefly imagines for himself is predicated, at least in part, upon the future recitation of his verse and pronunciation of his name by the aged Hélène in the presence of her startled maid-servants. Indeed, the scene of Hélène's eventual old age, initially sketched out in the quatrains, can be seen to function incidentally as an emblematic representation of Ronsard's posthumous poetic fame, complete with its picture of an amazed as well as regretful Hélène and its caption: 'Ronsard me celebroit du temps que j'estois belle.' The question of the poet's suit for Hélène's elusive amatory favours is thus made immediately subordinate to the boast of the actual poetic ones already being bestowed by him upon the youthful Hélène. Furthermore, the very condition for Ronsard's writing in the first place has been, and ever must be, the frustration, not the fulfilment, of his desire for his mistress.

Therefore, what purports to be an urgent invitation to love under the threat of eventual old age may be no such thing. In fact, 'Quand vous serez bien vieille' displaces the desired act of love with an act of poetry, whose benefits are apparently to be appreciated in the long term, bestowing an immortality of sorts upon the poet-lover, if not upon his youthful, privileged subject as well. The young Hélène may well have been the indifferent inspirer and unwitting beneficiary of such poetry; in the end, however, when her youth has faded, she will be tempted to participate in that poetry — to re-create it — as an interested future reader, even performer. Indeed, one is led to wonder whether Hélène's imagined future *regret* as an old woman may be not so much for Ronsard's past love ('mon amour') as for his past celebration of her, which she strives to perpetuate in her 'singing' ('chantant mes vers').

---

4 Renaissance and classical examples of this topos are discussed below (cf. notes 14–19).

5 On which, see A. H. T. Levi, 'The Role of Neoplatonism in Ronsard's Poetic Imagination', in Cave (ed.), *Ronsard the Poet*, 121–58, pp. 128–37, and Dassonville, 'Avatars', p. 98.

6 The classical models for this in Tibullus and Ovid are discussed below (cf. notes 21, 23).

Thus, behind the desire for the immediate consummation of love in the realm of the physical and the ephemeral looms large the opposing desire for poetry and poetic immortality in the realm of Art — a desire realised in the very creation of the text of 'Quand vous serez bien vieille' itself, as in the rest of Ronsard's anti-Petrarchist and anti-Neoplatonist *Sonets pour Helene*, the purpose of whose composition was to outdo the rival Petrarchist and Neoplatonist love-poet Philippe Desportes.[7] Moreover, if in this particular sonnet multiple layers of illusion and delusion about love and love poetry are immediately apparent and invite exploration, love serving as a semi-transparent cover for love poetry,[8] this is no less true of the poem's multiple layers of intertextuality, to which we must now turn.

Text and Intertexts

Ronsard's relentless predictions in this piece set up, quite patently, a competitive relation between the poet, his poetry and future glory on the one hand, and the beloved, her beauty and future domesticity on the other hand. The somewhat barbed opposition between the poet's ageless repose amongst the shades of love poets in the Underworld and Hélène's continuing busyness in old age, among her maids, in the labour of spinning, is hardly flattering to his mistress. At the level of this surface read-ing of the text the implication is more generally one of the superiority of the (male) poetic activity over the (female) domestic one, the former having assured its exponent a privileged afterlife in Elysium. That said, the opposition with Hélène's spinsterly activities becomes markedly ironic as well as uncomplimentary when explored intertextually, for the image of spinning had traditionally been used as a metaphor for the ac-tivity of poetic composition itself. For example, Horace had boasted in his *Odes* of 'having spun out song' ('carmen...deduxisse'), a metaphor also applied by Virgil to the 'spun-out song' ('deductum...carmen') of his *Eclogues*, as it would be later by Ronsard's poetic rival (before Desportes), Joachim Du Bellay, to the Latin love poetry of his *Poemata*

---

7 On this generally, see Levi, 'The Role of Neoplatonism', pp. 135–7, and Dassonville, 'Avatars', pp. 96–8. Cf. also Ronsard, *Sonnets pour Helene*, ed. Smith, pp. 148–9, for the precise textual and intertextual link with Desportes furnished by the image of the 'vieille accroupie'; cf. below, n. 17.

8 The confusion of love(r) and love-poet(ry) is a traditional feature inherited from Roman love elegy.

(1558).[9] Indeed, Du Bellay had similarly placed the vernacular love poetry of his pioneering Petrarchist sonnet sequence *L'Olive* (1549; 1550) under the aegis of Minerva, patron goddess of the distaff, and so, by implication, firmly in the realm of technical artistic labour. Significantly, therefore, Hélène's imagined literal spinning of wool in her dotage is of an order quite different from that of Ronsard's past, metaphorical, artistic 'spinning' of verse in celebration of her youthful beauty. Indeed, the divorce between the two seems to be brought all the more home to Hélène in her own 'singing' of Ronsard's verse, with which she accompanies her labours ('devidant & filant'), and whose effect is to inspire in her an emotion approaching disbelief ('en vous esmerveillant').

A stranger to the poetic image that Ronsard has woven of her in her youth, the aged Hélène is also an ironised figure of destiny, recalling the 'spinning' one of the Fates: in the end she will have 'spun out' the course of her own destiny quite literally, in implicit contrast with Ronsard, who, for example, would later boast in his *Derniers vers* of having done so poetically, to the glory of his name and fame:

> C'est fait j'ay devidé le cours de mes destins,
> J'ay vescu j'ay rendu mon nom assez insigne...[10]

In this last respect it is worth noting also that in both the earlier and later versions of 'Quand vous serez bien vieille' it will be the mention of Ronsard's famed name itself ('Ronsard'/'mon nom') that will awaken the sleeping maid-servants and inspire them to bless the juxtaposed name ('vostre nom') of their mistress. Her fame may have been assured in its turn (being now 'de louange immortelle'), but only by virtue of Ronsard's fame,[11] and through a poetic image that no longer corresponds to what she is, dating as it does from the time of her beauty ('du temps que j'estois belle').

It should not be forgotten, of course, that the divorce between the time of Hélène's youth and the time of her old age, cruelly juxtaposed by the poet-lover, is as much an imaginative construct of the poet's as the pro-

---

9 Horace, *Odes* III. 30. 13–14; Virgil, *Eclogues* 6. 3–8; Joachim Du Bellay, *Poemata* (1558) I. 6. 61–2. Cf. G. H. Tucker, *The Poet's Odyssey: Joachim Du Bellay and the* Antiquitez de Rome (Oxford: Clarendon Press, 1990), p. 28.

10 'Sonets', VI. 5–6 ('Il faut laisser maisons & vergers & Jardins'), in Laumonier (ed.), Ronsard, *Œuvres complètes*, XVIII. 180–1.

11 Cf. Stone, *Ronsard's Sonnet Cycles*, p. 8: 'It is through Ronsard that Hélène's name will continue to be sung.'

jected divorce between his noble poetic destiny and her ignoble mortal one. Furthermore, this fiction of a future hindsight on Hélène's part from the perspective of old age is even used to confirm spuriously (as if prophetically true) the Epicurean wisdom of Ronsard's eventual command (in the final two verses) that she should live for the day and 'pluck the roses of life' immediately. This forceful advice from the (equally fictional) poet-lover could hardly be called disinterested, and invites the question, 'Who is plucking whom?'. In addition, the discrepancy between this double exhortation and the multiple intertexts that it recalls only serves to underscore the ironies and duplicities of Ronsard's ruse.

For example, the Horatian poem (*Odes* I. 11. 8) that similarly concluded with the famous advice to a girl, Leuconoë, to 'pluck the day' ('carpe diem') had opened by dissuading her from seeking to know either of their respective futures — a tactic quite the opposite of Ronsard's opening gambit, which is to sketch out manipulatively his own and Hélène's eventual destinies.[12] Likewise, another famous classical intertext — Catullus's exhortation to Lesbia, in the first person plural, that they should both 'live and love' (Catullus 5. 1: 'Vivamus, mea Lesbia, atque amemus') — had placed a very different emphasis on the shared enjoyment of erotic pleasure in the time of youth and in defiance of the crabbed, hypocritical disapproval of old men.[13] In Ronsard's sonnet such a sense of youthful complicity between the lovers is absent, replaced by an older man's lecturing of a younger woman, whom he threatens with the prospect of an old age from which he, the older poet, will have escaped by then.

The scenario is a familiar one, carefully reworked and condensed by Ronsard from an earlier ode 'A sa Maistresse' ('Jeune beauté, mais trop outrecuidée / Des presens de Venus...'), where the conjuring up of the young woman's future regret is the main manipulative strategy, and where the poet-lover's desire for revenge (even more than for conquest) is the prime motivation.[14] In Ronsard's sonnet the poet may well anticipate being dead by the time Hélène is old, but the marked difference in their ages is further suggested in the idiomatic qualification of 'Vivez' by 'si m'en croyez', suggesting a suitor endowed with superior wisdom and

---

[12] Horace, *Odes*, I. 11. 1–2: 'Tu ne quaesieris — scire nefas — quem mihi, quem tibi / finem di dederint, Leuconoë...'

[13] Catullus, 5. 2–3: 'rumoresque senum severiorum / omnes unius aestimemus assis.'

[14] Ronsard, *Le Troisième Livre des Odes*, XIII, in Ronsard, *Œuvres complètes*, ed. cit., Bibliothèque de la Pléiade, I. 761–2.

greater experience. Indeed, Ronsard had used this idiomatic device to similar effect in that other, more famous 'Ode à Cassandre', 'Mignonne, allons voir si la rose', which had at least begun with an exhortation in the first person plural (as in Catullus's poem). Like Ronsard's sonnet, however, this earlier ode concluded with a transparently self-interested imperative, 'Cueillez cueillez vostre jeunesse' (l. 16), whose familiar metaphor was likewise reinforced by mention of the woman's inevitable old age (ll. 17–18: 'Comme à ceste fleur la vieillesse / Fera ternir vostre beauté'), and by the assumption of a personal, prophetic authority (l. 13: 'si vous me croyez, mignonne').[15]

Editors and critics have noted and disputed many other possible classical and vernacular intertexts that serve only to amplify the literary resonances of the closing figurative command of Ronsard's sonnet: 'Cueillez...les roses de la vie.'[16] However, it is the suggestion of vindictiveness on the part of Ronsard's frustrated poet-lover that is of particular interest here. It informs the sonnet's conclusion in the immediate wake of the startling vehemence that momentarily erupts in the previous two verses (ll. 11–12); these portray Hélène as a regretful old crone crouching by the fire ('au fouyer une vieille accroupie') — a striking image of old age also developed by Ronsard's rival, Desportes, in conflation with Tibullus's portrait of his Delia's aged chaperone busy at her spinning and surrounded by her sleepy maids (*Elegies* I. 3. 83–8). The difference with Ronsard's poem is that the aged companion of the beloved has now become, ironically, the beloved herself.[17]

This aggressive, ironic evocation of old age is very different indeed from Petrarch's representation of the future time of Laura's grey hairs as

---

15 Ronsard, *Le Premier Livre des Odes*, XVII, in Ronsard, *Œuvres complètes*, ed. cit., Bibliothèque de la Pléiade, I. 667.

16 Notably, Ausonius, *Idylls*, 'De rosis nascentibus' 49–50 ('Collige, virgo, rosas, dum flos novus et nova pubes...'); Tibullus, *Elegies* I. 8. 41–8, emphasising the futile regret for the flower of youth, when it is lost all too soon, whose theme and flower metaphor are also developed by Ronsard in one of his *pièces retranchées* (cut out in 1578) from the *Second Livre des Amours* [VI]: 'Je vous envoye un bouquet, que ma main', in Ronsard, *Œuvres complètes*, ed. cit., Bibliothèque de la Pléiade, I. 270. On this and other intertexts, see the notes on 'Quand vous serez bien vieille' in the following: Ronsard, *Œuvres complètes*, ed. cit., Bibliothèque de la Pléiade I. 1391; *Œuvres complètes*, ed. Laumonier, XVII[2], 265–7; *Les Amours*, ed. H. & C. Weber, p. 757; and *Sonnets pour Helene*, ed. Smith, pp. 148–9. See also Smith (ed.) on *Sonnets pour Helene*, I. 62 (ed. cit., pp. 99–100), listing numerous classical and vernacular intertexts for this topos.

17 See Ronsard, *Œuvres complètes*, ed. cit., Bibliothèque de la Pléiade, ad loc. (I. 1391); and *Sonnets pour Helene*, ed. Smith, ad loc. (pp. 148–9).

a possible locus of consolation and reconciliation in *Canzoniere* 12 ('Se la mia vita da l'aspro tormento / Si può tanto schermire e dagli affanni'). Rather, it seethes with a resentment and menacing violence that recalls Propertius's wish for a painfully regretful age to befall his cruel Cynthia (*Elegies* III. 25. 11–18), or Ronsard's similar curse upon Hélène in *Sonets* I. 56 [62] ('Je ne veux point la mort de celle qui arreste / Mon cœur en sa prison...'), which had likewise concluded that 'Les beautez en un jour s'en-vont comme les Roses'(l. 14). Editors have even noted a witty parallel with another possible intertext: Horace's pederastic ode to the cruel boy Ligurinus (*Odes* IV. 10), where the vindictive wish of the poet for his uncompliant beloved is not so much hoary old age as hairy manhood (thus providing an ironic counterpoint to the standard topos).[18] However, a more damning and more consonant Horatian intertext would be the scornful and vengeful diatribe against the ageing beauty Lydia (*Odes* I. 25), already less besieged by young men, and soon to be (so the poet predicts) a weeping, frustrated, and regretful old woman, locked out in the cold north wind like one of her erstwhile suitors. The intertextual link with Ronsard's sonnet is underpinned in the ode's closing stanza, which associates the aged Lydia with withered leaves consigned to the winter's wind, of little interest to the carefree young, who delight more in the green ivy-leaf of Bacchus and the dark myrtle of Venus.[19]

The joyful, youthful, amatory associations of the myrtle lend a further point to Ronsard's preceding self-depiction (l. 10) as taking his rest in Elysium among the 'myrtled' shades of deceased love-poets. Editors have invariably pointed to possible echoes of the myrtle grove ('myrtea... / silva') of a less happy, more gloomy part of the Virgilian Under-world, in which tragic lovers (including Dido, after her abandonment by Aeneas and subsequent suicide) are condemned to roam.[20] However, in Tibullus, *Elegies* I. 3, the myrtle furnishes the distinctive garlands ('myrtea serta') proudly worn by young men, the deceased yet eternally youthful poet-lovers, caught by Death in the midst of their loving and their love-poetry — and still making such love and love-poetry in Elysium; the ailing love-elegist Tibullus anticipates joining their number, should he succumb to his illness whilst abroad and away from his

---

[18] The view on 'Quand vous serez bien vieille' in Ronsard, *Œuvres complètes*, ed. cit., Bibliothèque de la Pléiade, I. 1391.

[19] Horace, *Odes* I. 25. 17–20: 'laeta quod pubes hedera virenti / gaudeat pulla magis atque myrto, / aridas frondes hiemis sodali / dedicet Euro.'

[20] Virgil, *Aeneid*, VI. 440–55.

beloved Delia.[21] Pointedly, also, for Tibullus in the same elegy (in contrast with Ronsard's sonnet and the gloomy scene of its second quatrain), the alternative scenario ardently wished for by the love-poet, should he recover, is his joyful, unannounced safe return to Delia; he hopes to surprise her as she waits for him faithful and chaste (like Ulysses' Penelope) in the company of her aged, weaving chaperone and assisting, sleepy maidens.[22]

Significantly, also, it is the immediate classical intertext of this Tibullan intertext, one directly relating to it, that provides a helpful gloss upon Ronsard's ghostly evocation of himself as 'fantaume sans os' — and so, upon an emphatic, strangely tautologous detail which appears to qualify the French love-poet's assumption of a continuing, hedonistic, quasi-corporeal after-life awaiting him in the poet-lovers' Elysium. Alluding to Tibullus's elegy, Ovid in his own *Amores* (III. 9) concluded a lament for the recently deceased Tibullus with moving speculation about his fellow love-poet's possible afterlife in Elysium in the company of the other love-elegists (including the ivy-crowned Catullus): that is, 'if anything remains of us other than a name and a shade' (ll. 59–60: 'Si tamen e nobis aliquid nisi nomen et umbra / restat'), or (more drastically) 'if only there survives the shade of the body' (l. 65: 'Siqua est modo corporis umbra'), whose solid bones by contrast remain buried in a funeral urn and invite Ovid's compassionate prayer for their safe rest.[23] If Ronsard imagines himself as surviving also in Elysium in the boneless shade of his body, apart from in his name and fame, implicitly it will be like the deceased Tibullus pictured by the mourning Ovid.

The contrast between Ronsard's hedonistic, amatory 'repose' and Hélène's imagined lot in the preceding quatrain could not be greater, just as that unflattering representation of her enfeebled future is pointedly at odds with the Tibullan intertext, already noted, distorting as it does the pleasant image of the Roman love-elegist's longed-for, joyful reunion with Delia. Indeed, the note of menace, and the contrasting, depressing sense of a perpetuated, unbridgeable divide between the French love-poet and his beloved, resonates in sympathy with a competing classical intertext, also supplied by Ovid, *Heroides* 19.

This elegiac letter by Hero to her lover Leander, for whom she is anxiously waiting, and of whose drowning in the Hellespont (as he swam to

---

21 Tibullus, *Elegies* I. 3. 57–66.
22 Tibullus, *Elegies* I. 3. 83–94, mentioned above.
23 Ovid, *Amores* III. 9. 67–8: 'ossa quieta, precor, tuta requiescite in urna, / et sit humus cineri non onerosa tuo.'

join her) she is as yet unaware, supplies in its turn a tragic female voice of desire for a lost lover — one which might correspond putatively to the silent thoughts of the regretful Hélène, still coming to terms with her lost opportunity for Ronsard's love in her youth. Like Hélène, Hero 'beguiles the slow hours of waiting' with the 'woman's art of weaving' (ll. 37–8) — and no less futilely so. Hero is also accompanied by a servant, an aged nurse, upon whom slumber steals in the process, whilst she (like Hélène) speaks aloud of her beloved (ll. 45–6). Indeed, as in Ronsard's preceding sonnet, night has brought for Hero an illusory, erotic dream of her lover, as she herself succumbs to sleep (ll. 55–66). The scene of Hero's lonely vigil is similarly graced by a light, the agreed signal for Leander to come (ll. 35–6), whose sputtering may portend his imminent arrival (l. 151), but whose hopeful promise is qualified by her memory of a previous, ominous dream that had come to her (on dozing from her spinning) at dawn, when dreams are wont to be true (ll. 191–204). As with Hélène, too, Hero's frustrated waiting generates a poetic performance (the composition of her elegiac epistle), which must act as a substitute for the lover's presence, but which, as she knows only too well, cannot deliver him to her. Indeed, for Hero, as for the aged Hélène, reunion has in fact already been made an impossibility through a death which still has to make its impact upon her.

Ultimately, the intertext supplied by Ovid's *Heroides* amplifies a major irony latent in the French poet's textual posturing at erotic engagement with a female other. The figure of Hélène imagined in the guise of Ovid's isolated tragic heroine Hero (rather than of Tibullus's beloved Delia) may be seen to function as a mirror image of the male love-poet himself lucidly indulging in the phantasm of a love whose consummation is ever awaited yet ever displaced by the accompanying weaving of both wool, poetry, and a destiny of sorts. In contrasting Hélène's decrepit, spinsterly, reflective lot in a future old age with his own future privileged poetic and erotic immortality, and in so warning her of the consequences of her present resistance to him, Ronsard has in fact created no more than a figure of his own poetic self, albeit a feminised one. Moreover, it is neither safely ensconced in Elysium, nor even 'living and loving', but deluding and consoling itself with the wiles of poetry.

For the shadowy, Narcissistic figure that is the love-poet of 'Quand vous serez bien vieille' as much as for his auto-erotic counterpart, the persona of the dreamer-lover in the previous sonnet, 'S'abuser en amour' is all that really counts.[24] The actual, physical enjoyment of the other is either an impossibility or an irrelevance — an empty space inviting, perhaps inexorably, the self-reflexive gaze of the self-involved, self-projecting poet.[25]

---

24 A conclusion which coincides in part with that of Stone, *Ronsard's Sonnet Cycles*, p. 224: 'the poet himself counted for little his sources of inspiration as long as the immortal, poetic monument was secure.'

25 Cf. O. de Mourgues, 'Ronsard's Later Poetry', in *Ronsard the Poet*, ed. Cave, 287–318, p. 314, commenting on this sonnet and other late Ronsardian texts: 'More than once Ronsard looks at himself at a distance measured by pride and intimations of future glory.'

6

Ronsard and Yeats

Elizabeth Guild

Thiard, chacun disoit à mon commencement
Que j'estoi trop obscur au simple populaire:
Aujourd'hui, chacun dit que je suis au contraire,
Et que je me dements parlant trop bassement.   4
   Toi, qui as enduré presqu'un pareil torment,
Di moi, je te suppli, di moi que doi-je faire?
Di moi, si tu le sçais, comme doi-je complaire
A ce monstre testu, divers en jugement?   8
   Quand j'escri haultement, il ne veult pas me lire,
Quand j'escri bassement, il ne fait qu'en médire:
De quel estroit lien tiendrai-je, ou de quels clous,   11
   Ce monstrueux Prothé, qui se change à tous cous?
Paix, paix, je t'enten bien: il le faut laisser dire,
Et nous rire de lui, comme il se rit de nous.   14

(Ronsard, 1555)

   Tyard, on me blasmoit à mon commencement
Dequoy j'estois obscur au simple populaire:
Mais on dit aujourd'huy que je suis au contraire,
Et que je me dements parlant trop bassement.   4
   Toy, de qui le labeur enfante doctement
Des livres immortels, di moi, que doi-je faire?
Di moi (car tu scais tout) comme doi-je complaire
A ce monstre testu, divers en jugement?   8
   Quand je tonne en mes vers, il a peur de me lire:
Quand ma voix se desenfle, il ne fait qu'en mesdire:
Dy-moy de quel lien, force, tenaille, ou clous   11
Tiendray-je ce Proté, qui se change a tous coups?
Tyard, je t'enten bien: il le faut laisser dire,
Et nous rire de lui, comme il se rit de nous.   14

(Ronsard, 1584)[1]

---

[1] P. de Ronsard, *Œuvres completes*, ed. P. Laumonier (Paris: Librairie Hachette, 1934), VII. 115–6. I have given two texts, from the first edition and the edition of 1584, because at least two of Yeats's editors (Albright and Jeffares) appear to be

At the Abbey Theatre

(Imitated from Ronsard)

Dear Craoibhin Aoibhin, look into our case.
When we are high and airy hundreds say
That if we hold that flight they'll leave the place,
While those same hundreds mock another day   4
Because we have made our art of common things,
So bitterly, you'd dream they longed to look
All their lives through into some drift of wings.
You've dandled them and fed them from the book   8
And know them to the bone; impart to us —
We'll keep the secret — a new trick to please.
Is there a bridle for this Proteus
That turns and changes like his draughty seas?   12
Or is there none, most popular of men,
But when they mock us, that we mock again?

(Yeats)[2]

The first of these two sonnets about reception and the poet's relations with his public cannot be described as welcoming the reader. What reader other than Tyard would Ronsard consider worthy of his poetry?

Well, let us suppose that Ronsard might have considered Yeats a competent reader, a man of honour who would not let him down, always be asking for more, or for what was not on offer. He has the credentials, after all: a fellow poet; prolific; a brother in the desire for, and working towards, national cultural renewal; a lover of myths; canonised, for his sublimity. Here, it seems, Ronsard has even met his match.

And I? An academic reader, a latecomer, in what sense could I be competent? Perhaps precisely by being like neither a member of the audiences pilloried in both Ronsard's and Yeats's sonnets, nor the intended reader, the desired reader, the brother, the like-minded one. Not Protean, nor monstrously many-headed (*testu(e)* in Huguet means only that: *pourvu de testes*); but, taking my cue from a shift in meaning in *testu* as it crossed the Channel, and arrived at Cotgrave's door: 'testie, headie, headstrong, wilfull, obstinate'; (also 'headed or having many heads') — a somewhat resistant reader, reluctant to stay in her

---

referring to the 1584 text, although without giving a reason for choosing that edition.

2 W. B. Yeats, *The Poems*, ed. D. Albright (London: J. M. Dent & Sons, 1990), p. 145.

place, or at least in a place allocated and circumscribed by masculine prescription. (Cotgrave's first example of *testu* is 'femme testue: a domineering or maisterfulle housewife; one that (at least) would be her husband's maister; one that hath too much head'.)[3] But not masterful, no, that's not my intention: rather, resistant to both Ronsard and Yeats's representation of their readers or audience, and to their implicit desire to master them and — in Ronsard's case — to locate in that mastery his own mastery of the future meaning of his work. To expand a little on what I mean by this reading, I propose to consider not just the two poets' representations of their theme of reception and of the poet's relations with his public, but also the consequences initially of Ronsard's reading of his own text and then of Yeats's reading of Ronsard.

Yeats had perhaps here turned to Ronsard to license his representation of his own stance as poet, a stance not without arrogance; Ronsard a heroic figure from the past of poetry, whose authority Yeats may have longed for. Fitting, then, to turn to his sonnet 'en vers héroïques' as a model for a poem which speaks a disaffection, a sense of loss and betrayal, the failure of a poet's and poetic dream, to find in a hero a fellow-sufferer. Fitting, too, to write an imitation which runs true to the tenets Ronsard would recognise: neither translation nor copy, but reworking, reorientation, reinflection, renewal of the original. And thematically fitting, too, to invoke a conversation over four hundred years old between two poets, both a ghostly echo of, and a complement to, the conversation Yeats stages,[4] suggesting that the song remains the same whilst it is amplified over time. Yeats would presumably have recognised, besides, that Ronsard was already in a similar intertextual relationship with Horace.[5] But does this replication and amplification add resonance and authority, or rather intensify a hint of futility?

For Ronsard and Yeats, having converged on the theme of their audience's failures towards them, both close on the idea that the relation between the poet and his public, his simple, foolish, vulgar audience, remains, in an endless repeating present, one of mutual mockery. This seems to leave little to say. And yet, it is also perhaps a bait, a nice 'trick' — not to please, but to prompt further reflection on both sonnets

---

3 R. Cotgrave, *A Dictionarie of the French and English Tongues* (London, 1611), facsimile, English Linguistics, 82 (Menston, 1986).

4 An echo, too, in that like Pontus de Tyard, who for many readers has become scarcely more than a footnote in Ronsard's story, Craoibhin Aoibhin may well not be identified as Douglas Hyde, Yeats's fellow-writer, without an editor's help.

5 Laumonier notes the works in question: *Satires* II. 1 and *Epistles* I. 1.

and the different inflections they give their complaint, and to resist this settlement. Mutual mockery? Or, *pace* Yeats, later, as babies are 'self-born mockers of man's enterprise' ('Among School Children'),[6] there is room perhaps outside this apparently exhaustive symmetry for new readings, quizzical, questioning readings which, if they mock, mock only in that they speak from a different time and place, from among a new generation of readers, which wonders at and about the cultural inheritance it might, but need not, shoulder, perhaps more alert than its makers to some of its limits. Perhaps more ready to travel beyond, to where meanings emerge: for meanings and new possibilities of meaning lie not so much *in* the text as between it and the readings to which it lends itself, or which engage it. Just such an engagement has already happened between Ronsard and Yeats — and let's not overlook the range of possible relationships that the verb 'engage' affords: from binding both marital and contractual or promissory, through charm and attraction, to interlocking and holding fast, and lastly, entering into conflict (*Concise Oxford Dictionary*). More than mockery, then, whilst it may be that the potential complexity and duration of the relationship mocks the reader's callow expectation that she or he might get off with a brief flirtation with the text.

Yeats engages Ronsard's sonnet to write a moment of frustration and loss, a moment in itself perhaps ambivalent (certainly more than Ronsard's text allows), and certainly not his constant mood. In the same volume of poems, 'At Galway Races' allows the existing possibility of a culture which unites all, maker (here the riders) and public in their enjoyment: 'delight makes all of one mind' and, whilst mourning poetry's loss of this shared delight in a 'timid' world given over to mercantilism and accounting, has not lost hope that it may yet have 'hearers and hearteners' again.[7] What is already lost, and mourned, is the idealised immediacy of speech — a doubly derived illusion of immediacy contrived by Yeats the playwright at the Abbey Theatre? This complex context already unsettles the hold of that present-tense exchange of mockery. And yet we need not look beyond the sonnet for difference. It is already there in Yeats's inflection and displacement of two aspects of Ronsard's sonnet: the verb *enfanter*, and the characterisation of his relation with his public, beyond its Protean character.

Before exploring Yeats's 'imitation', however, it is worth considering what precisely he read. His sonnet 'At the Abbey Theatre' is 'imitated

---

6 Albright, pp. 261–3.
7 Albright, p. 146.

from Ronsard'; in their notes to the poem, two of Yeats's editors refer his readers to Ronsard's sonnet, 'Tyard, on me blasmoit, à mon commencement', that is, a 1584 version of a 1555 sonnet which was still to be subject to further changes. Without further evidence, this does not guarantee that this was the text Yeats read; nor do I know whether he knew of the variants of the text. I would only go so far as to suggest that, in the light of Yeats's poem, it is more likely that he had in mind editions of the sonnet which incorporate the verb *enfanter*, that is, those from 1560 onwards, than the earliest editions of 1555 and 1557.

What, then, did Ronsard read of his own writing that he chose to change? It has to do with changes of emphasis and detail rather than of structure or founding theme and development, but some of the changes are interesting in relation to what Yeats in turn will read and change. Originally the attacks on Ronsard are attributed to 'chacun' rather than 'on': more acute, more differentiated and accusatory. The substitution of 'on' suggests that some of the sting has faded; however, the verb *blasmer* comes to replace *dire* in the 1578 version in the first line and subsequently (in 1587) in both the first and third lines, indicating no loss of impact; rather, relocation of impact in the line. What is lost, on the other hand, in all post-1555 versions, is the original's insistence that the situation is one of torture: 'Toi [Tyard], qui as enduré presqu'un pareil torment, / Di moi, je te suppli…' (ll. 5–6), a change which allows the following speculation: that this rhetoric is recognised as excessive and therefore alienating — whilst the desire to torment is then reserved for the poet in his revenge on his Protean adversary, his never-satisfied public. More than that, it allows a change of emphasis which has interesting implications for Yeats's reading/writing.

Gone is the reference to mutual 'torment'; in its place: 'Toy, de qui le labeur enfante doctement / Des livres immortels': the written word is what remains and is where meaning is. This privileging of writing over speech is perhaps diminished by what might be read as a compensatory reversal in ll. 9–10, where 'j'escri' (l. 9) becomes 'je tonne' (1584–87) or 'je brave' (1578–87) and 'ma voix se desenfle' (l. 10) or in 1587 (with possibly less emasculating associations) 'rabaisse'; in the Ronsard sonnet the hierarchy remains undecided, all the more so because, if we were to posit a deliberate insistence on the enduring value of Ronsard's writing as opposed to the constant inconstancies and inconsistencies of the public's words of reproach, his own rewriting of his words suggests otherwise. Yeats, however, seems more inclined to mourn the loss of (a mythical) oral immediacy — 'hearers and hearteners'.

In later versions it seems enough to refer to the public as 'Proté'; the original adjective 'monstrueux' goes, to be replaced by further emphasis on the impossibility of holding it, that is, on the quality that makes it monstrous. That Proteus is monstrous can perhaps be taken for granted — Yeats treats him this way.

Almost all of Ronsard's changes, then, have to do with his self-repre-sentation, a representation in which he himself is seamlessly identified with his words, be they speech or writing. There is one last variant to note in this respect, however: from 1587, the sonnet begins: 'Ma Muse estoit blasmée à son commencement': gone is the conversation between the two men, although it emerges later in the sonnet as before; gone too is the seamless identity of poet and creation — and the feminine figure is left to shoulder the blame whilst the two men then get together to act on the situation. (Such a reading of the narrative is at least a possibility, if perhaps too ideologically marked, or testy.)

Ronsard's changes to his sonnet over time *may* be symptomatic of reader-response, prompted by the sonnet's reception; but they are not an effective barometer, and offer no evidence that Ronsard responded to any reading of his work other than his own. The changes neither clarify nor elevate the original; they do not engage the issues of reception that the poet confronts in the work. Besides, what remains largely constant is the structure of the relation between Ronsard and his monstrous pub-lic: the lines are simple, deliberately polarised: this public is a mon-strous, monolithic other, as if the poet has little interest in exploring its nature in any detail, and is determined to allow no differentiation or specificity to attenuate the hostility. In fact, the loss of the notion that the poet might find the situation a torment serves to mark this as a hos-tility which remains rigidly in place but leaves him cold, his intractable assailants other than or less than human — and himself more: not one to argue with the idea of his sublimity as a poet, here he reminds his fellow-poet Tyard and his reader of his ascendancy, his inspiration (in the 1587 version, 'Ma Muse'), and his capacity for god-like thunder.

This representation of his public might be read as Ronsard's revenge on his public's betrayal: for failing to appreciate his sublimity, being ungrateful for his more accessible writing, never satisfied, its appetite contrary, exorbitant, excessive. His revenge is this representation, par-ticularly his closure on mutual mockery: for the apparent symmetry conceals another closure, on an implicit asymmetry: Ronsard's mock-ery, lofty, prescient; his public's, product of and subject to monstrous, blind whim.

Whilst Yeats's sonnet seems to reproduce this closure, it already takes some distance by not asserting the relationship of mockery but rather, casting it as a question. And this final attenuation has been anticipated by other differences in the representation of the relation between poet and public, which I shall now consider. Ronsard offers Yeats a verb, *enfanter*; in the original sonnet, its meaning and context is strictly regulated: Tyard *produces* books. The use of *enfanter* in this context is familiar enough, falling within an ancient discourse of writing, a discourse renewed by Ronsard and his contemporaries, in which the writer (male) plays with the fantasy that writing is analogous to giving birth. In Ronsard's sonnet, the book is the infant, ideally graced with immortal life; life and meaning are in the words. Yeats, however, suggests both a different model of meaning and a different relationship with the reader. Not so alien and subsidiary an other but, rather, engaged somewhat in the production of meaning and as much the poet's child as any words might be ('You've dandled them and fed them from the book / And know them to the bone...'). With this recasting of his public, its excessive appetites and contrariness seem less those of a monster than those of a child; no less frustrating, perhaps, but no longer unnatural and purely other to the poet. The public's/child's endless need and curiosity, or desire for poetic (and theatrical) nurture which can never be satisfied, it seems, engage and correspond to the poet's insatiable desire to be read, heard, and to feed — and shape — the public's cultural desires.

Nor are the public's desires dismissed as nothing other than contrary and excessive, merely infantile. Yeats's figures are more elaborated and sympathetic than Ronsard's use of opposition: here the public shares its dreams of flight with the poet, whose sometimes 'high and airy flight' mirrors its desire to 'look...into some drift of wings'. And when this shared rhetoric is put alongside the ideal that 'delight makes all of one mind', whilst this intensifies the pathos and tension of the mutual failing in this moment of the poet's relationship with his public, it also reminds of the public's participation in the work's meaning.

If a 'trick' were enough, this public would be put in its place. As would the poet: resorting to tricks out of a desire to please, or turning tricks to seduce. Ironically the trick in this sonnet — the last line's trick of rhetorical symmetry — works: but then, it is more than a trick, it has a place in a culture of rhetoric, and once recognised no longer tricks, but rather, engages the reader.

What of the Protean cast of Yeats's public? — for the figure remains. Given the other differences, the place of this mythological creature changes accordingly; although the desire is to 'bridle...this Proteus', it is less emphatically a desire to master it, that is, future meaning. Ronsard's 'Proté' earns a note from his commentator Belleau, reproduced in the Laumonier edition. This sea-god could predict the future; his shape-changing was designed 'pour plus aisement decevoir ceus qui s'adressoient à luy, desireux de scavoir les choses futures: mais pour en avoir la raison il le failloit [*sic*] surprendre de toute force et luy garoter piez et mains, et alors il reprenoit sa forme naturelle et annonçoit le futur à ceus qui le luy demandoyent'.[8] For the future to be known, Proteus must be subject to horrible violence ('surprendre de toute force et luy garoter'), grabbed and bound: what order of knowledge is this that it can be uttered only by an other so brutally subjected to one's will to know? Ronsard's implicit desire to master the future and future meaning, to ensure that the meaning that endures ('immortels') is none other than he dictates, discredits itself here; the public's resistance to his will gains validity. This desire for mastery does not re-emerge with such unbridled vigour in Yeats's sonnet. Proteus has changed his form, the significance of Ronsard's original sonnet has changed, beyond his mastery; and precisely because of this, it could and can engage readers who want neither less nor more (as Ronsard cast them), but who enjoy the play of language and potential meanings, and who will suggest diverse, unbridled readings, finding a place for the sonnet here and now in an unmastered future. And not only for this sonnet, but for all of Ronsard's writing: resilient writing for resilient readers. It does not take an academic or a poet to offer a new, renewing reading; not even a very *testu(e)*/'testie' reader; but the more resilient and the more interested the reader is in opening up the exclusive conversation between the fellow-poets to a wider public, perhaps, the richer the engagement will be.

---

8 See Laumonier, p. 116, n. 3

7

The Androgyne Myth in Montaigne's
De l'amitié

Philip Ford

[A] Au demeurant, ce que nous appellons ordinairement amis et amitiez, ce ne sont qu'accoinctances et familiaritez nouées par quelque occasion ou commodité, par le moyen de laquelle nos ames s'entretiennent. En l'amitié dequoy je parle, elles se meslent et confondent l'une en l'autre, d'un melange si universel, qu'elles effacent et ne   5 retrouvent plus la couture qui les a jointes. Si on me presse de dire pourquoy je l'aymois, je sens que cela ne se peut exprimer, [C] qu'en repondant: Par ce que c'estoit luy; par ce que c'estoit moy.

[A] Il y a, au delà de tout mon discours, et de ce que j'en puis dire particulierement, ne sçay quelle force inexplicable et fatale, mediatrice de   10 cette union. [C] Nous nous cherchions avant que de nous estre veus, et par des rapports que nous oyïons l'un de l'autre, qui faisoient en nostre affection plus d'effort que ne porte la raison des rapports, je croy par quelque ordonnance du ciel: nous nous embrassions par noz noms. Et à nostre premiere rencontre, qui fut par hazard en une grande feste et   15 compagnie de ville, nous nous trouvasmes si prins, si cognus, si obligez entre nous, que rien des lors ne nous fut si proche que l'un à l'autre. Il escrivit une Satyre Latine excellente, qui est publiée, par laquelle il excuse et explique la precipitation de nostre intelligence, si promptement parvenue à sa perfection. Ayant si peu à durer, et ayant si tard commencé,   20 car nous estions tous deux hommes faicts, et luy plus de quelque année, elle n'avoit point à perdre temps, et à se regler au patron des amitiez molles et regulieres, ausquelles il faut tant de precautions de longue et preallable conversation. Cette cy n'a point d'autre idée que d'elle mesme, et ne se peut rapporter qu'à soy. [A] Ce n'est pas une speciale   25 consideration, ny deux, ny trois, ny quatre, ny mille: c'est je ne sçay quelle quinte essence de tout ce meslange, qui, ayant saisi toute ma volonté, l'amena se plonger et se perdre dans la sienne; [C] qui, ayant, saisi toute sa volonté, l'amena se plonger et se perdre en la mienne, d'une faim, d'une concurrence pareille. [A] Je dis perdre, à la verité, ne nous reservant rien   30 qui nous fut propre, ny qui fut ou sien ou mien.

(Montaigne, *Essais* I. 28, 'De l'amitié')

When I was a young research student in 1974, I attended a conference at King's College organised by Robert Bolgar and Patrick Wilkinson at which Dorothy Gabe Coleman gave a paper on Montaigne.[1] In it, she explored the use of quotations from Martial in *Essais* III. 5, 'Sur des vers de Virgile', showing that what had traditionally been thought of as misquotation due to Montaigne's poor memory was in fact deliberate *adaptation* on his part, and that the original contexts of the quotations provided a coded subtext for sensitive readers, alerting them to a homoerotic context in his comments on sexual experiences. Dorothy did not use the term 'intertextuality', but this is what she had in mind, and at the time I was convinced, excited, and inspired by her paper, which moved the rather sterile hunt for sources common until then in much criticism of Renaissance writing onto a far more productive level of analysis.

The passage from 'De l'amitié' which I have chosen to consider does not contain any direct quotations, yet Dorothy's approach can be applied to intertextual allusions to a work which I feel Montaigne did have in mind when he wrote this moving tribute to his friendship with Étienne de La Boétie: Plato's *Symposium*.[2] The meaning of the term 'amitié', as it is here conceived by Montaigne, is at the heart of this chapter, and as is so often the case in the *Essais*, what at first sight appears to be obvious rapidly gives way to gradations of nuances, and it soon becomes clear that he has something very particular in mind. Cotgrave offers 'Amitie, friendship, love, kindnes, good will; concord; correspondencie' as translations of *amitié*, and 'A friend; a lover, a Paramor; a loving mate, a deere companion' to translate *ami*.[3] We shall see in the course of this reading of the passage that Montaigne has something rather closer to 'love' than to 'friendship' in mind.

Earlier in the chapter, Montaigne had considered, only to reject them, the 'quatre especes anciennes' of *amitié*: 'naturelle, sociale, hospita-

---

[1] This was subsequently published as 'Montaigne's "Sur des vers de Virgile": Taboo Subject, Taboo Author', in R. R. Bolgar, ed., *Classical Influences on European Culture, AD 1500–1700* (Cambridge: Cambridge University Press, 1976), 135–40.

[2] The text is taken from *Les Essais de Montaigne*, edited by Pierre Villey, revised by V.-L. Saulnier, 2 vols (Paris: PUF, 1978), I. 188–9. All references to Montaigne will be to this edition. The translation of the *Symposium* cited here is by W. R. M. Lamb in the Loeb edition of Plato, vol. III (Cambridge, MA and London: Harvard University Press and Heinemann, 1975).

[3] *A French-English Dictionary, Compil'd by Mr Randle Cotgrave* (London, 1650), first edition 1619.

liere, venerienne' (I. 184). Natural bonds, such as those between father and son or brother and brother, do not depend upon the will and are purely fortuitous. Even marriage, which ought to offer a total union of body and soul made on the basis of choice, is excluded from providing a truly fulfilling relationship because 'la suffisance ordinaire des femmes n'est pas pour responde à cette conference et communication, nourrisse de cette saincte couture; ny leur ame ne semble assez ferme pour soustenir l'estreinte d'un neud si pressé et si durable' (I. 186). He also rejects the relationship between a man and a beautiful boy advocated not only in the *Symposium* but also in Marsilio Ficino's influential commentary, [4] 'laquelle pourtant, pour avoir, selon leur usage, une si necessaire disparité d'aages et difference d'offices entre les amants, ne respondoit non plus assez à la parfaicte union et convenance qu'icy nous demandons' (I. 187).

Montaigne spends even less time, at the beginning of this passage, in rejecting merely social bonds, 'ce que nous appellons ordinairement amis et amitiez' (ll. 1–2). Such relationships are dependent upon external factors such as chance circumstances or mutual interest, and are therefore unworthy of the title *amitiez*. His ideal *amitié* involves a total coming together of souls, and to express this, he employs a series of images. The souls 'se meslent' — mingle together — 'se confondent' — literally pour or melt together — so completely (and now we move on to a sewing image) 'qu'elles effacent et ne retrouvent plus la *couture* qui les a jointes'. Montaigne, as we have seen, had already used this metaphor — 'cette saincte couture' — in discussing marriage, and in considering the relationship between father and son, he had spoken of 'philosophes desdaignans cette cousture naturelle' (I. 185). For him, it is only when the marks of this sewing together have completely disappeared that a relationship can truly be described as *amitié*.

It seems to me that what he has in mind here is the witty but perversely influential contribution attributed to Aristophanes in the *Symposium* on the nature of love, which gave rise in the Renaissance to the popular androgyne myth.[5] Originally, Plato has Aristophanes say,

---

4 Throughout his commentary on the *Symposium*, Ficino speaks in terms of the masculine nouns *amator* and *amatus*; see *Commentaire sur le Banquet de Platon: Texte du manuscrit autographe*, edited and translated by Raymond Marcel (Paris: «Les Belles Lettres», 1956).

5 On the use of this myth see, for example, Edgar Wind, *Pagan Mysteries in the Renaissance* (Oxford: Oxford University Press, 1980), pp. 201 sq. Although the commonly used term 'androgyne' is rather inappropriate in the predominantly homoerotic context of Plato and Ficino, I shall nevertheless use it in this paper.

all humans were double, not single, beings, and were of three sexes: all male, all female, or male and female. Their arrogance, however, led them to try to overthrow the gods, and in order to punish them, Zeus cut them in half:

> Well, when one of them — whether he be a boy-lover or a lover of any other sort — happens on his own particular half, the two of them are wondrously thrilled with affection and intimacy and love [φιλία, οἰκειότης, ἔρως], and are hardly to be induced to leave each other's side for a single moment. These are they who continue together throughout life, though they could not even say what they would have of one another.
>
> (Plato, *Symposium* 192 C)

Alluding, no doubt, to this last sentence, Montaigne writes (ll. 6–7): 'Si on me presse de dire pourquoy je l'aymois [Montaigne has not mentioned La Boétie for several pages, but feels no need to specify whom he means], je sens que cela ne se peut exprimer.' It is only fifteen years later, in the 1595 edition, that we have the additional simple yet moving words: 'qu'en respondant: Par ce que c'estoit luy; par ce que c'estoit moy.'

Aristophanes goes on to say:

> Suppose that, as they lay together, Hephaestus should come and stand over them, and showing his implements should ask: 'What is it, good mortals, that you would have of one another?' — and suppose that in their perplexity he asked them again: 'Do you desire to be joined in the closest possible union, so that you shall not be divided by night or by day? If that is your craving, I am ready to fuse [συντῆξαι] and weld [συμφυσῆσαι] you together in a single piece, that from being two you may be made one; that so long as you live, the pair of you, being as one, may share a single life...' Not one on hearing this, we are sure, would demur to it or would be found wishing for anything else: each would unreservedly deem that he had been offered just what he was yearning for all the time, namely, to be so joined and fused with his beloved that the two might be made one.
>
> (*Symposium*, 192 E)

In other words, love — *amitié* — can make men whole again. There is a world of difference between the crude knots of banal acquaintances ('accoinctances et familiaritez *nouées* par quelque occasion ou commodité', ll. 2–3) and the seamless union of two soul mates so that 'elles effacent et ne retrouvent plus la couture qui les a jointes' (ll. 5–6). The images that Montaigne uses (*se mesler* and particularly *se confondre* (l. 4)) deliberately echo Plato's 'fuse and weld...together'.

In the 1580 text of the *Essais*, published seventeen years after the death of La Boétie, Montaigne only speaks in fairly general terms here about his relationship with his friend, yet even then he says that it was predestined: 'Il y a...ne sçay quelle force inexplicable et fatale, mediatrice de cette union' (ll. 9–11). With the passing of time, but with no blunting of his original feelings, and true to his statement in *Essais* III. 2: 'Je dy vrai, non pas tout mon saoul, mais autant que je l'ose dire; et l'ose un peu plus en vieillissant' (II. 806), he reveals more about this 'force fatale' which led to their meeting. Aristophanes, in the *Symposium*, describes what happens when the two separated halves of the men that Zeus had cut in two meet up again:

> Now when our first form had been cut in two, each half in longing for its fellow would come to it again; and then they would fling their arms about each other and in mutual embraces [συμπλεκόμενοι] yearn to be grafted together, till they began to perish of hunger and general indolence, through refusing to do anything apart.
>
> (*Symposium*, 191 A–B)

Once more, Montaigne appears to have this passage in mind in the 1595 text when he writes: 'Nous nous cherchions avant que de nous estre veus,...nous nous embrassions par noz noms. Et à nostre premiere rencontre..., nous nous trouvasmes si prins, si cognus, si obligez entre nous, que rien dès lors ne nous fut si proche que l'un à l'autre' (ll. 11–17). Montaigne and La Boétie are two halves of a whole being who had been searching for each other all their lives and who, on being reunited, recognise one another and became inseparable.

It is clear from what Montaigne goes on to say that each of them was taken by surprise at the suddenness and violence of their emotions — 'la precipitation de nostre intelligence, si promptement parvenue à sa perfection' (ll. 19–20) — and that they felt that some explanation was called for, with La Boétie obliging in the form of his 'Satyre Latine'. At the same time, the term 'intelligence' indicates that this attraction involves a perfect understanding of each other, going beyond 'amitiez molles et regulieres' (ll. 22–3). The adjective 'molles' is problematic here next to the far more general 'regulieres'. Cotgrave translates it as : 'Soft; supple, tender; lithe, limber, pliant; easie, gentle, yeelding; mild, effeminate, remisse; dainty, delicate.' Given the clearly negative context, the semantic group 'mild, effeminate, remisse' appears to correspond most closely to Montaigne's meaning here, and this reading is in line with his dismissal of marriage as a suitable form of *amitié* because the soul of a woman 'ne semble assez *ferme*' to maintain such a long-lasting relationship. Such relationships, with all their imperfections, nevertheless require 'tant de precautions de longue et preallable conversation' (ll. 23–4), emphasising both the length of time and the care needed to prepare for even an inferior form of friendship.[6] This contrasts with the immediate sense of recognition in the meeting between Montaigne and La Boétie. The Platonic subtext of this passage is further confirmed by Montaigne's statement concerning the uniqueness of his relationship with La Boétie: 'Cette-cy n'a point d'autre *idée* que d'elle mesme' (l. 24, my emphasis), where the word 'idée' has the Platonic sense of idea or essence, the original form of things contained in the cosmic mind, which all earthly things seek to imitate.

Montaigne explains retrospectively the extreme haste with which their relationship developed by a further appeal to the notion of a preordained fate: 'Ayant si peu à durer...elle n'avoit point à perdre temps' (ll. 20–2). Yet despite this sense of predestination, this 'force...fatale', the will is also involved, as he writes in the 1580 text, where he speaks of a 'quinte essence de tout ce meslange, qui, ayant saisi toute ma volonté, l'amena se plonger et se perdre dans la sienne' (ll. 27–8). This formulation later suggested to Montaigne a certain disparity between the experiences of himself and his friend, implying perhaps that the lesser will of Montaigne plunged and was lost in the sea of his friend's will. The image is retained in the 1595 text, but is now applied to La Boétie equally (ll. 28–9), thus providing an example of parallelism similar to the 1595 addition at the close of the first paragraph: 'Par ce que c'estoit luy; par ce que c'estoit moy.' The mutual character of this process, central as it is to Aristophanes' representation of love, is further emphasised by Montaigne in the phrase 'd'une faim, d'une concurrence pareille' (ll. 29–30). At the end of this paragraph, in order to underline the importance which these images of fusion have for the author, he stresses that his choice of the verb 'perdre' is not an otiose one and, in another effective use of possessive pronouns, that the friends' altruism for each other was total, 'ne nous reservant rien qui nous fut propre, ny qui fut ou sien, ou mien' (ll. 30–1). This last comment is perhaps intended to conjure up a kind of personal Golden Age shared by the two, a time, in Ronsard's words, 'Quand ces mots, *Tien* &

---

6 Cotgrave's glosses on the key words in this phrase are useful: for *precaution* he offers 'A precaution; a foreseeing, bewaring, or providing for beforehand; also, a premonition, or warning'; *conversation* is translated as 'conversation, commerce, great acquaintance, familiarity, association, with'.

Mien, en usage n'estoient' (*Hymne de la Justice*, l. 53).[7] These images of mutual affection also bring to mind Marsilio Ficino's comments on reciprocal love in his commentary on the *Symposium*:

> But when the loved one loves in return, the lover leads his life in him. Here, surely, is a remarkable circumstance that whenever two people are brought together in mutual affection, one lives in the other and the other in him. In this way they mutually exchange identities; each gives himself to the other in such a way that each receives the other in return.[8]

Montaigne creates, then, in this text the picture of a unique relation-ship, 'cette amitié que nous avons nourrie, tant que Dieu a voulu, entre nous, si entiere et si parfaite que certainement il ne s'en lit guiere de pareilles, et, entre nos hommes, il ne s'en voit aucune trace en usage. Il faut tant de rencontres à la bastir, que c'est beaucoup si la fortune y ar-rive une fois en trois siecles' (I. 184).

In looking at this passage, it is both interesting and instructive to consider the balance between the original printed text of 1580 and the additions made to the *exemplaire de Bordeaux* published posthumously in 1595, as well as to note the absence of 1588 additions. (In fact, in this whole chapter, there are only three 1588 additions, of which two are Latin quotations.) With the majority of the text dating from between 1588 and 1592, the year of his death, it seems that Montaigne could only bring himself to write fully about his feelings for La Boétie as his own life was drawing to a close. While the 1580 text speaks in general terms of their mutual feelings, the 1595 version adds flesh to the bones, recalling in moving detail a first meeting, an *innamoramento*, which had taken place over thirty years previously, and the still vivid memories of a friendship that lasted only five years.

The Platonic references to fusion which we have considered in the first paragraph seem to be confirmed in later additions: 'Nous nous cherchions avant que de nous estre veus...nous nous embrassions par noz noms...rien dès lors ne nous fut si proche que l'un à l'autre' (ll. 11–17). The long paragraph preceding this passage which had dealt with the Greeks' ideal of pederasty was also largely a late addition, other than the opening sentence: 'Et cet' autre licence Grecque est justement ab-horrée par nos meurs.' In fact, it is the age difference between the lover

---

7 See the Laumonier edition of Ronsard, vol. VIII, p. 50 (Paris: Droz, 1935).

8 Translated in *Marsilio Ficino's Commentary on Plato's 'Symposium': The Text and a Translation, with an Introduction*, Sears Reynolds Jayne, University of Missouri Studies, 19 (Columbia, 1944).

and beloved, as we have noted, and the lover's attraction to the purely physical beauty of the beloved that Montaigne finds objectionable. He identifies a great deal of value in the relationship in other respects, citing, for example, but without comment, 'les salutaires amours de Hermodius et d'Aristogiton' (I. 188), lovers who attempted to rid Athens of the tyrants Hipparchus and Hippias. Athenaeus (probably Montaigne's source) cites Hieronymus the Peripatetic as declaring that 'these love affairs with boys became widespread because it often happened that the vigour of the young men, joined to the mutual sympathy of their companionship, brought many tyrannical governments to an end'.[9]

It is clear, then, that Montaigne's idea of *amitié* goes far beyond the normal notion of friendship. It is a unique relationship between two men, based on spiritual and intellectual, rather than physical attraction, and involving the total absorption of the one in the other. Is it really so different, then, from 'cet' autre licence Grecque' which, in the final years of his life, Montaigne does not bring himself to condemn without prevarication? And is it legitimate to wonder whether there was a physical dimension to Montaigne and La Boétie's love for each other? Montaigne, after all, did not marry until two years after the death of his friend, and then not because he wanted to but because he was constrained to do so. As he writes in 'Sur des vers de Virgile': 'De mon dessein, j'eusse fuy d'espouser la sagesse mesme, si elle m'eust voulu...Toutesfois je ne m'y conviay pas proprement, on m'y mena, et y fus porté par des occasions estrangeres' (II. 852).

Montaigne does not discount the importance of physical intimacy as part of a full and loving relationship, but regrets that this relationship is not possible in marriage because, as we have seen, of the lack of firmness of women's souls:

[A] Et certes, sans cela, s'il se pouvoit dresser une telle accointance, libre et volontaire, où, non seulement les ames eussent cette entiere jouyssance, mais encores où les corps eussent part à l'alliance, [C] où l'homme fust engagé tout entier: [A] il est certain que l'amitié en seroit plus pleine et plus comble. Mais ce sexe par nul exemple n'y est encore peu arriver, [C] et par le commun consentement des escholes anciennes en est rejetté.

(I. 186–7)

---

9   The translation is that of Charles Burton Gulick in the Loeb edition of Athenaeus, *Deipnosophistae*, vol. VI (Cambridge, MA and London: Harvard University Press and Heinemann, 1980), 602a.

The 1595 additions, in line with what Montaigne has to say about his own marriage in III. 5, 'Sur des vers de Virgile', strengthen rather than mitigate this idea that real intimacy is impossible between a man and a woman. If, then, there is to be any place for physical union beyond merely physical pleasure and, of course, the procreation of children, then it would be in the sort of *amitié* which Montaigne describes in this chapter. Unlike Ficino, in his commentary on the *Symposium*, Montaigne does not explicitly reject the idea of physical intimacy, which is in any case more than implicit in the images of union in the androgyne myth. Moreover, whereas the main thrust of the *Symposium*'s discussion of love is to maintain that the love of another beautiful mortal is merely a stepping stone to the love of ideal Beauty and Truth, Aristophanes' idiosyncratic intervention sees the reunion of the lovers as an end in itself. It is no doubt this that particularly appealed to Montaigne, and which he picks up in the words: 'Cette cy n'a point d'autre idée que d'elle mesme' (l. 24).[10]

At the end of the chapter, Montaigne uses one final image to repre-sent his relationship with La Boétie. Although, as we have seen, he re-jects the idea that the natural bonds between brothers can offer real *amitié*, he nevertheless writes: 'C'est, à la verité, un beau nom et plein de dilection que le nom de frere, et à cette cause en fismes nous, luy et moy, nostre alliance' (I. 185). Apart from fitting in with Aristophanes' Siamese-twins idea of lovers as two separate halves of one body searching for each other, it also allows Montaigne to take leave of his friend at the end of the chapter with the words of Catullus' moving farewell to his own dead brother (I. 194):

> ...O misero frater adempte mihi!
> Omnia tecum una perierunt gaudia nostra,
> Quae tuus in vita dulcis alebat amor.

(Oh brother, snatched away from me in my sorrow! With you perished at the same time all of our joys, which your sweet love nourished while you were alive.)

---

[10] In any case, Montaigne feels that we are cut off from such transcendental knowledge, cf. II. 601: 'Nous n'avons aucune communication à l'estre', and Odette de Mourgues's comments on this in her essay 'Passé, présent, futur dans les *Essais*', in *Montaigne in Cambridge: Proceedings of the Cambridge Montaigne Colloquium, 7–9 April 1988*, edited by Philip Ford and Gillian Jondorf (Cambridge: Cambridge French Colloquia, 1989), 1–6, p. 4.

Moreover, Montaigne would probably not have been ignorant of the fact that the term 'frater' was also used as a term of endearment between lovers in Latin, which, like the allusions to the largely homo-erotic context of the *Symposium*, would provide another hint to the 'lecteur suffisant' of Montaigne's meaning.[11] As Dorothy wrote of Montaigne's use and adaptation of quotations, 'the implicit suggestions are more pregnant than the explicit statements — which is what one would expect from Montaigne' (art. cit., p. 140).

---

[11] Cf. Tibullus III. 1. 23, Martial II. 4. 3, and in a homosexual context, Martial X. 65. 14 and Petronius 9. 2, 10. 6, 129. 8.

8

François de Sales:
The Writer and his Reader

Elisabeth Stopp

1) La douceur des lecteurs rend douce et utile la lecture; et pour t'avoir plus
favorable, mon cher Lecteur, je te veux icy rendre rayson de quelques pointz
qui autrement, a l'aventure, te mettroyent en mauvaise humeur.

...Certes, j'ay eu en consideration la condition des espritz de ce siecle, et
je le devois: il importe beaucoup de regarder en quel aage on escrit....   5

Un grand serviteur de Dieu m'advertit n'a guere que l'addresse que
j'avois faite de ma parole a *Philothee*, en l'*Introduction a la Vie devote*,
avoit empesché plusieurs hommes d'en faire leur proffit, d'autant qu'ilz
n'estimoyent pas digne de la lecture d'un homme les advertissemens faitz
pour une femme. J'admiray qu'il se trouvast des hommes qui, pour vouloir   10
paroistre hommes, se monstrassent en effect si peu hommes; car je te laisse
a penser, mon cher Lecteur, si la devotion n'est pas egalement pour les
hommes comme pour les femmes...Mays outre cela, c'est l'ame qui aspire
a la devotion que j'appelle *Philothee*, et les hommes ont une ame aussi bien
que les femmes.   15

Toutefois, pour imiter en cette occasion le grand Apostre qui s'estimoit
redevable a tous, j'ay changé d'addresse en ce Traitté, et parle a *Theotime*:
que si d'aventure il se treuvoit des femmes (or cette impertinence seroit plus
supportable en elles) qui ne voulussent pas lire les enseignemens qu'on fait
a un homme, je les prie de croire que le *Theotime* auquel je parle est l'esprit   20
humain, qui desire faire progres en la dilection sainte, esprit qui est
egalement es femmes comme es hommes.

Ce Traitté donq est fait pour ayder l'ame des-ja devote a ce qu'elle se
puisse avancer en son dessein, et pour cela il m'a esté force de dire
plusieurs choses un peu moins conneües au vulgaire et qui par consequent   25
sembleront plus obscures: le fond de la science est tous-jours un peu plus
malaysé a sonder, et se treuve peu de plongeons qui veuillent et sachent aller
recueillir les perles et autres pierres precieuses dans les entrailles de l'ocean.
Mays si tu as le courage franc pour enfoncer cet escrit, il t'arrivera de vraye
comme aux plongeons, lesquelz, dit Pline, «estans es plus profonds   30
gouffres de la mer y voyent clairement la lumiere du soleil»; car tu treuveras
es endroitz les plus malaysés de ces discours une bonne et aymable clareté.

(Traitté de l'Amour de Dieu: Préface)

2) Un musicien des plus excellens de l'univers, et qui jouoit parfaitement du luth, devint en peu de tems si extremement sourd qu'il ne luy resta plus aucun usage de l'ouïe; neanmoins il ne laissa pas pour cela de chanter et manier son luth delicatement a merveilles, a cause de la grande habitude qu'il en avoit, que sa surdité ne luy avoit pas ostee. Mais parce qu'il n'avoit [5] aucun playsir en son chant ni au son de son luth, d'autant qu'estant privé de l'ouïe il n'en pouvoit appercevoir la douceur et beauté, il ne chantoit plus ni ne sonnoit du luth que pour contenter un prince duquel il estoit né sujet, et auquel il avoit une extreme inclination de complaire, accompaignee d'une infinie obligation pour avoir esté nourri des sa jeunesse chez luy: c'est [10] pourquoy il avoit un playsir nompareil de luy plaire, et quand son prince luy tesmoignoit d'aggreer son chant il estoit tout ravi de contentement. Mais il arrivoit quelquefois que le prince, pour essayer l'amour de cet aymable musicien, luy commandoit de chanter, et soudain, le laissant la en sa chambre, il s'en alloit a la chasse; mais le desir que le chantre avoit de [15] suivre ceux de son maistre luy faisoit continuer aussi attentivement son chant comme si le prince eust esté present, quoy qu'en verité il n'avoit aucun playsir a chanter: car il n'avoit ni le playsir de la melodie, duquel sa surdité le privoit, ni celuy de plaire au prince, puisque le prince estant absent ne jouissoit pas de la douceur des beaux airs qu'il chantoit...Certes, le cœur [20] humain est le vraye chantre du cantique de l'amour sacré, et il est luy mesme la *harpe* et le *psalterion*...

(*Traitté de l'Amour de Dieu*, Livre IX, Chapitre IX)[1]

François de Sales (1567–1622), the eldest son in a family of the Savoyard nobility, was educated first at Annecy and then at one of the outstanding humanist schools in Paris, the Collège de Clermont, which has survived into the twentieth century as the Lycée Louis le Grand. To obey his father he then studied law at the University of Padua, and to follow his own bent he read theology, leaving Padua with a double doctorate in 1591. Two years later he was ordained, then sent on a mission to the Calvinist Chablais region where he wrote his first important book, *Défense de l'Estendart de la Saincte Croix* (1600), a theological inquiry into the nature of pictorial representation in the context of Christianity. He then went to Paris on ecclesiastical and state business and was acclaimed

---

[1] *Œuvres de Saint François de Sales*, Édition complète, 27 volumes (Annecy, 1894–1964). The preface is to be found pp. 3–22. Hereafter, references to the Annecy edition are by the initial 'A' followed by volume and page number, thus (for the first passage quoted here): A. IV. 8, 9, 12–13, and for the second passage A. V. 137. See also: Saint François de Sales, *Œuvres*, ed. André Ravier and Roger Devos, Bibliothèque de la Pléiade (Paris: Gallimard, 1969), Préface, *Traité de l'Amour de Dieu*, pp. 335–49.

as a preacher at the court of Henri IV who wanted him to stay in Paris, as did the Pietist circles gathered in the salon of Madame Acarie. Soon after his return to Savoy he was consecrated Prince Bishop of Geneva, an an-cient See of the Holy Roman Empire, exiled to Annecy after the Reformation. Together with Madame Jeanne-Françoise de Chantal, of Dijon, a spiritually-inclined widow who had lost her husband in a tragic hunting accident, François de Sales founded (in 1610) a new and quite originally orientated contemplative order for women, the Visitation de la Sainte Marie, which spread rapidly throughout France, Italy, and Spain. The remaining years of his life were filled to overflowing with ecclesias-tical and state business, but he found time to write what turned out to be a best-seller of great spiritual and social influence, *Introduction à la vie dévote* (1608), and a mystical treatise, *Traitté de l'amour de Dieu* (1616). In 1622 he died in Lyon, where he had been officiating in the presence of Louis XIII at the marriage of Christine of France to a duke of Savoy — to which royal house in Turin the Bishop of Geneva was subject.[2]

* * *

In the Preface to each of his main works François de Sales gives a pre-cise idea of what he is going to do, and after introducing himself to his reader in this way he gives what amounts to a structural analysis of the work offered; he tells how best to set about reading it, omitting, in the case of the *Traitté*, certain rather more complex sections at a first reading: but he expects texts to be studied, and studied attentively and prayerfully. At the same time he makes a point of forming an immediate and warm relationship with his 'très cher lecteur', calling her by name as 'Philothee' in the *Introduction* and him as 'Theotime' in the *Traitté*. The woman's name means 'one who loves God', while the man is 'one who fears God', not in the sense of being afraid but of having sovereign respect for God's will and authority.

The passage from the Preface to the *Traitté*, chosen to give some idea of his attitude to his reader, shows a nice awareness of the need for in-clusive language and for the thinking that underlies this by no means modern notion. The irony is patent, the long opening sentence carefully structured to work up to a neat final point. This tone continues in the sec-

2 See also Elisabeth Stopp, *Madame de Chantal, Portrait of a Saint* (London and Westminster, Maryland: Faber and Faber, 1962); and by the same author, *St François de Sales, a Testimony,* (London and Hyattsville: Faber and Faber and Salesian Press, 1967).

ond paragraph. In spite of the completely serious compliment to women readers this also has a slight mocking edge to it, but all ends in a reconciling conclusion which unites both Philothée and Théotime in the one simple designation of a shared humanity (ll. 20–2).

In the next paragraph François clearly states the aim of his work (ll. 23–4) and warns the reader that there might be difficulties because of the rather more complex, and indeed mysterious, aim of the theological area of the soul's deeper relationship to God in ever greater love that is now being explored. But he begs his reader to persevere, proceeding to what could be seen as a *petitio benevolentiae* (ll. 24–8). There is then a parallel from Pliny's *Natural History*, telling of the marine diver in the depths of the ocean who is aware that even in this apparent darkness he can some times see the sun and that it suddenly gives him brilliant light (ll. 30–1). Either the final sentence can be taken as a compliment to the reader's readiness to face an intellectual challenge, or there may again be just another subtle touch of benevolent irony, depending on what precisely one considers to be 'la condition des esprits de ce siècle' (l. 4).

Where, in the *Introduction*, comparisons and images had been used as ornament helping to make moral analysis and religious instruction attractive, and constituted 'une grande variété de bouquets et le meslange des fleurs' to please Philothée, in the *Traitté* Théotime is taught, especially at important stages of the exposition, by metaphor rather than by image and parallel. He is told what might be called, in C. S. Lewis's terms, a 'fable', a brief story having a simple narrative shape and making its impact at a deeper level of consciousness where there is no need for explanation in logical terms: the fable conceals and at the same time reveals its own answer. The fable of the musician tells of someone who is in a state of spiritual darkness and complete unknowing.

The story is told simply and clearly in three carefully structured sentences; a relatively short opening statement tells of the musician's dilemma, his inability to hear and enjoy his own beautiful music, then in two long sentences of simple, clear narrative we are told about the prince, so greatly loved, who abandons the musician so that there is then no pleasure left for him, either in his music, his profession, or in the presence of his master. Finally there is a brief, almost epigrammatic definition which, however, holds no answer to the mystery.

In the emblematic thinking of the time François de Sales was seen as a writer who was 'revealed by his own portent': 'Indicio proditur ille suo', that is, by the phenomenon of fire and flashing light said to have appeared to him in the sky as he was writing the *Traitté*. An emblem in the emblematised life of St François shows this portent and also the table with the quill pen poised ready for writing on the as yet blank pages of the book on its stand, the writer's doctrine being 'all on fire with divine love' (Fig. 1). In the next emblem (Fig. 2) what he wrote is shown as sweet but also useful, of much help and profit for all its delight: 'Miscuit utile dulci.' The brief phrases were meant as a memorable summary of the writer's impact. Perched right at the top of the beehive as a further visual aid, there is the actual book, the pages now covered with writing. By his skill as a writer François de Sales has prepared and distilled what is sweet to the mind and heart of those who read his books, of Philothée and of Théotime.

A most percipient and also beloved Théotime was Claude Favre de Vaugelas (1585–1650), author of the *Remarques sur la langue française*, a writer closely associated with the early days of the French Academy. He was a fellow-Savoyard, the son of the eminent lawyer, President Antoine Favre, who was responsible for the 'Code Fabrien', the major revision of Roman law then still internationally valid. He was also a poet and an amateur of the arts who was François de Sales's closest friend, with whom from 1593 onwards he conducted an attractive and amusing correspondence in Latin, in the best humanist manner and style (A. IX). Together the friends founded a literary and learned Academy at Annecy, the *Académie Florimontane* (1606). As a young student Claude Favre attended meetings and absorbed the traditions of the Italian Academies that served as models for the *Florimontane*. In the constitutions it is written:

> Le stil de parler ou de lire sera grave, exquis, plein, et ne ressentira en point de fasson la pedanterie. Dans les leçons on traictera de l'ornement des langues, et surtout de la françoise...Les lecteurs tascheront de tout leur pouvoir d'enseigner bien, beaucoup et en peu de temps.[3]

In 1627 Vaugelas was a witness at the first canonisation inquiries for François de Sales. He chose to speak specifically about his manner and style as a speaker and writer, and of a certain striking immediacy which made both listener and reader feel that what was being said or written was addressed to him or her alone. Another witness at this same inquiry at Annecy, Madame de Chantal, for whom the 'fable' of the Deaf Musician was written, also stressed the clarity and immediacy of François's method and style which made people grasp readily 'the most delicate and subtle truths of the spiritual life':

---

[3] A. XIV. 48.

Il usait toujours des termes communs et des paroles propres à se faire bien entendre, mais jamais recherchées. Il était merveilleusement clair, en sorte qu'en expliquant les plus obscures questions de philosophie ou de théologie qu'on lui posait, il les rendait intelligibles aux plus idiots [that is, in the connotation of that word in its time, 'to the simple and unlearned'].[4]

While this clarity and immediacy may well be a special charisma, it is also, quite realistically, linked with actual expertise and training in the art of rhetoric, of literary and artistic skills. The *Académie Florimontane*, in its humble way, was helping people to prepare for their chosen profession in the service of the state, the law, or the church. It is clear from the correspondence of both the founders of this Academy that they were very much aware of their responsibility, and through the young Vaugelas there was, in a sense, a link with the formation (and the traumas) of the *Académie française* later on, in the 1630s.

François's writings, like his life, form a close-knit unity in themselves and in relation to his apostolate as a declared 'doctor', or teacher, of the Church, and also, since 1923, as the declared Patron Saint of Writers and Journalists. His main works, with the letters as a background, are the varied facets of a unified spiritual doctrine, that of mysticism in action, which informed his own life and would, as he hoped, inform the mind and heart of his readers.

A Note

'Il a fait de la théologie une matière de littérature' was the dictum about François de Sales that Dr F. W. Stewart used to quote in his course of lectures on 'French Literature in the Seventeenth Century'. Dr Stewart, a great Pascal scholar and translator, was the first holder of a Readership in French in the Faculty of Modern and Medieval Languages, the office held also by Dorothy Gabe Coleman. This Faculty had only been established in the University of Cambridge in 1923, after long and acrimonious debate as to whether Modern Languages, as compared with Classical Greek and Latin, could rightly be regarded as a subject worthy of serious academic study and a Tripos examination. Dr Stewart himself taught Classics before he turned to French, and his doctorate was, in any case, a doctorate of Divinity: he was Dean of Chapel in Trinity College. He used to lecture in the Hall of his college, presided over by King Henry VIII as

---

4 Roger Devos, *Saint François de Sales par les témoins de sa vie* (Annecy, 1967), p.156.

portrayed by Holbein, an impressive and memorable juxtaposition to what was being said, more especially about texts that, as was inevitable in the seventeenth century, were so deeply informed by theological belief.[5]

---

5 Sadly, Elisabeth Stopp died before the publication of this volume, on 4 November 1996.

Fig. 1. *La Vie Symbolique du bienheureux François de Sales, comprise sous le voile de 52 emblèmes.* Par Adrien Gambart (Paris, 1664), p. 112

116   *La vie Symbolique*

❋◟✿❋◟✿❋◟✿❋◟✿❋◟✿❋◟✿❋◟✿❋◟✿

EMBLEME XXX.

La douceur & l'vtilité de ses écrits.

Elle r'enferme, elle distille
Le doux, l'agreable, & l'vtile.

Fig. 2. *La Vie Symbolique du bienheureux François de Sales, comprise sous le voile de 52 emblèmes*. Par Adrien Gambart (Paris, 1664), p. 116

9

Bear Words

Gillian Jondorf

Deux compagnons pressés d'argent
A leur voisin Fourreur vendirent
La peau d'un Ours encor vivant,
Mais qu'ils tueraient bientôt, du moins à ce qu'ils dirent.
C'était le Roi des Ours au compte de ces gens.   5
Le Marchand à sa peau devait faire fortune.
Elle garantirait des froids les plus cuisants.
On en pourrait fourrer plutôt deux robes qu'une.
Dindenaut prisait moins ses Moutons qu'eux leur Ours:
Leur, à leur compte, et non à celui de la Bête.   10
S'offrant de la livrer au plus tard dans deux jours,
Ils conviennent de prix, et se mettent en quête,
Trouvent l'Ours qui s'avance, et vient vers eux au trot.
Voilà mes gens frappés comme d'un coup de foudre.
Le marché ne tint pas; il fallut le résoudre: 15
D'intérêts contre l'Ours, on n'en dit pas un mot.
L'un des deux Compagnons grimpe au faîte d'un arbre;
    L'autre, plus froid que n'est un marbre,
Se couche sur le nez, fait le mort, tient son vent,
    Ayant quelque part ouï dire   20
    Que l'Ours s'acharne peu souvent
Sur un corps qui ne vit, ne meut, ni ne respire.
Seigneur Ours, comme un sot, donna dans ce panneau.
Il voit ce corps gisant, le croit privé de vie,
    Et de peur de supercherie   25
Le tourne, le retourne, approche son museau,
    Flaire aux passages de l'haleine.
C'est, dit-il, un cadavre; Ôtons-nous, car il sent.
A ces mots, l'Ours s'en va dans la forêt prochaine.
L'un de nos deux Marchands de son arbre descend,   30
Court à son compagnon, lui dit que c'est merveille
Qu'il n'ait eu seulement que la peur pour tout mal.
Eh bien, ajouta-t-il, la peau de l'animal?
    Mais que t'a-t-il dit à l'oreille?
    Car il s'approchait de bien près,   35

Te retournant avec sa serre.
— Il m'a dit qu'il ne faut jamais
Vendre la peau de l'Ours qu'on ne l'ait mis par terre.

When this fable was set for commentary in Part II of the Cambridge Modern and Medieval Languages Tripos some years ago the resulting scripts were disappointing, enlivened only by the candidate who supported her theory that the bear was Louis XIV with the argument that 'a skinned bear looks like a man'. In examining the fable, I shall concentrate on three aspects: comparison with other versions, La Fontaine's humour, and the question of the moral.

Editors cite three precursors for La Fontaine's treatment of this story, Aesop, Abstemius, and Commynes.[1] By far the closest of these is Commynes, so close indeed that there can be little doubt that La Fontaine knew Commynes's version. However, rather than studying sources, I shall be looking at various versions of the fable to draw out what is special about La Fontaine's.

The first thing that strikes the reader who begins to browse among these versions is that in the earliest ones, although the middle of the story is the same (one man climbing a tree and the other playing dead, and the bear being taken in by this ruse), the opening plot device and the moral are quite different. In Aesop the men are simply travellers (*hodoiporoi*) and friends (*philoi*). Their meeting with the bear is unintentional. When the tree-climbing friend asks his fellow-traveller what the bear said, the answer is: 'Not to travel in future with friends who do not stand by you in danger.' The narrator's moral is: 'This fable shows that genuine friends are to be recognised when tested in misfortune.' This is still the

---

[1] 'Aesop' is used here to refer to the body of Greek prose fables generally ascribed to a legendary sixth-century BC Samian slave mentioned by Herodotus, Aristophanes, and Plato. The bear fable can be found as no. 254 (p. 113) in Ésope, *Fables*, éd. et trad. par Émile Chambry (Paris: Société «Les Belles Lettres», 1921), or as no. 255 (vol. II, pp. 420–1) in *Aesopi fabulae recensuit Aemilius Chambry*, 2 vols (Paris: Société «Les Belles Lettres», 1925 and 1926). Abstemius was a fifteenth-century Venetian humanist who published a collection of one hundred Latin fables (*Hecatomythion*) in 1495, with an enlarged edition in 1499. The work continued to be reprinted: for example, there was an edition in Frankfurt in 1660. Philippe de Commynes's version of the bear fable can be found in the *Mémoires* (first six books published posthumously in 1524) for the year 1476. This book was also frequently reprinted in the seventeenth century, for example in Paris in 1662.

theme in Avianus.[2] In this more expansive version, one traveller (the one who is later obliged to feign death) felt safe because he believed he could depend on the support of the other whatever might befall them:

> securus, quodcumque malum fortuna tulisset,
> robore collato posset uterque pati.

This strengthens the force of the moral, and it is strengthened even further in the translation of a selection of Avianus' fables known as *L'Avionnet*, which formed part of some of the medieval fable-collections called *Isopets*:

> Deus hommes ensemble se mistrent
> Et par les fois s'entrepromistrent
> Qu'am tous cas s'entracorderoient
> En tous les lieus ou il vendroient.[3]

In Caxton's tale of the 'two felawes', the emphasis in preamble and moral is less on misfortune as the test of friendship than on the destruction of trust by deception.[4] 'Man ought not to hold felawship with hym / whiche is acustommed to begyle other', we are told before the story begins. The two men, like those in the *Avionnet*, 'were sworne eche one to the other / that none of them both shold leve other unto that the tyme of dethe shold come and departe them', and the disappointed friend says that the bear taught him 'many fayre secretes / but among alle other thinges he sayd to me that I shold never trust hym who ones hath deceyved me'.

With Commynes and Abstemius the bear-story changes, and the moral changes too. We now have the story more or less as La Fontaine will tell it. Both texts were accessible when La Fontaine was composing the *Fables*. The two characters in Abstemius are a hunter and a dealer in hides. Having paid in advance for the bearskin, the dealer out of curiosity

---

2 Avianus (fl. *c*. AD 400) wrote forty-two Latin fables in elegiac metre. Most, and perhaps all, are derived from the Greek verse fables of Babrius. Babrius published, probably in the second century AD, ten books of (mainly Aesopic) fables, of which one complete and one incomplete book survived in the manuscript tradition.

3 Quoted from *Recueil général des Isopets*, ed. Julia Bastin, Société des Anciens Textes Français (Paris: Honoré Champion, 1929), 2 vols, II. 355.

4 William Caxton, *The History and Fables of Aesop* (London: The Scolar Press, 1976), a facsimile of a copy of the 1484 edition in the Royal Library, Windsor, f. Cx^r–Cx^v.

(if rather improbably) accompanies the hunter and climbs a tree so as to have a good view of the 'sport'. The hunter sends his dogs into the bear's cave, the bear rushes out, the hunter misses his aim and is knocked over by the bear. Neither man is presented as frightened. Commynes's version tells of three men rather than two setting out to kill the bear (one runs back to town when the bear turns up) but otherwise resembles La Fontaine's even to the use of the word 'compagnons' for the men, and in the fact that they are short of money — to be precise, they owe money to an innkeeper and want to extend their credit. However, unlike La Fontaine's fable, Commynes's comes with a context and a strong political application. The fable, according to Commynes, is the reply given by the Emperor (Frederick III) to ambassadors from Louis XI who put to him a scheme to confiscate the lands and titles held by the last great duke of Burgundy (Charles le Téméraire) both from the Emperor and from the French crown. Plainly, the bear (which 'faisoit beaucoup de mal' in the neighbourhood of a German town) represents the duke of Burgundy. The Emperor's fable is glossed by Commynes:

> Et avec cette fable paya l'empereur nostre roy, sans faire autre responce à son homme, sinon en conseil, comme s'il vouloit dire: «Venez icy, comme vous avez promis, et tuons cet homme, si nous pouvons, et puis départons ses biens.»[5]

There are plenty of fables where La Fontaine proposes a political application; perhaps here he scarcely needs to since the Commynes version would probably have been known to a good many of his readers, who would recognise it as a story susceptible of political reading. Maybe a trace of the Emperor's use of the fable can be seen in La Fontaine's references to 'le Roi des Ours' and 'Seigneur Ours' — a grand and even regal personage, very different from the uncouth 'Ours montagnard, Ours à demi léché' of La Fontaine's 'L'Ours et l'Amateur des jardins' (VIII. 10). The *recueil* in which our bear fable appears was published in 1668 (*privilège* 6 June 1667; *achevé d'imprimer* 31 March 1668). Contemporary readers wishing to devise a political application could take their pick between the War of Devolution still in progress when the book appeared (it began 24 May 1667 and ended 2 May 1668), previous hostilities with Spain, like those ending with the Peace of the Pyrenees

---

5 Philippe de Commynes, *Mémoires sur Louis XI (1464–1483)*, ed. Jean Dufournet, Collection Folio 1078 (Paris: Gallimard, 1978), pp. 279–80.

(November 1659), or episodes from the turbulent career of the prince de Condé.

What, above all, distinguishes La Fontaine's version from any of the others is that it is funnier and cleverer. Most other versions are straight-forward and plain, even though there are some enlivening details such as the unusual verb (*periosphrainesthai*) used by Aesop for the action of the bear sniffing round the man on the ground. Many editions (including those of Caxton and Croxall) have charming woodcuts or engravings of the bear smelling the man on the ground while the companion watches from a tree (usually a very small tree, to fit into the frame). La Fontaine has other means of charming his reader. One of the sources of his hu-mour is the variation between concision and expansiveness. The opening three lines set up the situation very rapidly and the phrase 'encor vivant' even enables us to predict the outcome (as does the reference to Dindenault: praising his sheep led him to a deal that brought about his death).[6] Guessing the outcome (our guess strengthened by the narratorial comments in lines 4 and 10), we are amused as the text expands into the exuberantly inflated sales-talk of the 'compagnons'. In purely narrative terms, nothing happens between lines 2 and 12, then comes another burst of rapid narrative in lines 12–14, followed by a slowing of the pace for the rest of the events until the bear's departure. These changes of pace are more entertaining than a straightforward evenly-paced narrative like Aesop's.

The expansive passages are also full of comic devices. In the sales-talk, for example, there is a wealth of conditional verbs, used to represent the future in reported speech, but also the appropriate tense for a fantasy which will never be realised, so that there is a sort of grammatical pun here. This flight of eloquence, marked by hyperbole ('des froids les plus cuisants', 'plutôt deux robes qu'une') and by the culminating string of repetitions of 'leur' (ll. 10–11), is punctured twice by the narrator, first with the cautionary note of line 4, then by the demurral in the second part of line 10, commenting on the repeated 'leur' ('non à celui de la Bête'). These strengthen the reader's expectations of the outcome, without halt-ing the 'compagnons' who are plainly completely captivated by their own advertising.

The presentation of the bear is much more complex here than in earlier fables. Aesop simply tells of a bear suddenly coming into view ('arktou de autois epiphaneises'). The Greek noun *arktos* is feminine, and is used

---

6 The death of Dindenault is in Rabelais, *Le Quart Livre*, chapter VIII ('Comment Panurge feist en mer noyer le marchant et les moutons').

for bears of either sex; some Latin fabulists use 'Ursa', others 'Ursus' for their bear. Apart from that, there is little to choose between them. With Commynes and Abstemius, the bear gets a little more interesting. In Commynes, the bear is a known pest, causing damage like a fairy-tale dragon: 'auprès d'une ville d'Allemagne y avoit un grand ours, qui faisoit beaucoup de mal.' In Abstemius, the meeting with the bear is dramatic, and the bear's intentions hostile. As Lestrange's translation of Abstemius engagingly puts it, the bear when disturbed by the hunter's dogs 'Rustled out Immediately, and... Overturn'd him'.[7] In La Fontaine, we have only the *Compagnons*'s word for it that there is anything exceptional about the bear, but we certainly form a mental picture of a very large animal. This makes for a comic effect when the bear appears, for he appears 'au trot'. The trot is the second slowest gait of a horse, and the command 'au trot' tells the horse to speed up, or slow down, to a brisk, controlled, and elegant movement. No wonder the men are 'frappés comme d'un coup de foudre' at the sight of a trotting bear.

In spite of being thunderstruck, both men are able to devise evasive action. Climbing a tree is perhaps no safer than playing dead, since bears are good tree-climbers, but if you climb 'au faîte d'un arbre' then a very large bear will not be able to follow you, so the reader is relieved of worry about Tree-climber and is free to concentrate on Death-feigner.[8] Appropriately, fear of death has made him resemble his own funerary effigy — 'plus froid que n'est un marbre', 'le corps gisant' — but he nevertheless has enough self-possession to remember something he has heard about bears (ll. 20–1) and to take pains over his act ('tient son vent': the three clauses of line 19 are neatly echoed and explained by the three verbs of line 22).

Here we come to La Fontaine's boldest divergence from his predecessors. In other versions (later as well as earlier) the bear is taken in by the man's stillness. In La Fontaine, he is misled by the man's smell into thinking that he is sniffing a cadaver. The narrator stresses that it is after sniffing 'aux passages de l'haleine' that the bear comes to this conclusion: this certainly implies a formidable case of halitosis but protects the polite narrator from the suspicion that he might be suggesting another kind of smell (extreme fear loosens the bowels...). On the other hand Death-feigner 'tient son vent', so how can the bear smell his breath? This is a puzzle for the reader which La Fontaine does not solve. Another

---

[7] Roger L'Estrange, *Fables of Æsop and Other Eminent Mythologists; With Morals and Reflexions* (London: for R. Sare, T. Sawbridge, B. Took, etc., 1692), p. 261.

[8] I label the two men thus for brevity.

innovation follows. I think it is unique for the bear to speak at this point in the story, but the fact that this bear does so sets up La Fontaine's last joke. As readers, we 'hear' the bear say that the man must be dead because he smells so bad. But when Death-feigner is asked by Tree-climber what the bear said to him, instead of repeating what we 'heard' the bear say to him, Death-feigner saves the narrator a job by producing the moral of the fable. Why? Did he not hear what the bear said? Was he embarrassed by it? Did the bear not say it? Did the bear say what Death-feigner says he did?

Something odd is happening here. In other versions of the fable, I imagine most readers would assume that they are to understand that the bear said nothing at all to the man, but that he is communicating his own hard-won wisdom and (in many versions) expressing his sense of betrayal by his friend. If the bear had thought the man was alive (and therefore worth speaking to) he would have killed him, not given him good advice. Dialogue between humans and other species is not very frequent in La Fontaine's fables, occurring in only about a dozen (it is impossible to be precise because sometimes it is not clear whether we are to think that an animal has spoken and been understood or not). In some cases, La Fontaine seems to go out of his way to justify the device by indicating the special circumstances in which animals could speak to humans: 'Du temps que les bêtes parlaient' (IV. 1); 'On vous rend déjà la parole' (Ulysse to his transmogrified crewmen, XII. 1). Here we are given no such guidance. Perhaps the bear's first reported utterance was incomprehensible to Death-feigner, although clear to the privileged narrator and therefore to his reader. The bear was certainly talking to himself ('Ôtons-nous', using a grand plural form as befits this lordly bear), and this can be done either aloud or silently. If we think Death-feigner heard and understood it, then it follows that the bear didn't say what Death-feigner attributes to him in the last two lines of the fable. Yet there is a sense in which the bear *did* say precisely that, since this is the lesson that Death-feigner has learnt from his encounter with the bear; it is what the bear taught him, and therefore in a non-literal sense it is indeed what the bear said to him. It is also, of course, what the fabulist is saying to us, so three voices are involved here, those of the bear, the *compagnon*, and the fabulist.

But there are few if any La Fontaine fables where the moral content (in the widest possible sense) is restricted to a lesson summed up in a proverbial moral tag. Sometimes the moral tag is withheld so that the reader is forced to discover the moral meaning of a fable for herself, and may well discover two or three (this is conspicuously true of the opening fable of Book I). Sometimes the wording of the tag itself creates ambiguity or opens up the fable to multiple interpretation — this is most strikingly the case in 'Le Pot de terre et le Pot de fer' (V. II):

> Ne nous associons qu'avecque nos égaux.
> Ou bien il nous faudra craindre
> Le destin d'*un de ces Pots.*

(My emphasis.) The last four words transform the fable. In other versions of this fable it is clear that the earthenware pot's fate is the one to be feared, but La Fontaine with these four short words makes us wonder which is really worse, to suffer an accident or to cause one.

In the bear fable, readers familiar with other versions will be conscious of a sort of 'ghost-moral', that of the oldest versions: friendship is not proved genuine until tested; pick your friends carefully; never trust again someone who has deceived you or let you down. But while these morals may occur to some readers (and they are stated or implied elsewhere in La Fontaine, in for example V. 2: 'Le Pot de terre et le Pot de fer'; VIII. 10: 'L'Ours et l'Amateur des jardins'; XII. 2: 'Le Chat et les deux Moineaux'), La Fontaine has made clear that he is not following the line of older fabulists who cast blame on Tree-climber. He makes no moral distinction between the two men, nor does the story from the start seem to concern one more than the other (as it does in Avianus). They are referred to in the plural until their actions diverge, with a tone of affectionate banter applied to both ('Voilà mes gens frappés'; 'nos deux Marchands'). But if La Fontaine suppresses one possible dimension of the story, he introduces others which nudge the reader into thinking about human behaviour and thus form part of the *moraliste* baggage of the fable.

The question of the bear's words (did he speak once, twice, or not at all?) has already been raised, but associated with it is another one: was the bear stupid? La Fontaine says that he was taken in by Death-feigner 'comme un sot' (l. 23), but a foolish action is not necessarily proof of stupidity (as La Rochefoucauld tells us[9]), and the bear acts very intelligently. He sees a body on the ground, forms a hypothesis (l. 24), but cautiously ('de peur de supercherie', l. 25) tests it by careful observations (ll. 26–7) which seem to confirm his hypothesis, and so concludes (erroneously but logically) that it is indeed a dead body. A scientific,

---

[9] See, for example, Maxime 415: 'L'esprit nous sert quelquefois hardiment à faire des sottises.'

indeed a Cartesian bear. That he misinterprets the evidence is hardly his fault.

What about the *compagnons*? Are they cleverer or less clever than the bear? In a sense they and the bear make the same mistake: the men were at fault in anticipating the bear's death, but similarly the bear wrongly assumed the man to be dead. Of course it is unwise to 'Vendre la peau de l'Ours qu'on ne l'ait mis par terre', but the *compagnons* were clever in their persuasive sales-talk, and resourceful in escaping from the bear. Although it may seem silly to be completely flabbergasted by the appearance of a bear which you are actually looking for, the unexpected arrival of a large bear moving fast perhaps justifies their fright (remember 'au trot', slowish for a horse but terrifyingly fast for an approaching bear), and perhaps also it is a surprise to find that the bear is as big as they said he was.

They are certainly incompetent hunters: but whether or not they are also inept businessmen is another question that we cannot answer. La Fontaine seems to want us to keep it in mind, as the narrator introduces business terms at the moment of greatest drama (ll. 15–16), and again in line 30 when the *compagnons* become 'nos deux Marchands'. But who has been the more unwise, whether the *compagnons* or the 'voisin Fourreur' (l. 2), is not clear because we do not know whether the 'Fourreur' paid in advance for the skin. The use of 'vendirent' in line 2 suggests that he did, but in line 12 they merely 'conviennent de prix' before setting out, and lines 16–17, humorously suggesting that the bear might be liable to pay compensation for failing to be killed, do not tell us whether the unfulfillable 'marché' included a cash payment. Some fabulists are less ambivalent: 'A *Currier* bought a *Bear-skin* of a *Hunts-man*, and laid him down ready Money for't', runs Lestrange's translation of Abstemius, and in his 'Reflexion' he points out that 'with the Moralist's Leave, the Uncertainty was on the Other Hand, and he that *Bought* the Skin ran a Greater Risque than T'other that *Sold* it; and had the Worse End of the Staff'.[10]

La Fontaine often leaves a good deal to the reader; here we must work out for ourselves not only who, if anyone, is stupid and who is clever, but even the meaning of individual lines. For example, when Tree-climber says 'Eh bien...la peau de l'animal?', what tone of voice should we hear this in, what intention should we read into it? A proposal to resume the hunt? A reluctance to believe what he saw happen? A question as to whether the skin was really worth risking their lives for? La

---

[10] Roger L'Estrange, *Fables of Æsop*, p. 262

Fontaine's relationship with his reader is never discourteous but it is often teasing, and to tease us is one of his ways of amusing us. The balance between humour and the invitation to thought is one form of that 'equilibrium of wit', so characteristic of *moraliste* thought and practice, which Dorothy Gabe Coleman and Peter Bayley chose as the theme and title of the volume of essays they edited in honour of Odette de Mour-gues.[11] Perhaps no-one exemplifies it better than La Fontaine.

[11] *The Equilibrium of Wit: Essays for Odette de Mourgues*, ed. Dorothy Gabe Coleman and Peter Bayley (Lexington, KY: French Forum, 1982).

10

Reading the Signs:
With the Princesse de Clèves at Coulommiers

Jonathan Mallinson

M. de Clèves ne douta point du sujet de ce voyage, mais il résolut de
s'éclaircir de la conduite de sa femme et de ne pas demeurer dans une
cruelle incertitude. Il eut envie de partir en même temps que M. de
Nemours et de venir lui-même caché découvrir quel succès aurait ce
voyage. Mais, craignant que son départ ne parût extraordinaire, et que M. de   5
Nemours, en étant averti, ne prît d'autres mesures, il résolut de se fier à un
gentilhomme qui était à lui, dont il connaissait la fidélité et l'esprit. Il lui
conta dans quel embarras il se trouvait. Il lui dit quelle avait été jusqu'alors
la vertu de Mme de Clèves et lui ordonna de partir sur les pas de M. de
Nemours, de l'observer exactement, de voir s'il n'irait point à   10
Coulommiers et s'il n'entrerait point la nuit dans le jardin.

Le gentilhomme, qui était très capable d'une telle commission, s'en
acquitta avec toute l'exactitude imaginable. Il suivit M. de Nemours jusqu'à
un village, à une demi-lieue de Coulommiers, où ce prince s'arrêta, et le
gentilhomme devina aisément que c'était pour y attendre la nuit. Il ne crut   15
pas à propos de l'y attendre aussi. Il passa le village et alla dans la forêt, à
l'endroit par où il jugeait que M. de Nemours pouvait passer. Il ne se
trompa point dans tout ce qu'il avait pensé. Sitôt que la nuit fut venue, il
entendit marcher, et, quoiqu'il fît obscur, il reconnut aisément M. de
Nemours. Il le vit faire le tour du jardin, comme pour écouter s'il n'y   20
entendrait personne, et pour choisir le lieu par où il pourrait passer le plus
aisément. Les palissades étaient fort hautes, et il y en avait encore derrière
pour empêcher qu'on ne pût entrer en sorte qu'il était assez difficile de se
faire passage. M. de Nemours en vint à bout néanmoins. Sitôt qu'il fut dans
ce jardin, il n'eut pas de peine à démêler où était Mme de Clèves. Il vit   25
beaucoup de lumières dans le cabinet; toutes les fenêtres en étaient ouvertes,
et, en se glissant le long des palissades, il s'en approcha avec un trouble et
une émotion qu'il est aisé de se représenter. Il se rangea derrière une des
fenêtres, qui servaient de porte, pour voir ce que faisait Mme de Clèves. Il
vit qu'elle était seule; mais il la vit d'une si admirable beauté qu'à peine fut-   30
il maître du transport que lui donna cette vue. Il faisait chaud, et elle n'avait
rien, sur sa tête et sur sa gorge, que ses cheveux confusément rattachés.
Elle était sur un lit de repos, avec une table devant elle, où il y avait plusieurs

corbeilles pleines de rubans; elle en choisit quelques-uns, et M. de Nemours
remarqua que c'étaient des mêmes couleurs qu'il avait portées au tournoi. Il   35
vit qu'elle en faisait des nœuds à une canne des Indes, fort extraordinaire,
qu'il avait portée quelque temps et qu'il avait donnée à sa sœur, à qui Mme
de Clèves l'avait prise sans faire semblant de la reconnaître pour avoir été à
M. de Nemours. Après qu'elle eut achevé son ouvrage avec une grâce et
une douceur que répandaient sur son visage les sentiments qu'elle avait   40
dans le cœur, elle prit un flambeau et s'en alla proche d'une grande table,
vis-à-vis du tableau du siège de Metz, où était le portrait de M. de Nemours;
elle s'assit et se mit à regarder ce portrait avec une attention et une rêverie
que la passion seule peut donner.

On ne peut exprimer ce que sentit M. de Nemours dans ce moment. Voir   45
au milieu de la nuit, dans le plus beau lieu du monde, une personne qu'il
adorait, la voir sans qu'elle sût qu'il la voyait, et la voir tout occupée de
choses qui avaient du rapport à lui et à la passion qu'elle lui cachait, c'est ce
qui n'a jamais été goûté ni imaginé par nul autre amant.

(La Fayette, *La Princesse de Clèves*[1])

This famous vision of the Princesse de Clèves at Coulommiers has often
been seen as one of the novel's defining moments. For the heroine, it
suggests a moment of freedom from the constraints of the court when
she can be herself and openly express her feelings; for Nemours it offers
an incontrovertible sign of love, previously seen only fleetingly or indirectly; and for the reader, it is a rare glimpse of truth in a text dominated
by deception. In different ways critics have implied the clarity of the
scene and have been quick to extract from it evidence of the heroine's
passion. Butor, famously, attested to the phallic symbolism of the *canne
des Indes*;[2] Didier has come to similar conclusions about the potency of
the scene, exploring contemporary belief in the powerful, quasi-magical
properties of objects which represent or belong to another;[3] and Miller
has seen here a prefigurement of the heroine's final retreat in which erotic
longings are fulfilled in daydream.[4] Such apparent transparency, though,

---

[1] The text cited is that of the *Œuvres complètes*, ed. Roger Duchêne (Paris: Bourin,
    1990), pp. 367–8.

[2] 'Il n'est, certes, pas besoin d'un diplôme de psychanalyse pour percer et goûter le
    symbolisme de toute cette scène...' ('Sur *La Princesse de Clèves*', *Répertoire*, 1
    (Paris: Minuit, 1960), 74–8).

[3] B. Didier, 'Le Silence de la Princesse de Clèves', *Écriture-femme* (Paris: PUF,
    1981).

[4] N. K. Miller, 'Emphasis Added: Plots and Possibilities in Women's Fiction',
    Publications of the Modern Languages Association of America, XCVI (1981),
    36–48.

is deceptive. The gestures of the *princesse* may suggest her passionate thoughts, but the account of her actions is much more complex and misleading than these retrospective analyses may imply. We, like the characters, may be confident that we can read the signs, but the narrative offers a rather sterner test of, and lesson in, interpretation.

There can be little doubt that we are encouraged to see the scene as a moment of revelation. The narrative traces a series of interconnected actions leading steadily to the *princesse*: Clèves is keen to 's'éclaircir de la conduite de sa femme' (l. 2); the *gentilhomme* follows Nemours as part of Clèves's 'commission'; and Nemours himself enters the garden to watch the heroine. Furthermore, there is clearly every confidence on the part of the characters that truth can be attained through their actions. Clèves, we read, is resolved to shake off 'une cruelle incertitude' (ll. 2–3) and the *gentilhomme* is seen to be perfectly capable of fulfilling the task given him. The relationship of these two characters is seamless: Clèves can trust (*se fier à*) a man of unquestioned *fidélité* (ll. 6–7); he enjoins him to 'observer exactement' (l. 10), and the *gentilhomme* obeys the order 'avec toute l'exactitude imaginable' (l. 13). He is seen to make a number of correct judgements about Nemours's behaviour ('devina aisément' (l. 15), 'jugeait que' (l. 17)) and in spite of the darkness he can see exactly what Nemours is doing ('il reconnut aisément' (l. 19), 'il le vit' (l. 20)), even to the extent of being able to interpret his thoughts ('comme pour écouter' (l. 20)). The repetition of 'aisément' underlines his skill and suggests his reliability.

The representation of Nemours's activities significantly mirrors that of the *gentilhomme*; the same pattern of difficulties faced but overcome is to be found. Just as the *gentilhomme* is confronted with darkness but is able to see Nemours clearly, so Nemours is faced with a double row of fences but is nevertheless able to find a way into the garden; just as the 'gentilhomme reconnut aisément M. de Nemours', so Nemours 'n'eut pas de peine à démêler où était Mme de Clèves' (l. 25). Furthermore, once he has entered the garden the dominant images are of clarity: there is light everywhere and the windows are open. No further impediments, it seems, are to be found; Nemours has a direct view, and details of the heroine flood the narrative in a sequence of notations reflecting what he sees: 'Il vit beaucoup de lumières' (ll. 25–6), 'Il vit qu'elle était seule' (ll. 29–30), 'il la vit d'une si admirable beauté' (l. 30), 'Il vit qu'elle en faisait des nœuds' (ll. 35–6).

Just as the characters are confident that what they see reveals the truth, the reader is encouraged to trust the narrator's words. Clèves's position is clearly depicted in a series of authoritative statements ('M. de Clèves ne

douta point' (l. 1), 'il résolut' (l. 1), 'il eut envie' (l. 3), 'il résolut' (l. 6))
and the same is true of the *gentilhomme* whose own thoughts and deduc-
tions are unambiguously presented to us ('ne crut pas à propos' (ll. 15–
16), 'ne se trompa point' (ll. 17–18)). Similarly, when Nemours first
sees the heroine, he has feelings 'qu'il est aisé de se représenter' (ll. 28);
the narrator has the same easy assurance that the characters can be understood, and this assurance is passed on to the reader. We see the heroine at
a moment of privacy, rare in novels of the period, the naturalness of her
'cheveux confusément rattachés' (l. 32) seemingly reflecting her inner
state. The uninterrupted flow of verbs as we too watch her in action ('elle
était' (l. 33), 'elle…choisit' (l. 34), 'elle prit un flambeau et s'en alla'
(l. 41), 'elle s'assit et se mit à regarder' (l. 43)) further enhances the impression of a clear and direct vision of events. For all these signs of certainty, though, the passage has a more complex narrative texture; things
are not quite as they seem.

At one level, of course, it depicts a fundamental error on the part of the
gentilhomme, and through him, of Clèves. Both focus their attention on a
single action — Nemours's entry into the garden — and draw from this
general conclusions about his character and that of the *princesse*. Their
analysis, though, is flawed, and signs which appear to incriminate both
parties are shown to be misleading. Significantly, however, the reader is
also drawn into this error: we are led to misjudge the *gentilhomme* just as
he misjudges Nemours, to characterise him on the basis of evidence
which is only partial. When we are told that 'il ne se trompa point dans
tout ce qu'il avait pensé' (ll. 17–18) we inevitably assume that the infal-
lible judgement demonstrated in the past will continue into the future, that
the *gentilhomme*, once defined as a reliable judge, will continue to act in
accordance with this character. However, just as Nemours's later actions
diverge from the image of him created by his earlier deeds, so too apparently absolute statements are seen, in retrospect, to have a more limited
force. The ease with which the *gentilhomme* predicts Nemours's first actions is no guide to his future insight, and the authority of the statement
that '[il] devina aisément que c'était pour y attendre la nuit' (l. 15) invites
confidence in a skill which, in fact, is not to be sustained. The *gentilhomme*'s demonstration of 'toute l'exactitude imaginable' (l. 13) has a
validity simply for the moment, but it does not extend beyond the
present, beyond Nemours's entry into the garden. The confidence embedded in the narrative is seen in retrospect to reflect the *gentilhomme*'s
own over-confidence: he sees what he expects to see. And what is true of
him is true also of the reader. Not for the only time in the text, our implicit faith in the narrator's language is shown to be misplaced.

Significantly, the narrative slips unobtrusively from the *gentilhomme*'s perspective to that of Nemours, precisely at the point where the *gentilhomme* seemingly enters Nemours's thoughts: 'Il le vit faire un tour du jardin, comme pour écouter' (l. 20). His sight and insight are clear, and yet he loses both as Nemours enters the garden, leaving the *gentilhomme* behind, absent from the narrative. The transition is so discreet that it temporarily conceals the fact that what we see is no longer what the *gentilhomme* himself sees; we may be misled, even as he is.

However, the account of what Nemours himself sees is also in its own way misleading. If the representation of the *gentilhomme*'s movements had in part reflected his own angle of vision, the same is true of this next section. This perspective is suggested in the density of references to *voir* as Nemours first catches sight of the heroine and it is embedded in other ways in the narrative. Apparently neutral statements of fact simultaneously suggest the character's own perception: narrator and character blend. The observation, for instance, that 'Il faisait chaud' (l. 31) may be an objective statement about the ambient temperature, but following as it does a reference to Nemours's barely contained 'transport' at the sight of the heroine, it carries an additional force; in this balmy atmosphere, fantasy and reality may merge. Similarly, the observation that 'elle n'avait rien, sur sa tête et sur sa gorge' (ll. 31–2) does not merely represent fact, but suggests too the degree of attention which Nemours pays to the heroine as he fixes his gaze on her. His intention may have been to 'voir ce que faisait Mme de Clèves' (l. 29), but it is her physical presence which first catches his attention, her 'admirable beauté' (l. 30).

Similar hints of subjectivity characterise the analysis of the heroine's actions. The final sentence of the paragraph brings together verbs of action ('Après qu'elle eut achevé…, elle prit un flambeau et s'en alla…' (ll. 39, 41)) and interpretative statement ('avec une grâce et une douceur que répandaient sur son visage les sentiments qu'elle avait dans le cœur' (ll. 39–41)). At one level the analysis, like the narrative, might seem to have unequivocal authority. However, in a paragraph dominated at the start by its subjective references, the actions depicted are still dependent, by implication, on 'Il vit'. Similarly, the terms 'grâce' and 'douceur', attributed so categorically to the heroine, may express the narrator's judgement but also reflect that of the observer, whose own earlier 'trouble' and 'émotion' had been recorded at the sight of her 'admirable beauté'. The same uncertainty of focus characterises the next observation. A seemingly unequivocal statement is made that the heroine's 'attention' and 'rêverie' are unambiguous signs of 'passion' (l. 44); however the same possibility of contamination by context is apparent. This is further enhanced by the next paragraph where the renewed, insistent repetition of *voir* underlines the character's perspective. His observation of a 'passion qu'elle lui cachait' (l. 48) picks up the earlier reference to 'passion' and adds a subjective cast to the conclusion about the heroine's feelings. To this extent, it is not clear how far we see the heroine at all; what we see may just be Nemours's perception of her, reality mediated through his own desires. The narrator may simply be recording Nemours's own conclusions about the heroine, presenting them with the same semblance of authority as Nemours himself invests them with. This is the paradox of the passage: just like the *gentilhomme* who appears to get directly to the truth but stops short, the narrative appears to lead unequivocally and relentlessly to the *princesse*, but it too may not get beyond Nemours. Apparent omniscience blends then with an implied *style indirect libre*, destabilising the narrative perspective and casting doubt on the authority of statements whose authority seems absolute.

The scene, though, is misleading in other ways. Nemours believes that the signs of passion he detects in the *princesse* are a guide to the future: she loves him, his happiness is therefore assured. He may end the passage in a state of delight unknown to any other lover, but, as we shall subsequently discover, this moment of promise is not to be fulfilled; the lovers will not exceed all others in their shared bliss. The hero's joyful assumptions, too, are cast into doubt by the narrative, and signs of happiness are accompanied by other, contradictory signs. At one level, it is clear that the characters' perception of the scene is quite different from reality: the *princesse* does not realise that she is being observed, and Nemours does not know that he has been followed. The same possibility of error is implied, too, in their perceptions of each other. What may appear to depict the love of these two characters is as much a scene of separation as it is of mutual passion. Nemours and the *princesse* are not only physically separate, but metaphorically alone, too. Both look at an ideal, idealised representation of the other. Nemours is seen to be entranced by an image of the *princesse*, alone, beautiful, and absorbed in thoughts of him; the *princesse*, too, is seen to be captivated by an image of Nemours, heroic and chivalrous. Such images may correspond in part to the 'truth' of the characters, but the extent to which they reflect the whole person is left in doubt. The *princesse* may at this moment be full of passion, but this tells us nothing about how she may subsequently behave; the *portrait* of Nemours may depict him in a heroic context, but this reveals nothing for certain about his nature. What dominates the narrative is not so much the authenticity of these images as their status as images. The verb *voir* regularly recurs in the account of Nemours's thoughts, and the *princesse* herself is caught in the same light, seen to *regarder*, obsessed by a *portrait* of Nemours. Such references to sight may suggest clarity and certainty, a reflection of reality, and yet they simultaneously throw attention back on the perceiver; they do not denote togetherness but separation, they do not guarantee the future but only reflect the present. Significantly, there is no dialogue in this scene; the characters communicate only with themselves.

At one level, the reader may be led to believe that he is in a privileged position, aware of the ironies, knowing more than the characters. And yet we are not privy to everything. On the contrary, the signs which we are given are no less equivocal than those which confront the others. If the characters gain little reliable insight into each other, neither does the reader learn much about them. For all its apparent clarity, the scene in fact tells us very little. As far as the *princesse* is concerned, critical attention has traditionally concentrated on the force of the *canne des Indes* as the focus for her passion. Less time has been given to the statement that 'Mme de Clèves l'avait prise sans faire semblant de la reconnaître pour avoir été à M. de Nemours' (ll. 37–9). This observation may suggest the narrator's openness and omniscience, introducing information in order to explain her possession of the *canne*. In other ways, though, it is a subversive statement and paradoxically draws attention to the narrator's unreliability. This fact about the heroine has been concealed from the reader until now, even though it is an act no less significant than Nemours's own appropriation of her *portrait*; its disclosure at this point underlines what has previously been concealed. Furthermore, it serves simultaneously to lead the reader astray. By drawing attention to an act of surreptitious theft equivalent to that of Nemours, it encourages us to see in both characters the same manifestation of love, a parallel which seems to imply and prefigure a future harmony. However, the expectation thus aroused will not be fulfilled, and the knowledge we may think we gain from the narrator will prove to be unfounded.

Other problems arise from the different and conflicting intertextual associations of this kind of scene. In *L'Astrée*, Celadon's regular furtive glimpses of Astrée while in disguise are marks of his passionate and ideal love; in the same text, though, Climanthe is seen to spy on Galathée and Leonide in a much more villainous manner. The act of secret observation may be a sign of true love, or it may equally suggest some kind of tyrannical desire for possession, an intrusion, a rape. Literary antecedents do not allow us any kind of certainty. The passage, in fact, offers us two visions of Nemours, but the relationship between the two is not clarified. At one level we may see here the two classic roles of the fictional hero, the soldier and the lover. Alternatively, the two may be juxtaposed in a more provocative way, suggesting a distinction between the character in the painting, open, stable and unchanging, and the character in the garden, secretive and stalking. Are the two visions complementary or self-contradictory? Which is the 'real' Nemours? Both are presented to us with no further narratorial comment, and with no guidance as to how they should be read.

The same is true of the terms with which Nemours is presented to us by the narrator. Language can neither fathom nor convey the complexity of his character. We are told that 'à peine fut-il maître du transport que lui donna cette vue' (ll. 30–1), but this comment tells us little about Nemours. The term *transport* refers merely to the intensity of his feelings rather than to their nature; nor is it a reliable guide to their durability, focusing simply on the emotion aroused at a particular moment, by a single stimulus, 'cette vue'. It neither confirms nor denies that he is in love. We may see more of Nemours than the *gentilhomme*, but in fact we are little wiser about what he is like. The beatific vision of the final sentence is characteristically ambiguous, containing insistent references to the self alongside evocations of the heroine. Such references may imply the selfish, predatory nature of the hero; they may suggest the essentially subjective and misleading nature of his conclusions; or they may reflect simply the extent of a joy which brings together the self and the other. Clarity, though, is impossible to find in the text. This makes the final phrase so difficult to read; it may express hitherto unattained heights of joy in love, but it may equally well imply the difficulty of interpreting or categorising the character in a situation unlike that of any other lover. Such is the narrator's language that it remains on the surface of characters and events, undermining its own apparent authority, leaving open the possibility of different readings. The language of absolutes may be common in the *roman*, but here we are made to be on our guard. Different possibilities coexist in the narrative as they coexist perhaps in the character, who remains as opaque as the terms which describe him. Nowhere is this more apparent than in the sentence 'On ne peut exprimer ce que sentit M. de Nemours dans ce moment' (l. 45). This negative formulation may be a classic way of expressing sublime love, but it also suggests the impenetrability of the character; nobody, not even the narrator, can say for certain what he feels.

To a certain extent Coulommiers stands, like the passage itself, as the location of an impenetrable truth. It does not willingly admit intruders, and has a double row of fences 'pour empêcher qu'on ne pût entrer en sorte qu'il était assez difficile de se faire passage' (ll. 23–4). There is a certain measure of confidence on the part of those who attempt to break into it. The *gentilhomme*, like Nemours, is confident that he knows the answers, and yet both come away with no firm grip on reality. At the end of this passage the reader too is arguably no wiser. The signs are no easier to interpret for the reader than they are for the characters, and what appears straightforward is in practice much less so. We may think that what we see in this apparently privileged moment will give us some insight into the characters, some idea of how the novel will end; but if we do, we are going to be disappointed. For all involved, *gentilhomme*, Nemours, *princesse*, reader, seeing may be believing; but, the text shows us, to see is not to know. Characters turn out to be unpredictable, unfathomable, and the language which describes them loses its authority. This scene of apparent openness and disclosure is in fact one of deception and confusion. The reader, like the characters, is caught seeing what he wishes or expects to see. The text does not simply represent a scene of misunderstanding, it enacts it, inviting us to read the signs while simultaneously blurring what they signify.

11

The Divine Sentence

Henry Phillips

Prêtez-moi l'un et l'autre une oreille attentive.
Je ne veux point ici rappeler le passé,   465
Ni vous rendre raison du sang que j'ai versé.
Ce que j'ai fait, Abner, j'ai cru le devoir faire.
Je ne prends pas pour juge un peuple téméraire;
Quoi que son insolence ait osé publier,
Le ciel même a pris soin de me justifier.   470
Sur d'éclatants succès ma puissance établie
A fait jusqu'aux deux mers respecter Athalie.
Par moi Jérusalem goûte un calme profond.
Le Jourdain ne voit plus l'Arabe vagabond
Ni l'altier Philistin, par d'éternels ravages,   475
Comme au temps de vos rois, désoler ses rivages;
Le Syrien me traite et de reine et de sœur.
Enfin de ma maison le perfide oppresseur,
Qui devait jusqu'à moi pousser sa barbarie,
Jéhu, le fier Jéhu, tremble dans Samarie;   480
De toutes parts pressé par un puissant voisin,
Que j'ai su soulever contre cet assassin,
Il me laisse en ces lieux souveraine maîtresse,
Je jouissais en paix du fruit de ma sagesse,
Mais un trouble importun vient, depuis quelques jours,   485
De mes prospérités interrompre le cours.
Un songe (me devrais-je inquiéter d'un songe?)
Entretient dans mon cœur un chagrin qui le ronge.
Je l'évite partout, partout il me poursuit.
C'était pendant l'horreur d'une profonde nuit.   490
Ma mère Jézabel devant moi s'est montrée,
Comme au jour de sa mort pompeusement parée.
Ses malheurs n'avaient point abattu sa fierté;
Même elle avait encore cet éclat emprunté
Dont elle eut soin de peindre et d'orner son visage,   495
Pour réparer des ans l'irréparable outrage.
«Tremble, m'a-t-elle dit, fille digne de moi;
«Le cruel Dieu des Juifs l'emporte aussi sur toi.
«Je te plains de tomber dans ses mains redoutables,

«Ma fille». En achevant ces mots épouvantables,   500
Son ombre vers mon lit a paru se baisser;
Et moi je lui tendais les mains pour l'embrasser,
Mais je n'ai pu trouvé qu'un horrible mélange
D'os et de chair meurtris et traînés dans la fange,
Des lambeaux pleins de sang et des membres affreux   505
Que des chiens dévorants se disputaient entre eux.

(Racine, Athalie, II. v, lines 464–506)

Athalie makes her first entrance in Act II, scene 3, appearing alone with Abner in scene 4, joined by Mathan in scene 5. She is thus in the presence of two representatives of the Jews, one who serves his queen having remained faithful to his religion, and one who has abandoned his religion to serve the queen.

Athalie has of course been present in the play before this point in the descriptions of her by other characters. It is no surprise that the epithets used are negative, like 'Cette reine jalouse' (l. 31), 'la superbe Athalie' (l. 51), 'l'injuste Athalie' (l. 206) and 'de Jézabel la fille sanguinaire' (l. 59). This latter reference is particularly supported by a vivid portrayal of the queen as the killer of children (ll. 243–6). Other details help to situate the words which are the subject of this commentary. First, we are prepared for the state of mind of Athalie by the news that she 'Dans un sombre chagrin paraît ensevelie' (l. 52). Secondly, she has been ejected from the inner sanctum of the temple where women are forbidden to enter (ll. 398–406). Thirdly, she has been reduced to silence by the sight of Joas (ll. 411–14). The beginning of her first speech in Act II, scene 5 is indeed a reaction to Mathan noticing that the queen is still in a state of agitation, thus suggesting that something in her appearance betrays her condition.

Athalie opens by interrupting Mathan, since she does not wish to be reminded of what has just happened. Her use of the imperative seeks to regain the speech initiative which has been interrupted by Joad's brutal intervention and by the sight of Éliacin. Her command is thus an attempt to remind her interlocutors of her authority, of which the reaffirmation of voice is a mark. She refocuses attention on herself as queen and not as troubled individual.

The situation of speech at this point is worthy of note. 'Ici' (l. 465), implying that this is neither the time nor the place, is an example of how words have resonances beyond their seeming innocence. Time and place are each relevant to the day on which the action of the play takes place. It is the day of sacrifice when the Jews are celebrating God's communication of the Ten Commandments to Moses and is thus a symbol of the antiquity of the Jewish religion, as is the temple, a place where Athalie's presence is a stain on its purity. None of this can be lost on either Athalie or Mathan, the one whose political authority ensures the continuing worship of Baal, the other who is an apostate Jew. Moreover, the first commandment is 'Thou shalt have no other gods before me' and the second 'Thou shalt not make unto thee any graven image' (Exodus 20. 3–4), both of which are relevant to the idea of idolatry contained in the worship of Baal. The celebration of this religious past is in itself a reminder to Athalie at a moment when she is about to propose herself as the creator of a modern history. The tenses themselves project the past into the present through the use of the perfect. This is not a past which can so easily be forgotten, even in the manner of speaking of it. The day of sacrifice is in addition the occasion for blood as a sacred offering, whereas the blood to which Athalie refers in line 466 has been shed in a sacrilegious act, the murder of the children of David's line.

However imperious her opening line may be and however authoritative her refusal to justify herself may appear (ll. 465–6), the imperative is immediately undermined by the negative 'Je ne veux point', since it refers to the possibility that justification is what is expected of her. It sounds like an answer to a question that has not been asked but which she is aware of in her mind. After placing others in the situation of listening as a mark of her authority, she does implicitly the same for herself, admitting to an authority outside her own with which she can be compared. The very need to enunciate a refusal to speak underlines her recognition that it is both necessary and inescapable. 'Je ne veux point' emerges here as a wish rather than a refusal since lines 471–84 demonstrate that her need to justify herself, itself a sign of uncertainty, outstrips her desire not to. That she may indeed have something on her conscience is further implied by her direct address to Abner whom she clearly wishes to recuperate. She recognises him as different, as someone to take account of, as someone to justify herself to. In his person he represents the unspoken question which I alluded to earlier.

Indeed, the text is dominated by ways in which Athalie's attempt to set herself up as her own authority and as the creator of a modern history independent of Jewish history are constantly undermined by her own words. This manifests itself in constant references to the Jewish people and how she relates to them. Despite the personalisation of history and politics apparent in the text, a personalisation which contrasts with the Jews as God's chosen people, as the instrument of God's will, these references deny her the possibility of putting herself forward as an absolute authority. The negative in her refusal to take the Jewish people as her judge is important. Who suggests that she should? Her authority is further undermined by the admission that the Jewish people offer a counter-voice in their public insolence. We know this voice to be in the minority (ll. 5–12), but it concerns Athalie sufficiently for her to need to refer to it.

The use of the negatives 'Je ne veux point' and 'Je ne prends pas', along with the use of the first-person pronoun which pervades the text, especially in the expression of the 'political' self of the queen, point to the competing themes of self-isolation and self-recuperation. On the one hand Athalie desires to arrogate to herself an absolute authority, that is to say an authority requiring no legitimation. On the other, she is aware of a sense of herself in relation to the Jewish people and Jewish history. This leads to the need for self-justification evident not only in her almost apologetic address to Abner but in the audacious suggestion (having just described the Jewish people as 'téméraire') that 'le ciel même a pris soin de me justifier' (l. 470). By availing herself of the authority of heaven, Athalie seeks legitimation within history. But Athalie can never avoid conveying an idea of self-isolation in her sense of relationship with others. The queen identifies herself as an outsider, hence as the usurper she is. In this speech she personalises her crime, thereby admitting to having acted on her own authority and, in spilling blood in her own name, she is seen in direct opposition to the blood being shed on the day of sacrifice in the name of God, a higher authority. Even if one interprets her appeal to heaven as a challenge to the God whose people she has appropriated as queen, this challenge is a further sign of that isolation of the self, the self as set apart, but one which can never be seen as autonomous. Her awareness of that difference is at the root of her anxiety, an anxiety which constantly undermines her attempts to establish herself as the source of her own legitimacy.

Nowhere are the themes of self-recuperation and self-isolation more apparent than in Athalie's promotion of herself as the originator of a modern history. In lines 471–83 Athalie presents a picture of herself as a successful and efficient queen, a picture giving rise to a self-evident right to her position. She suggests by the choice of 'ma puissance' that all this has been achieved on her own from a position of personal strength. In her own mind she realises a fusion of the personal and the historical. This fusion is further reflected in her objectivisation of herself in line 472 whereby she presents a counter-image to the image

Mathan has on seeing the queen. It will amount however to an image in words only.

The facts of the political situation do have some substance. As the re-sult of her 'éclatants succès', the political realities of the region evince some sense of stability and order. Deliberately her first example is Jerusalem itself, the seat of the Jewish religion, and provocatively 'Par moi' is placed in the strongest position. Hence what she has achieved through her own personal authority is implicitly contrasted with what others have not, even though their authority has derived supposedly from God. Is this an attempt on Athalie's part to deny in her mind the existence of that God whose authority she has flouted in taking over the reins of power? Indeed, Athalie never invokes the name of Baal to legit-imise her political authority so that this speech can be read as a secular political manifesto, perhaps reflected in 'respecter' (l. 472), a verb used in a human rather than a divine context.

The peace and stability which now exist in the region are further em-phasised as her own work when she alludes to the absence of marauding bands of Arabs and Philistines, and describes the current situation as preferable to 'Comme au temps de vos rois' (l. 476), a phrase in which, yet again, she cannot help but situate herself in relation to the kings whose place she has unjustly occupied. This contrasts with her desire to promote her image as 'modern', and indeed the use of 'éternels' (l. 475) suggests that Athalie has put an end to endlessness and instituted a new beginning. It is another sense of the word 'éternel' which Joad has in mind, for Athalie is isolated in time, isolated in history. She interrupts the continuum of Jewish history: in this perspective the idea of a secular history in the making is meaningless.

Athalie's attempts to elevate herself to the level of history cannot conceal an intensely personal aspect. Athalie's father, Ahab, was killed in a battle against 'Le Syrien' (l. 477) — the reference is to Azaël — and she now clearly sees it as a tribute that he should treat her well both politically and personally. The real sense of this relationship is however revealed in lines 478–83 when she informs her listeners that she has been able to persuade Azaël to rise up against Jéhu, the murderer of her son Ochosias (Ahaziah). This section of the narrative of her political successes, the longest devoted to a single individual and the most de-monised of her foes, is unquestionably the most bitter and the most per-sonal. Jéhu is invoked as 'le perfide oppresseur' (l. 478), 'cet assassin' (l. 482), and as the perpetrator of 'barbarie' (l. 479). Athalie in fact ex-poses herself even more to self-isolation and to the charge that she acts not out of authority as such but out of hatred and revenge. Her career is

seen to culminate in what she has done to Jéhu, not in terms of the efficient ruler or the maker of a modern history described earlier, but in
terms of a spiteful person. Her authority is her revenge. Revenge is not
absent from the Old Testament, but it is the vengeance of God.

The fact remains that Jéhu 'me laisse en ces lieux souveraine
maîtresse' (l. 483). The latter term is interesting not least because all her
rivals and allies are men. Athalie stands out as the *woman* of power.
Athalie represents at the same time the limits of power in the hands of
someone of her sex. As a woman she can exert influence, even fear,
over a vast expanse of territory, but the ruler of Jerusalem is forbidden
to enter the inner sanctum of the temple because she is a woman. The
male power that she comes up against here, not only in the context of
the Jewish religion but in the insistence on patriarchy in the line of
David, excludes her as queen, as follower of another religion, and as a
woman. Mathan later casts doubt on her authority as queen by explain-
ing her conduct precisely in terms of her nature as a woman (ll. 875–6).
She is a corrupt woman of power, a heretic, and vulnerable by virtue of
her gender.

But 'souveraine maîtresse' turns out to be particularly ironic when
Athalie turns to the intensely private world of her dreams where her
powers of control desert her. She can control neither what appears to
her in her dreams nor the way in which they continue to pursue her.
Racine marks the transition that takes place in Athalie's narrative by
introducing the imperfect tense ('jouissais') which acts as a clear break
from the present and perfect tenses of the previous lines. Athalie's ascendancy has now come to a halt, almost as if the political rhetoric is
now exhausted or has exhausted her. The historical text, focused on the
control of others, has reached a terminus, whereas, as we shall soon find
out, God's word, signified by the book on which Joas swears, is truly
eternal. But within the context of the imperfect, the present tenses of
lines 485–9 suggest a personal time of some duration in that the effects
of the dream still function even during her waking hours. That the
content of this personal time undermines our impression of the queen's
authority and self-control is also marked by the self-interrogation, isolated among so much affirmation, which isolates her within her own
history.

The dream is seen by Athalie herself as an interruption in time ('De
mes prospérités interrompre le cours'). The word 'fruit', while not rare
in Racinian tragedy (it appears in all 39 times), would have a particular
resonance here since it is so often used in the context of the vine in the
Old Testament. The vine is a frequent metaphor for Israel: the vine's

failure to flourish is seen as a sign of God's abandonment of Israel (Psalm 80. 8–13), or a lack of fruitfulness is seen as a consequence of Israel's faithlessness and disobedience towards God (Isaiah 5. 1–7). The idea that Athalie should avail herself of an image of fruitfulness reflects the appropriation of heaven's favour in line 470 and cries out therefore for God's revenge. The dream translates itself into the withering of Athalie's vine. This would especially be the case in view of the fact that Athalie conceives of her success as the result of 'sagesse'. Apart from one reference in *Les Plaideurs*, this word appears uniquely in the context of God's wisdom or that of the individuals he inspires (Esther). Just as Athalie has no right to 'fruit', as a heathen she has no right to 'sagesse', especially since she clearly interprets it as a secular quality.

The change in Athalie's fortunes can be interpreted in terms of a relationship between the spaces mentioned in her historical narrative and the world of the dream. The space of her power is indeed wide, stretching from the Red Sea to the Mediterranean (l. 472). In particular terms she moves from the confines of Jerusalem to the wider spaces of Jordan, and has the power to confine rulers like Jéhu to their own space. But at the same time as representing a political reality, her evocation of space is a rhetorical device which compensates for the way in which the narrow confines of the temple now seem to threaten her. Her reputation in the wider expanse, emphasised by what her name represents, contrasts strongly with her exclusion in the holy place of the Jewish religion. The temple as the space of belief and the focus of the legitimacy of David's line suggests that no amount of influence over geographical space, however extensive, can compensate for the power that emanates from the place over which Joad rules. In that sense, the temple is a spatial compression of the limitlessness of God's power.

The dream, the only one of its type in the whole of Racinian tragedy, is symbolic of another sort of space. Athalie may be able to 'lose' herself in her considerations of the wider territory, but this proves impossible in the unsounded depths of her conscience. The mention of 'paix' (l. 484) is inclusive of the two spaces of the political and the personal. What price peace in the wider space if Athalie finds it impossible to achieve peace of mind? This contrast once again highlights the rhetorical importance of her earlier narrative. In this way the enunciation of her narrative is more important than what it contains because it prevents her from reaching what she would rather not recount. Structurally, it is framed by the word 'trouble' used by both Mathan and Athalie herself (l. 460 and l. 485).

Athalie's dream continues the theme of self-isolation. Her political successes can be shared. They represent a space others can inhabit. A dream cannot. It is a space Athalie inhabits alone. Nor can she escape the dream which pursues her everywhere: 'Je l'évite partout, partout il me poursuit' (l. 489). The space of her conscience is as vast as the lands over which she wields influence: it also has depth, as the reference to 'une profonde nuit' (l. 490) implies. The space of the queen's conscience has the effect of an anti-space whose negativity is illustrated by the vocabulary of extreme feelings such as 'chagrin' (l. 488) and 'horreur' (l. 490). Athalie's anxiety is further emphasised by the paradoxical nature of the space of conscience she now inhabits. It may be vast but it is also being eaten away ('un chagrin qui le ronge' (l. 488)). Just as she becomes entrapped in the narrow confines of the temple, her habitable space is in the process of contraction.

The image of Jézabel reinforces Racine's concentration on time and space. Athalie's mother comes to represent in her body all the spaces I have evoked hitherto. Jézabel, we are told, is 'pompeusement parée' (l. 492). This is considerably qualified in lines 494–6 when Athalie describes her as bearing 'cet éclat emprunté' which immediately brings to mind the phrase employed by Athalie in the context of her achievements ('éclatants succès'). Jézabel's make-up was supposed to 'réparer des ans l'irréparable outrage' (l. 496). Jézabel's image is thus a parallel to the way in which Athalie's authority is borrowed or appropriated, and covers up the underlying state of affairs. However impressive the description of Athalie's success in rhetorical terms, she cannot wish away the illegitimacy of her power. She has no right to the appearance she gives of political authority. Indeed, the polyptoton of line 496 reminds us of the ultimate failure of her enterprise despite Athalie's unceasing efforts. Jézabel's person collapses, in the space of her body, the geographical expanse earlier described by Athalie at a time when this space itself collapses into the private space of her consciousness. In a sense, Jézabel also collapses the historical space since there is no escape for those who incur God's wrath. That 'outrage' is accompanied by 'irréparable' only serves to recall the unforgivable nature of Athalie's murder of her son's children, a crime which will be punished by 'le cruel Dieu des Juifs', especially since Athalie's mother considers her 'fille digne de moi' (l. 497). Athalie's arrogant belief that she is untouchable flies in the face of the example made of her mother which Athalie has seen in all its horror in the course of her dream.

But the last four lines of this speech do not mark out the space of conscience as an abstract space. Description of the kind we read here is exceedingly rare in Racine, especially in the terms used and especially be - cause animals make exceptional appearances in the tragedies. This space can also be conceived of as more real than the world outside her dream because it symbolises the justice of which she will soon be a vic- tim. It is the eternal promise of punishment for God's enemies as op- posed to the spurious peace of the modern history Athalie has attempted to create, especially when her actions in the wider expanse were meant to liberate her from Jewish history. The lasting image is one of physical dissolution. Just as Jézabel's body represents a symbolic collapsing of space, it now points to a bloody dispersal of everything Athalie has tried to put together.

Lines 464–506 reflect a number of themes found in other Racinian tragedies, particularly in the domain of speech. In the same way that Athalie eventually becomes entrapped in the temple, speech offers an- other form of trap. Athalie begins by endeavouring to say little but ends up saying a lot. Speech runs away with her. The more you say in Racine, the more you give away. In effect what she says undermines the very position from which she speaks. Her speech is an attempt to reassert her authority but simply underlines the way in which she has no right to it. Her loss of control is evident in the nature of the speech as self-address, despite the order to listen delivered at the beginning to her two interlocutors. Athalie has no need to remind either Mathan or Abner of her successes. But she needs to convince herself. She must establish her own text in opposition to another text which becomes prominent in the play, holy scripture. But her text is purely rhetorical and not yet written. It is God's word in scripture which represents what Athalie will never achieve in the simple reiteration of her successes in the ephemeral form of speech, especially in what is 'unspoken'. That is another way in which Athalie cannot aspire to the status of the creator of a modern history. The shadow of the history of the Jews is present at every stage, and concretised in the image of her mother's punishment. The very per- sonalisation contained in the political *récit* is placed in a context where divine providence denies personalisation, where personalisation is a mark of defiance and dissidence.

This text, then, provides us with a good example of the speech as a space in itself, a space which constantly reaches beyond itself. But, like Athalie's power, the more the speech extends its own space, the more likely it is that speech will collapse in on itself. All speech in Racine is fragile at the centre. Perhaps *Athalie* is the real culmination of Racinian tragedy in its assertion that the personal pronoun has no place in the divine sentence.

12

Diderot and the 'Modèle idéal'

Edward James

Mais, me direz-vous, il est donc impossible à nos artistes d'égaler jamais les anciens? Je le pense, du moins en suivant la route qu'ils tiennent, en n'étudiant la nature, en ne la recherchant, en ne la trouvant belle que d'après des copies antiques, quelque sublimes qu'elles soient, et quelque fidèle que puisse être l'image qu'ils en ont. Réformer la nature sur l'antique, c'est 5
suivre la route inverse des Anciens qui n'en avaient point; c'est toujours travailler d'après une copie. Et puis, mon ami, croyez-vous qu'il n'y ait aucune différence entre être de l'école primitive et du secret, partager l'esprit national, être animé de la chaleur, et pénétré des vues, des procédés, des moyens de ceux qui ont fait la chose, et voir simplement la chose faite? 10
croyez-vous qu'il n'y ait aucune différence entre Pigalle et Falconet à Paris, devant le *Gladiateur*, et Pigalle et Falconet dans Athènes, et devant Agasias? C'est un vieux conte, mon ami, que pour former cette statue vraie ou imaginaire que les anciens appelaient la règle, et que j'appelle le modèle idéal ou la ligne vraie, ils aient parcouru la nature, empruntant d'elle dans 15
une infinité d'individus les plus belles parties dont ils composèrent un tout. Comment est-ce qu'ils auraient reconnu la beauté de ces parties? De celles surtout qui, rarement exposées à nos yeux, telles que le ventre, le haut des reins, l'articulation des cuisses ou des bras, où le *poco più* et le *poco meno* sont sentis par un si petit nombre d'artistes, ne tiennent pas le nom de belles 20
de l'opinion populaire, que l'artiste trouve établie en naissant, et qui décide son jugement. Entre la beauté d'une forme et sa difformité, il n'y a que l'épaisseur d'un cheveu; comment avaient-ils acquis ce tact qu'il faut avoir, avant que de rechercher les formes les plus belles éparses, pour en composer un tout? Voilà ce dont il s'agit. Et quand ils eurent rencontré ces 25
formes, par quel moyen incompréhensible les réunirent-ils? Qu'est-ce qui leur inspira la véritable échelle à laquelle il fallait les réduire? Avancer un pareil paradoxe, n'est-ce pas prétendre que ces artistes avaient la connaissance la plus profonde de la beauté, étaient remontés à son vrai modèle idéal, à la ligne de foi, avant que d'avoir fait une seule belle chose? 30
Je vous déclare donc que cette marche est impossible, absurde. Je vous déclare que, s'ils avaient possédé le modèle idéal, la ligne vraie, dans leur imagination, ils n'auraient trouvé aucune partie qui les eût contentés à la rigueur. Je vous déclare qu'ils n'auraient été que portraitistes de celle qu'ils

auraient servilement copiée. Je vous déclare que ce n'est point à l'aide 35
d'une infinité de petits portraits isolés, qu'on s'élève au modèle original et
premier ni de la partie, ni de l'ensemble et du tout; qu'ils ont suivi une
autre voie, et que celle [du tâtonnement] que je viens de prescrire est celle
de l'esprit humain dans toutes ses recherches. Je ne dis pas qu'une nature
grossièrement viciée ne leur ait inspiré la première pensée de réforme, et 40
qu'ils n'aient longtemps pris pour parfaites des natures dont ils n'étaient
pas en état de sentir le vice léger, à moins qu'un génie rare ne se soit élancé
tout à coup du troisième rang, où il tâtonnait avec la foule, au second. Mais
je prétends que ce génie s'est fait attendre <et qu'il n'a pu faire lui seul ce
qui est l'ouvrage du temps et d'une nation entière>. Je prétends que c'est 45
dans cet intervalle du troisième rang, du rang de portraitiste de la plus belle
nature subsistante, soit en tout, soit en partie, que sont renfermées toutes
les manières possibles de faire avec éloge et succès, toutes les nuances
imperceptibles du bien, du mieux et de l'excellent. Je prétends que tout ce
qui est au-dessus est chimérique, et que tout ce qui est au-dessous est 50
pauvre, mesquin, vicieux. Je prétends que, sans recourir aux notions que je
viens d'établir, on prononcera éternellement les mots d'exagération, de
pauvre nature, de nature mesquine, sans en avoir d'idées nettes. Je prétends
que la raison principale pour laquelle les arts n'ont pu, dans aucun siècle,
chez aucune nation, atteindre au degré de perfection qu'ils ont eu chez les 55
Grecs, c'est que c'est le seul endroit connu de la terre où ils ont été soumis
au tâtonnement; c'est que, grâce aux modèles qu'ils nous ont laissés, nous
n'avons jamais pu, comme eux, arriver successivement et lentement à la
beauté de ces modèles; c'est que nous nous en sommes rendus plus ou
moins servilement imitateurs, portraitistes, et que nous n'avons jamais eu 60
que d'emprunt, sourdement, obscurément le modèle idéal, la ligne vraie;
c'est que, si ces modèles avaient été anéantis, il y a tout à présumer
qu'obligés comme eux à nous traîner d'après une nature difforme,
imparfaite, viciée, nous serions arrivés comme eux à un modèle original et
premier, à une ligne vraie qui aurait été bien plus nôtre qu'elle ne l'est et ne 65
peut l'être; et, pour trancher le mot, c'est que les chefs-d'œuvre des
Anciens me semblent faits pour attester à jamais la sublimité des artistes
passés, et perpétuer à toute éternité la médiocrité des artistes à venir. J'en
suis fâché; mais il faut que les lois inviolables de Nature s'exercent; c'est
que Nature ne fait rien par saut, et que ce n'est pas moins vrai dans les arts 70
que dans l'univers.

(Diderot, Salon de 1767, 'A mon ami Mr Grimm'[1])

The series of *Salons* which Diderot produced from 1759 to 1781 show
him to be the most gifted art critic of eighteenth-century France. His

---

[1] See Diderot, *Salons*, Texte établi et présenté par Jean Seznec, Second
Edition,Volume III, 1767 (Oxford, 1983), 52-65, pp. 61-63. The passage between
angle brackets < > is a later addition of Diderot's.

Salon of 1767 is particularly notable for a preamble addressed to 'Mon ami Mr Grimm' in which he develops an aesthetic theory of some com-plexity and great interest. Early in that preamble, Diderot imagines him-self putting to 'un de nos artistes les plus éclairés' the question whether a scrupulously accurate depiction of the most beautiful woman known to the artist would be a true representation of beauty.[2] His negative answer is inspired by the famous theory of imitation set out by Plato in the tenth book of *The Republic*. Plato takes as the object of his analysis the bed or table, and makes his celebrated tripartite distinction between (1) the idea and form of the bed, the bed as it really is in itself, as created by God; (2) the particular bed as made by a craftsman according to the idea or form of the bed; (3) the imitation by the artist of the particular bed made by the craftsman.[3] The artist's representation of a bed is therefore the imitation of an imitation, the phantasm of a phantasm and third in the order of creativity. But there is a major difference between Diderot's thesis and Plato's inasmuch as Diderot explicitly envisages the possibility of the artist's attaining to 'la ligne de beauté'[4] or 'ligne idéale', as distinct from 'une ligne individuelle'. The status and potential of the great artist are at once set on a high plane. Diderot's great artists are ancient Greeks, and an imaginary dialogue with Grimm follows in which Diderot emphasises the extraordinariness of the ancient Greek achievement, leading Grimm to conclude that there is no possibility of its being equalled by modern artists. This conclusion prompts the tirade which is the subject of our commentary.

The preamble to the *Salon* of 1767 is ostensibly an informal epistle to a friend, as the confidential, between-you-and-me-old-boy nudgings go to show; but it nevertheless has a formal polemical and didactic aim. In the passage commented on, Diderot argues his case by reiteration with variation, allowing of nuance, revision, and expansion. Although he is of-fering a critique of idealist conceptions of beauty, he is nonetheless de-fending an ideal, and there is an intriguing interplay between the empirical thrust of his argument and the ideality of the conception he defends. The structure of his argument does not appear preconceived, but rather to de-velop *ad hoc* as he becomes aware of the implications of his successive contentions — a process of 'tâtonnement' analogous to that which he at-

---

2 Seznec, p. 57.

3 In a later marginal addition (Seznec, p. 64), Diderot summarises Plato's principle bafflingly as 'secundus a natura; tertius ab idea'. Diderot surely intended to write: 'tertius a natura; secundus ab idea', but that is still not quite what Plato said.

4 For the notion of a 'line of beauty' see Hogarth, *The Analysis of Beauty* (1753), Preface and ch. vii.

tributes to the great artist. Diderot's rhetorical repetitiveness no doubt lacks subtlety — like his future pummelling of Catherine the Great's thighs to emphasise his points — and it sometimes replaces argument, but it is redeemed by the contagious enthusiasm which inspires it and the justified conviction it expresses that new light is being shed on a tangled and fascinating debate.

When Diderot speaks of modern artists studying and researching into nature and finding it beautiful only through the intermediary of ancient copies or imitations of nature, it is the fact that *copies* are being imitated which is important, not that they are ancient, even if modern artists (like the eighteenth-century sculptors Pigalle and Falconet) are not at the heart of the culture which produced such ancient artefacts as the *Gladiator* (or *Warrior*) of Agasias, and lack intimate understanding of, or feeling for, them. Ancient sculptors had a model for their art in the statue of the Doryphorus (called the 'Canon') of Polyclitus; Diderot's 'modèle idéal' or 'ligne vraie', on the other hand, resides in the imagination of the artist. The notion of the ancient artist searching through nature for the most beautiful features of individuals and assembling them to form a beautiful whole is derived from a remark of Socrates (see Xenophon, *Memorabilia*, III. 10. 2), and is repeated by later theorists down to Diderot's own time. He rejects the idea outright. How could the artists have recognised the beauty of these features? Diderot cites parts of the human body rarely visible to the eye so that popular opinion, which determines the artist's judgement from the beginning, cannot tell whether his portrayal of them calls for *poco più* or *poco meno*. (The scraps of rudimentary Italian point vaguely to Renaissance or later Italian theorists of art of whom Diderot knew.) It is in any case a premise of the discussion that perceptive artists are few in number.

Diderot often speaks of his ideal model with a fervour which suggests that art for him is an object of worship, a substitute religion (compare Rameau's nephew on the trinity of goodness, truth, and beauty). On the other hand, the difficulty Diderot postulates of discerning subtle differences between beauty and deformity seems to be an empirical one. The dialectic continues. The capacity to weld the discovered individual beauties into a whole would itself, according to Diderot, require the artist to have a profound knowledge of beauty, and to have the ideal model (further described, remarkably, as the 'ligne de foi') present in his imagination before he had created a single beautiful thing. Diderot asserts that this is absurd, as indeed it is: if it would be necessary for an artist to have an ideal model in his imagination in order to recognise beauty, it is difficult, even impossible, to see how an artist could ever acquire such a model — or recognise beauty. Diderot argues that the possession by an artist of that ideal model in advance of any artistic production would have prevented him from being satisfied with any of the features of his actual subject. In reality he could only have been a slavish copyist of admired features, a mere 'portraitist', in Diderot's terminology. But it is not through the accumulation and combination of isolated copies and 'portraits' that the artist can arrive at the original and prime model of the whole or the part. How, then, does the artist rise to the level of the ideal model? Diderot's answer is that it is by a process of 'tâtonnement' — of trial and error. This differs from the method of selection of the most beautiful features of the subject in that it does not entail the advance possession of a defined model of beauty. Such a model is reached at the conclusion of a process of research or endeavour. It is significant for Diderot's philosophy generally that he holds the method of 'tâtonnement' to be inherent in all investigation by the human mind.

Inevitably Diderot comes round to a commonsensical or empirical account of the beginnings of the quest for an ideal model. He concedes that the artist may first have been prompted to his quest of the ideal by observation of natural defect. Here one might wonder why Diderot does not object that the recognition of defect entails the possession of an ideal model. In fact, such an objection would be unjustified. Diderot is plainly correct now in assuming in the early artist a natural capacity for the beginnings of aesthetic judgement, even if that early artist should take to be perfect what is in fact still somewhat imperfect (at any rate from an eighteenth-century standpoint). The fact remains that the early artist belongs to the third order of creativity, and there, according to Diderot, he will long remain unless a 'rare and powerful genius' succeeds in rising to the second order — that of the true creative artist. But such a creative leap, such imaginative advance, is possible only after prolonged experimentation not only by the artist of genius but also on the part of the whole culture from which he springs.

What is interesting, and at first sight paradoxical, is that, whereas the third order of creativity and the work of the 'portraitist' within it were earlier treated dismissively, Diderot goes on to insist that artistic progress is possible only through the persistent endeavours of the portraitist in that same third order. There is, however, this difference, that the portraitist previously disdained was a slavish imitator, whereas the potentially creative portraitist now in view is experimental in his treatment of his subject. Here Diderot's arguments are directed against those who imagine that the artist should imitate traditional models of artistic perfection when the only profitable models available are those offered by 'la plus belle nature subsistante'. As things are, therefore, all degrees of artistic excellence or failure are contained in this domain. All else is chimerical or mean. So a whole contemporary academicist theory of art is brushed aside as providing no clear and reliable criteria of artistic quality. It is, of course, possible to ask just how clear and reliable are criteria of natural beauty, but Diderot's critique of academicist aesthetics is nevertheless telling.

What distinguishes the special artistic achievement of the Greeks is that ancient Greece was the only place where the arts were subjected to a process of 'tâtonnement'. The existence of the supreme Greek models has in effect prevented modern artists and societies from producing ideal models of their own, so that they have become merely imitators. But even in depreciating modern art and artists, Diderot makes an implicit or unconscious, but certainly necessary, concession. From the ancient models, they (or we) have borrowed or derived only dimly and obscurely the ideal model, the 'ligne vraie'. If so, it is nevertheless clear that the effects of imitating ancient models are not totally pernicious as Diderot had seemed implausibly to be claiming, but such imitation is an inefficient and often stultifying way of pursuing high artistic achievement.

Of great interest is Diderot's favourable evocation of the likely or necessary result if these ancient models were to be destroyed, so that modern artists had to start again from scratch. Reduced to making slow and painful progress through the imitation of a nature deformed, imperfect, and flawed, we should arrive, like the Greeks, at an original and prime model which, Diderot asserts significantly, would be more our own than our present one is or can be. It seems, then, that there can be more than one ideal model and that it will vary from culture to culture. Diderot claims later in the preamble that experience through the ages shows it to be impossible for one and the same people to have several great ages of artistic achievement. That impossibility is not self-evident and is certainly not a natural inference from Diderot's arguments. The hypothesis of the dissolution of an existing order of things and the evolution of a new order out of deformity and imperfection recalls the transformist hypothesis formulated in Diderot's *Lettre sur les aveugles* (1749), which admits of variously structured possible outcomes of natural disasters and evolutionary processes.

Diderot comments that the inviolable laws of Nature must take their course. Nature does nothing by leaps — a principle which is as true in the arts as in the Universe as a whole. The principle is Leibniz's, but there is nothing obviously Leibnizian about Diderot's argument. Since Diderot was a professed materialist, it is tempting to interpret his account of natural processes in materialist terms. But a satisfactory materialist interpretation of cultural evolution could in Diderot's time be no more than a pious hope and remains a long way off. Rather than a directly materialist interpretation of the conception one might prefer Professor Wilson's view of it as Baconian and Newtonian. But the Baconian philosophy, however influential on the scientific thinking of the French Enlightenment, proposes a method of induction, experiment, and collection of empirical data quite different from the imaginative 'tâtonnement' advocated by Diderot for the artist. Diderot's reference to the 'inviolable laws of Nature', on the other hand, is too imprecise to be assigned to any particular system of thought. His use of an initial capital for 'Nature' is nevertheless noticeable. He does seem to make a distinction between 'nature' with a small 'n' — presumably corresponding to what he calls 'la nature subsistante' — and 'Nature' with a capital 'N' and without the article: Nature as a formative power with its own laws and designs. The creativity of the great artist obeys the laws of that formative power even as he seeks to achieve an ideal image of it in a work of art.

In any case, Diderot was inevitably attracted to Italian Renaissance reflection on the relation between art and nature. In his fascinating and seminal work on 'Idea' as a concept in art theory, Erwin Panofsky shows how the suprasensible entity which 'Idea' was for Plato became for some Renaissance thinkers a concept or an image in the mind of the artist, an image which might either guide his study of nature or be the product of such study — the two processes not being always clearly distinct. Among the later Italian treatises on this matter which Diderot had read was that of G. P. Bellori, *L'Idea del Pittore, dello Schultore e del Architetto, Scelta dalle bellezze naturali superiore alla Natura*, an address, the very title of which is a whole programme, given in 1664 and prefixed to his *Le vite de' pittori* of 1672. Bellori represents the artist's 'Idea' or ideal form as constituted by selection from existing natural beauties, but he also sees it as being or containing the principle of that selection. Diderot is at one with Bellori in rejecting the mere copying of nature and in conceiving of his ideal model as surpassing empirical nature, but he rejects all idea of composing an ideal model or form from existing natural beauties. It is not made clear by Bellori how an ideal form can be created out of a collection or selection of individual beauties and perhaps it is something that cannot be made clear.

Nearer in time to Diderot is the work of abbé Charles Batteux, who was disapproved of by the *philosophes* as belonging to the camp of the *dévots*. Batteux's *Les Beaux-Arts réduits à un même principe* (1746) takes as its 'one and only principle' the imitation of 'la belle nature'. But although Batteux's conceptions have much in common with his own, Diderot objects that it is not at all clear what 'la belle nature' is, and earlier in the preamble to the *Salon* of 1767, in answer to the question where the ideal model is to be found if it is nowhere to be found in nature, he replies that even if he cannot say, his contentions as to its existence remain true. The ideal model is not derived from nature by compilation or montage but by creation or re-creation.

Diderot's conceptions were also influenced by those of J. J. Winckelmann, himself influenced by Bellori. Winckelmann published a number of works on ancient art, and his epoch-making *Geschichte der Kunst des Alterthums* (1764) was translated into French in 1766 as *Histoire de l'art chez les Anciens*. Like Bellori, Winckelmann also appears to see the artist as extracting a model of beauty from diverse beauties of nature, and he holds up ancient Greek artists as models for imitation. But despite Winckelmann's academicism, Diderot can only have found congenial his admiration for the serene grandeur of classical art. In a later addition to the preamble (Seznec, p. 64), however, Diderot extends the scope of his own principles to the arts of poetry and drama. He quotes some advice on acting given by Garrick. When acting a part, the actor should take as model not the most perfect naturally occurring example of the character in question, but a hypothetical ideal person, who would be affected in a quite different way from the actor in the same situation. This recommendation, added at the time (1769) of germination of *Le Paradoxe sur le comédien*, which contrasts the detachment of the actor with the violent passions that he enacts, bears some analogy with Winckelmann's classicism in the calm it requires of the artist, but reveals a Romantic or primitive strain in its fascination with the dramatic power of elemental passion.

Although the role of the creative artist is paramount in Diderot's mind, his conception of the ideal model is not categorically subjectivist, since he retains a certain classical concern for objectivity. His ideal model is, however, genre-relative and culture-relative. And whereas in Montesquieu's thesis of the influence of climate on culture Winckelmann had found support for his insistence on the unique excellence of the culture of the Greeks, there is evidence in the preamble that Diderot saw in the variety of factors which, according to Montesquieu, make up the 'esprit général' of a nation a reason for potential diversity of high artistic achievement between diverse cultures.

Diderot's art theory is constructed out of the theories of others — Plato, Leonardo, Raphael, Bellori, Batteux, Hogarth, Winckelmann, and not only these, are laid under contribution — but Diderot's conception of the source and identity of the ideal model is finally his own. While the great artist follows nature, studies nature, imitates nature, his ideal model is a hard-won insight or vision which comes after sustained creative 'tâtonnement' on his part and on that of the whole culture from which he springs. As Diderot recognises when writing of chiaroscuro in his *Essais sur la peinture* (1766), through the eyes of the great artist we see nature as we had never seen it before.

Bibliography

A. Becq, *Genèse de l'esthétique française moderne*, 2 vols (Pisa, 1984)

Y. Belaval, *L'Esthétique sans paradoxe de Diderot* (Paris, 1950)

A. Blunt, *Artistic Theory in Italy 1450–1600* (1962) (Oxford, 1978)

F. Bollino, *Teoria e sistema delle belle arti, Charles Batteux e gli esthéticiens del secolo XVIII* (Bologna, 1979)

E. M. Bukdahl, *Diderot critique d'art*, 2 vols (Copenhagen, 1980)

J. Chouillet, *La Formation des idées esthétiques de Diderot, 1745–1763* (Paris, 1973)

—, *L'Esthétique des lumières* (Paris, 1974)

—, *Diderot* (Paris, 1977)

A. Fontaine, *Les Doctrines d'art en France de Poussin à Diderot* (Paris, 1909)

D. Funt, *Diderot and the Esthetics of the Enlightenment,* Diderot Studies XI (Geneva, 1968)

E. G. Holt, *Literary Sources of Art History* (Princeton, 1947)

J.-R. Mantion, *Charles Batteux, Les Beaux-Arts réduits à un même principe*, Édition critique (Paris, 1989)

E. Panofsky, *'Idea': ein Beitrag zur Begriffsgeschichte der älteren Kunsttheorie* (Leipzig and Berlin, 1924); second edition translated into English by Joseph J. S. Peake as *Idea: A Concept in Art Theory* (Columbia, 1968)

G. Sauerwald, *Die Aporie der Diderot'schen Ästhetik (1745–1781)* (Frankfurt am Main, 1975)

A. M. Wilson, *Diderot* (New York: OUP, 1972)

Winckelmann, *Writings on Art*, Selected & Edited by David Irwin (London, 1972)

13

The Sense of an Ending
in Stendhal's *Le Rouge et le Noir*

Alison Finch

Vivre isolé!... Quel tourment!...

Je deviens fou et injuste, se dit Julien en se frappant le front. Je suis isolé
ici dans ce cachot; mais je n'ai pas *vécu isolé* sur la terre; j'avais la puissante
idée du *devoir*. Le devoir que je m'étais prescrit, à tort ou à raison... a été
comme le tronc d'un arbre solide auquel je m'appuyais pendant l'orage; je   5
vacillais, j'étais agité. Après tout je n'étais qu'un homme... mais je n'étais
pas emporté.

C'est l'air humide de ce cachot qui me fait penser à l'isolement...

Et pourquoi être encore hypocrite en maudissant l'hypocrisie? Ce n'est ni
la mort, ni le cachot, ni l'air humide, c'est l'absence de madame de Rênal   10
qui m'accable. Si, à Verrières, pour la voir, j'étais obligé de vivre des
semaines entières, caché dans les caves de sa maison, est-ce que je me
plaindrais?

L'influence de mes contemporains l'emporte, dit-il tout haut et avec un
rire amer. Parlant seul avec moi-même, à deux pas de la mort, je suis   15
encore hypocrite... O dix-neuvième siècle!

...Un chasseur tire un coup de fusil dans une forêt, sa proie tombe, il
s'élance pour la saisir. Sa chaussure heurte une fourmilière haute de deux
pieds, détruit l'habitation des fourmis, sème au loin les fourmis, leurs
œufs... Les plus philosophes parmi les fourmis ne pourront jamais   20
comprendre ce corps noir, immense, effroyable: la botte du chasseur, qui
tout à coup a pénétré dans leur demeure avec une incroyable rapidité, et
précédée d'un bruit épouvantable, accompagné de gerbes d'un feu
rougeâtre...

...Ainsi la mort, la vie, l'éternité, choses fort simples pour qui aurait les   25
organes assez vastes pour les concevoir...

Une mouche éphémère naît à neuf heures du matin dans les grands jours
d'été, pour mourir à cinq heures du soir; comment comprendrait-elle le mot
nuit?

Donnez-lui cinq heures d'existence de plus, elle voit et comprend ce que   30
c'est que la nuit.

Ainsi moi, je mourrai à vingt-trois ans. Donnez-moi cinq années de vie
de plus, pour vivre avec madame de Rênal.

Et il se mit à rire comme Méphistophélès. Quelle folie de discuter ces
grands problèmes!   35
(Stendhal, *Le Rouge et le Noir*, Part II, Chapter 44[1])

Critics have often commented on the speed of the endings of both *Le
Rouge et le Noir* and *La Chartreuse de Parme* — whether to blame or
praise. They point to the brevity of Stendhal's remarks about Julien's execution ('Jamais cette tête n'avait été aussi poétique qu'au moment où
elle allait tomber. [...] Tout se passa simplement, convenablement et de
sa part sans aucune affectation', p. 697); and they cite the summary
dispatching of characters on the last page of *La Chartreuse*.[2] This
abruptness is undeniable. However, the above extract from Julien's
meditations in prison (about eight pages from the end of the novel)
shows — obviously — that a summum does not have to be at the literal
close of a work.

What is most immediately noticeable about this sequence is that it has
a deliberate concentration of imagery unusual in Stendhal. Within a page,
there are three separate and clearly-signalled images, somewhere between
metaphor, analogy, and fable: duty as the trunk of a solid tree against
which to lean during the storm (ll. 4–5); death as a hunter's boot destroy-
ing an ant-hill (ll. 18–24); life as the existence of a mayfly (ll. 27–31).
These images are not in themselves as original or bold as the kind of
figurative writing we might find in Balzac or Proust, and all would seem
to be adapted from other writers. Duty as a tree is a simile suggested by

---

[1] Stendhal, *Romans et nouvelles*, Bibliothèque de la Pléiade, ed. H. Martineau (Paris:
Gallimard, 1952), I. 691–2. In this passage, emphases and suspension points are
Stendhal's or the editor's; in all succeeding quotations, emphases are mine unless
otherwise indicated, and '[...]' are mine if enclosed in brackets.

[2] Thus, J. Prévost, in *La Création chez Stendhal* (Paris: Gallimard, 1951), says: 'Par
un excès de soudaineté et tout en énonçant le fait, il nous en dérobe la peine
physique. L'exécution de Julien [...] est glissée en une ligne au milieu de pensées
tout étrangères à l'échafaud. Cette vitesse souveraine, cette sorte d'euthanésie
littéraire [...] reparaîtra [...] à la fin de la *Chartreuse*' (p. 323). Prévost goes so far
as to say that once Julien has reached the height of his ambitions (the betrothal to
Mathilde and the accompanying change in social status), the reader 'ne trouve plus
guère qu'un sec résumé de la vie du héros' (p. 333). M. Wood, in *Stendhal*
(London: Elek, 1971) remarks that events towards the end of the novel are
recounted with 'extreme terseness', that the writing is 'extremely strange' (p. 85),
and that 'At moments of crisis he simply will not tell us how his heroes feel, or
how we are to respond' (pp. 85–6). R. Pearson, on the other hand, takes a subtler
view, bringing out 'the aesthetic benefit of abrupt conclusion' in *Stendhal's Violin:
A Novelist and his Reader* (Oxford: Clarendon, 1988), p. 241.

the Mme de Duras whose novels *Olivier* and *Édouard* helped Stendhal with the plots of *Armance* and *Le Rouge*.[3] The hunter image derives from Goethe's *Faust*, and Martineau traces the mayfly image back to Diderot.[4] But Stendhal recharges all of them; here, as often, he is turning apparently 'easy' adoption of others' usages into his own mode of allusive writing. (A similar process is apparent not only in his well-known plagiarisms but also in his use of common hyperbole or his swoops into raconteur's colloquialisms.)

In part, this recharging is achieved by Stendhal's through-composing of the images. All rural pictures, each modulates into the following one: the tree of the first becomes the forest of the second; the helpless insects of the second become the ephemeral insect of the third. More substantially, the recharging is achieved through the immediate context; through the resonances Stendhal sets up between the images and other parts of the novel; and through the explicit questions raised as to how to verbalise the unverbalisable. As is well-known, such questions recurrently amused and troubled the mature Stendhal.[5] But here they are put in their most extreme form, since Julien is groping towards expressing not just feelings about death but, impossibly, the experience itself.

Thus, leaning against a tree suggests a clinging not just to duty but to life — an attempt to find shelter against an elemental force, the death that could 'emport[er]' one (ll. 4–7). The hunter image emphasises this helplessness before death in a more brutal, urgent, and undignified mode (ll. 18–24). Julien is now no doubt attempting to imagine what his own

---

3 In the unpublished but widely-circulated *Olivier*, the impotent hero complains he has no sense of 'Devoir' (Duras's capitalisation) and that 'Plus misérable que le roseau, je plie et ne me relève pas' (C. de Duras, *Olivier ou le secret*, texte inédit établi, présenté et commenté par D. Virieux (Paris: Corti, 1971), p. 155). (There are shades of La Fontaine, of course, in both the Duras and the Stendhal images.) Virieux points out that Stendhal uses almost verbatim another metaphor from this same work in *Armance* (p. 147, n. 45).

4 Soon after Faust first appears, he complains: 'I am not like a god! Too deeply now I feel / This truth. I am a worm stuck in the dust, / Burrowing and feeding, where at last I must / Be crushed and buried by some rambler's heel' (Goethe, *Faust*, tr. D. Luke (Oxford: Oxford University Press, 1987), Part One, ll. 652–5). For the mayfly image, see p. 692, n. 1.

5 See, for example, his marginal notes to *Lucien Leuwen*, and key comments in the *Vie de Henry Brulard* (not least the famous last sentence 'On gâte des sentiments si tendres à les raconter en détail': *Œuvres intimes*, Bibliothèque de la Pléiade (Paris: Gallimard, 1955), p. 395). Pearson brings out the importance for Stendhal of suggestion, as opposed to statement, at many points in his *Stendhal's Violin*, and especially in his concluding chapter 'Reverie' (pp. 266–75).

death by guillotine will be like. The 'corps noir, immense, effroyable' is not only a symbolic figure of death, but is also imprecise enough to evoke the appearance of the erected guillotine. The 'bruit épouvantable' and the 'incroyable rapidité' (especially 'incroyable' with the adjective preceding the noun) are Julien's way of conceptualising the falling blade; the sprays of reddish fire are the spurting of the blood, and the pain as the nerves are assailed in an unimaginably explosive shock. (The phonetic patterning in this paragraph — [p] and [f] — denser than usual in Stendhal, intensifies the climax.)

The mayfly image does more than re-emphasise the incomprehensibility of death: its barely sketched-out physicality implies a yearning to have a little longer to enjoy sensation (ll. 27–31). Like other writers, Stendhal suggests this simple savouring of sensation through the pleasures of a summer's day, starting with the freshness of the morning, 'neuf heures du matin'. (And Julien, still a young man, is in the 'summer' of his life.) The 'night' which the mayfly cannot know is complex. Not merely death and the idea of death, it is also here the continuation of life, more particularly life with Mme de Rênal. ('Donnez-lui cinq heures d'existence de plus, elle voit et comprend ce que c'est que la nuit. [...] Donnez-moi cinq années de vie de plus, pour vivre avec madame de Rênal', ll. 30–3.) Night suggests, then, a long, intimate eroticism. This final image in fact concludes Julien's meditations: there are now (after this extract) a few brief thoughts, followed very shortly by the end of the chapter with its last sentence 'Julien se sentait fort et résolu comme l'homme qui voit clair dans son âme' (p. 693). The image is able to be conclusive precisely because it is a synthesising one, combining fear of death with love for a partner.

Stendhal, then, reanimates these three images through their immediate, and urgent, setting. They also recapitulate wider structures of the novel. First, they allude to the title, echoed in the 'noir' and 'rougeâtre' of the hunter image: here is how both colours are about to end (ll. 21, 24). Second, the hunter's gunshot echoes Julien's shooting of Mme de Rênal: now he is to be 'shot'.[6] Third, the country scenes evoked show Julien finally rejecting the urban not just in deed and thought but more involuntarily, too, in imagination. Fourth, the forest and mayfly refer indistinctly back to the summer days near the beginning when Julien and Mme de

---

6 We might also see here a connection with Stendhal's half-joking, half-serious comments on other pistol-shot disturbances (politics in the novel are like the pistol-shot at the concert): they are the ultimate disruption — and yet, are they? Dissonance has its part in aesthetic structures.

Rênal chased butterflies in the orchard with the children, preparing per-haps the shortly-following memory of these scenes at the moment of his execution: 'Les plus doux moments qu'il avait trouvés jadis dans les bois de Vergy revenaient en foule à sa pensée et avec une extrême énergie' (p. 697).[7]

More generally, Julien's stress on the difficulties of understanding con-trasts with the feats of empty intelligence that his virtuoso memory had allowed him to perform earlier (ll. 21, 25–6, 28–30, 34–5). Girard claims that many outstanding novelists show their heroes, at the moment of death, not just undertaking a retrospective assessment, but undergoing a moral transformation: hatred gives way to love, pride to humility.[8] As in Constant and Flaubert, then, reflections about language and understand-ing have moral implications, and can create a special sense of tragedy.

Still at a general level, we may, too, find in the hunter figure a culmi-nation of the historical and political considerations that permeate *Le Rouge*. Hunting has clear social meanings in this novel, where it is al-most always an upper-class activity. Underlings like Julien may partici-pate, but it is led by nobles such as M. de Rênal (pp. 273, 335–6) or by the king (p. 602). And here the hunter is 'higher' on the scale of creation than the ants he unwittingly treads on. So this is a picture of low-status creatures being destroyed by a well-equipped high-status creature who has already proved his ability to rule nature, having just successfully shot an animal. We know already that Julien has been condemned to death in part because he is a proletarian who has dared to leave his class. He has of course played a part in his own punishment by himself outlining this class-based analysis at his trial; but even if he had not, the conditions for his condemnation were already there, with the presence of Valenod who is jealous of Julien both sexually and socially. Now, in the figure of the hunter, we have a suggestion that Julien is being crushed not only by a penal code but also by a class system.

This interpretation is reinforced when we look at other uses in *Le Rouge* of key words in this passage, and contrast them with frequency and usage in *La Chartreuse*. Would Dorothy Gabe Coleman have approved of resorting to word-frequencies and concordances in close readings? Possibly not; she was too alive to the complexities of syntax

---

7 In the early sequence there are no fewer than three pitying references within two paragraphs to the fate these butterflies meet: they are twice said to be 'pauvres'; finally, 'On les piquait sans pitié' (like Julien himself?), p. 263.

8 R. Girard, *Mensonge romantique et vérité romanesque* (Paris: Grasset, 1961); as well as Stendhal, Girard cites Tolstoy, Proust, and others (e.g. pp. 234, 296–8).

and tone, and too wary of the potential aridity of formalism, to resort to such mechanical devices as a way of analysing her favourite works. But, keenly aware as she also was of patterning in poetry, she might not have entirely rejected tools that allow one to see structures which, deliberate and visible in verse, are normally diffuse and hidden in the novel. We can use the concordance of *Le Rouge* and *La Chartreuse* to trace briefly the fortunes of two lexical fields in the hunter image — it is important to have some means of comparison, since frequencies for one work only do not tell us much on their own.[9]

Let us, then, look at 'haut', with its range of meanings from physical to figurative — appearing here in the anthill 'haute de deux pieds'; and at the *chasseur/chasser* group, taking *chasser* in both its main meanings of 'to hunt' and 'to banish' (ll. 17–24).

The anthill, only 'haute de deux pieds', already conveys the insignificance of human achievement, and we are quite consciously ready to identify it with the social 'heights' encountered over the preceding 500 pages. Looking at the concordance, we find what we were not, however, likely to be so consciously aware of: that there are far more figurative uses of *haut* in *Le Rouge* than in *La Chartreuse*: high rank, high opinions of x or y, high sense of morality, lofty thoughts. In addition, *hauteur* as haughtiness, and the associated word *hautain*, are used more often in *Le Rouge*.[10] So, by the time we reach the two-foot high anthill, we bring to the word 'haute' not just pictures of physical height, but other images of moral and social height which this novel, markedly more than *La Chartreuse*, slowly draws together by its use of *haut* in other contexts. The cumulative *haut*s, *hauteur*s, and *hautain*s come together at not only obvious thematic levels but also subliminal lexical ones. They reinforce

---

[9] All figures in the following discussion are taken from my *Concordance de Stendhal:* Le Rouge et le Noir *et* La Chartreuse de Parme, *Compendia*, vol. 13 (Leeds: Maney, 1991).

[10] The two novels are almost exactly the same length, so raw frequencies will tell us all we need to know; they do not have to be expressed as percentages or put through the unnecessarily complicated tests of stylometrics. (See my 'Excitement and Astonishment in *Le Rouge et le Noir* and *La Chartreuse de Parme*', *Essays in French Literature*, XXVI (1989), 21–37, n. 8; and 'The Imagery of a Myth: Computer-Assisted Research on Literature', *Style*, XXIX (1995), 530–40.) In the following groups of figures, those for *Le Rouge* will always come first.

Haut/e/s/es: 119, 90. Of these, literally high or tall: 26, 50; figuratively high (thoughts, class, morality, etc.): 65, 34. (The other uses occur in, e.g., phrases meaning 'loud', 'high colour', etc.) *Hauteur/s*: 36, 26. Of these, literally high or tall: 8, 9; meaning 'haughtiness': 28, 17. *Hautain/e*: 18, 6.

here the idea of a catastrophic destruction of all kinds of control and aspiration, from the sublime to the silly.

Hunters appear in *La Chartreuse* as well as in *Le Rouge*, but with differences in usage. Whereas in *La Chartreuse* the noun *chasseur/s* always denotes 'real' characters, in *Le Rouge* the single use of the word before the two in this passage comes — as here — only in a figure of speech. (Julien is at a certain point 'content comme un chasseur' discovering a plain full of game, p. 346.) Therefore, there is a surprise here — this final hunter is almost as much of an intrusion into the lexis of the novel as his foot is into the anthill. When we look at the verb *chasser*, other complexities emerge. *Le Rouge* uses this verb rather more often than *La Chartreuse*, never to mean hunting of animals, but almost always as 'chasing someone away', banishing them — from, say, one's house or salon.[11] Such fears of chasing away or banning haunt Julien and determine many of his actions. In the seminary, he thinks that after Pirard's departure 'le parti du *Sacré-Cœur* va me dégrader et peut-être me *chasser*' (p. 409);[12] newly arrived in the Mole household, he finds Mathilde's brother unexpectedly charming: 'Est-il possible, se dit-il, que ce soit là l'homme dont les plaisanteries offensives doivent me *chasser* de cette maison!' (p. 449); and when Mathilde proposes revealing her pregnancy to her father, 'Mais', says Julien, 'il me *chassera* avec ignominie!' (p. 625). After such uses, we at last come upon what is by far the most physically realised embodiment of chasing or hunting in the novel: the hunter with the frighteningly noisy gun, the heavy black boot, the greedy grasping of his fallen prey. ('Il s'élance pour la saisir.') We are, by now, predisposed to see in this particular *chasseur* an embodiment of everything that has had the potential to *chasser* in the other sense, culminating with the 'exiling' of Julien himself and the crushing of his anthill edifices.

Pulling related meanings into the net in this way will strike some as far-fetched, others as exciting, depending on their estimation of the power of the signifier; we might cautiously conclude that it would be as wrong to dismiss entirely the case for subliminal links as to overstate it. At any rate, analysed with a combination of the naked eye and the mechanical

---

11 Other uses (few) would be, e.g., 'to banish an illusion/to banish boredom'.

   Chasser: 27, 21; of these 0, 3 refer to a 'real' hunt. *Chasse*: (noun) 9, 15; of these 8, 15 refer to a 'real' hunt. *Chasseur/s*: (noun) 3, 14. (Early in *La Chartreuse*, some of these *chasseurs* are members of the *chasseurs* military division.)

12 Stendhal's/editor's emphasis in '*Sacré-Coeur*'.

help of the concordance, this passage shows that the shortly following 'real' end of *Le Rouge et le Noir* is irreducibly elliptical still, of course — but is not foreshortened. It can afford to be brief because it refers back to this meditation, thus subsuming a prolonged network of associations. As we see here, the teleology which many critics view as a hallmark of the nineteenth-century novel can be unexpectedly dispersed in its nature.

The passage is significant at levels other than those of these three well-foregrounded images. Julien's final Mephistophelian laughter arises from his sudden recognition that he is trying to make a bargain — with whom? ('Donnez-moi cinq années de vie de plus [...]', ll. 32–5). He has, perhaps, always been a version of Faust, as the adoption of Goethe's worm/rambler metaphor suggests.[13] But he now becomes both Faust and a devil possessed of all-powerful rhetoric. For Julien has just performed a linguistic trick as clever as any of Mephistopheles's: through his mayfly analogy, he has turned the night of death into a night of sensuous enjoyment (ll. 30–3). As a multilateral Faust/Mephistopheles, then, Julien can appreciate the dramatic ironies that may quasi-aesthetically present themselves at the approach of death. (His laugh is comparable to Bette's silent savouring, on her death-bed, of the Hulots's still-firm conviction that she is 'l'ange de la famille'; even now, she does not disabuse them: dramatic irony, of the kind the author himself enjoys, is preferable to the revelation her earlier self might have desired.)[14]

The reflections on the damp air of the cell, and on the influence of contemporaries, create other kinds of ambiguities (ll. 8, 14–16). Julien at first claims that physical and cultural environment *do* affect the tenor and content of one's thoughts and feelings, even at those supreme moments when unclouded thought ought to be possible. But he then affirms that one can escape both the physical environment and the 'contemporary' hypocrisy apparently forced upon one: 'Ce n'est ni la mort, ni le cachot, ni l'air humide, c'est l'absence de madame de Rênal qui m'accable' (ll. 9–11). However, Julien's own interpretation here is perhaps too simple: when, a few pages later, he leaves his cell for execution, Stendhal writes:

---

13 See above, n. 4.

14 Balzac, *La Cousine Bette* (Paris: Librairie Générale Française, 1963), p. 442. Julien's Mephistophelian laugh and his earlier 'rire amer' (l. 15) also have a role in Stendhal's life-long search to define and create varying modes of comedy. Some thirty years previously, he had started to puzzle over how to reconcile the laughable with the *odieux*; here is one example of the blending he does often achieve in his mature works. See his comments on his own attempts at drama in *Théâtre* (Paris: Le Divan, 1931) (e.g. on his play *Les Deux Hommes*, written 1803–4: II. 178; or on *Letellier*, first version written 1804–5: III. 18, 270).

'Le mauvais air du cachot devenait insupportable à Julien. Par bonheur, le jour où on lui annonça qu'il fallait mourir, un beau soleil réjouissait la nature [...]. Marcher au grand air fut pour lui une sensation délicieuse [...]. Allons, tout va bien, se dit-il, je ne manque point de courage' (p. 697). The air of the cell was not so immaterial after all; at any rate, the reader is left in uncertainty on this point — an uncertainty which shows (if it still needed showing) that the nineteenth-century novel is not monolothic in its presentation of surroundings and causes.

The narrative pace of this passage is both atypical and typical of Stendhal. This is not a rapidly moving sequence, yet in Stendhal reflection and impetus are not incompatible: even here, unobtrusively, there is that illusion of events being pushed along, or collapsed into each other, that he creates so often elsewhere. [15] Action is fast — the storm might 'emport[er]' one (l. 7), the hunter *rushes* to *seize* his prey ('s'élance', 'saisir', l. 18), and his boot penetrates the anthill with, as we have seen, 'incroyable rapidité' (l. 22). The mayfly image too — that of the astonishingly short life snuffed out — is more than just an echo of a Romantic topos. It is an extreme example of the elided time-scale that creates the narrative speed *in excelsis* of Stendhal's two best novels. Five years become five hours; a life becomes a day.

Furthermore, Julien's meditation, rather than taking on an air of grave development, passes quickly from one idea to the next; these ideas, whether low-key or passionate in tone, are not formally structured but slip, apparently casually, from one point to another, then back again, in a mode characteristic of Stendhal. For example, the conclusion drawn after the paragraph about the hunter ('Ainsi la mort, la vie', etc., ll. 25–6) seems to be the moral of the fable, but it does not even have a main verb, and then, surprisingly, we come to another analogy, that of the mayfly. So we jump from illustration to conclusion back to illustration, in a manner which is at once disjointed and supple. This approach mirrors

---

15 For decades, critics have been trying to define this illusion, often seeking to express it through rather belle-lettrist metaphors of their own. To take only two examples from among very many, in the 1930s C. Du Bos remarks that 'Le style de Stendhal, c'est l'action d'un cheval de race' (*Approximations*, Deuxième Série (Corrêa, 1932), p. 2); in the 1950s, J.-P. Richard writes that '*Le Rouge* halète. C'est le roman d'un coureur qui oublie de reprendre souffle [...]. Le miracle demeure *La Chartreuse*: surprise d'un récit dont l'écoulement souple est nerveux comme une véhémence' ('Connaissance et tendresse chez Stendhal', in *Littérature et sensation* (Paris: Seuil, 1954), p. 102). R. Pearson comments sanely on this area in *Stendhal's Violin*: see the chapter 'Time and Imagination in *Le Rouge et le Noir*', especially the section 'The Passage of Time', pp. 102–7.

Julien's own many-pronged effort to come to terms with his situation, and also represents one way the mind works — dartingly and obliquely.

This brings us back to the most self-reflecting implications of this passage: the exceptional value it gives to metaphorical and analogical thinking. Stendhal's strictures against Chateaubriand's style, and against even Balzac's excesses and affectations, have made commentators, not unjustifiably, focus on his economies and ironies; they have been inclined to think that he does not 'believe in' figurative language.[16] In fact, Stendhal does use such language more than is sometimes realised, and when he does it is, as I have shown, both unpretentious and powerful. However, what is really unusual about this passage is not so much its density *per se* of figures of speech, but its interweaving of these figures with a discussion of the limits of understanding. Stendhal, far from being a 'metaphor-hater', is, at this near-final point, suggesting that there are certain feelings and thoughts that can be approached *only* by way of figurative language. The 'sense of an ending' could scarcely be more resonant than in this passage.[17]

---

[16] For example J. Attuel, who, in *Le Style de Stendhal: Efficacité et romanesque* (Paris: Nizet, 1980), tends to reproduce this view 'from the horse's mouth' without question (e.g. p. 345). A much subtler discussion is to be found in A. Jefferson, *Reading Realism in Stendhal* (Cambridge: Cambridge University Press, 1988), e.g. pp. 93, 99.

[17] I of course borrow my key phrase from F. Kermode's *The Sense of an Ending* (Oxford: Oxford University Press, 1967).

14

A Conversation Piece:
Baudelaire's *Causerie*

Felix Leakey

CAUSERIE

Vous êtes un beau ciel d'automne, clair et rose!
Mais la tristesse en moi monte comme la mer,
Et laisse, en refluant, sur ma lèvre morose
Le souvenir cuisant de son limon amer.   4

— Ta main se glisse en vain sur mon sein qui se pâme;
Ce qu'elle cherche, amie, est un lieu saccagé
Par la griffe et la dent féroce de la femme.
Ne cherchez plus mon cœur; les bêtes l'ont mangé.   8

Mon cœur est un palais flétri par la cohue;
On s'y soûle, on s'y tue, on s'y prend aux cheveux!
— Un parfum nage autour de votre gorge nue! ...   11

O Beauté, dur fléau des âmes, tu le veux!
Avec tes yeux de feu, brillants comme des fêtes,
Calcine ces lambeaux qu'ont épargnés les bêtes!   14
                         (Baudelaire, *Les Fleurs du Mal,* 1861)

The version chosen of this sonnet is the last one revised and approved by
Baudelaire himself. Of the four earlier texts known to us, the first is a
manuscript dating probably from 1854–5, whilst the other three
(including two proofs) relate to the first edition of 1857 of *Les Fleurs du
Mal.* (The 1868 text, in the Banville-Asselineau third edition, we may ignore, since it is identical to that of 1861.)[1] As to the woman to whom the

---

[1] The manuscript version was first revealed, in facsimile as well as in transcription,
    by Yoshio Abé in his translation into Japanese of Baudelaire's *Complete Works*
    (Tokyo: Chikuma-Shobo, 1983), I: *Les Fleurs du Mal,* pp. 711–12; six years later,

poem is addressed, she no doubt was Marie Daubrun;[2] what matters most for the reader, though, in biographical terms, is not so much her identity but rather, as we shall see, the *chronology* of the encounter with her recorded in these lines.

This encounter, as we immediately perceive, is as intimate as could well be imagined, since it takes place between two people in the very act of making love. Three other general features quickly engage our attention. Firstly, the poem's structure — more wayward and irregular than the sonnet medium traditionally allows: there is continuity, rather than division, between the second quatrain and the first tercet, and the third and final part of the poem overlaps from line 11 to line 12. A device of punctuation, secondly, the dash — much favoured by Baudelaire, in his prose writings as well as his poetry — is used not to differentiate the two speakers (there is only one) in the 'conversation', but to convey sudden changes of mood. A final general feature is the form of address Baudelaire adopts: this varies surprisingly as the poem progresses, from *vouvoiement* in the first, second, and third stanzas, to *tutoiement* in the second and last.

I have indicated already that the poem's title (to pass now to our detailed analysis) is in all strictness a misnomer: we certainly cannot speak of a true dialogue, since throughout we hear Baudelaire's voice only, without even any such brief, opening recall of his companion's questioning words or glance as we find in two later poems in the same 'conversational' genre, *Semper eadem* and *Sonnet d'automne*.[3] The title in *Causerie* (like so many of Baudelaire's titles) is in any case an afterthought — perhaps ironic; it was absent from the manuscript, and was

---

Professor Abé included the transcription alone in his edition for a French public of *Les Fleurs du Mal* (Paris: Orphée: La Différence, 1989), p. 176 (hereafter abbreviated: Abé). For full details of the textual variants in the other four versions of *Causerie*, see Baudelaire, *Œuvres complètes*, ed. Claude Pichois, Bibliothèque de la Pléiade, 2 vols (Paris: Gallimard, 1975–6), I. 933–4 (hereafter abbreviated: *OCP*); all my references to and quotations from Baudelaire's texts are to this edition.

[2] This presumed attribution has long been accepted, by virtue of Baudelaire's inclusion of the sonnet in the Marie Daubrun 'cycle', running from poems XLIX to LVII in the second edition of 1861 of *Les Fleurs du Mal*; see, in this connection, *OCP* I. 922, 936.

[3] Here are the two opening couplets in question (my italics, in both cases): '«D'où vous vient, *disiez-vous*, cette tristesse étrange, / Montant comme la mer sur le roc noir et nu?»' (*Semper eadem*; first published 1860, but no doubt drafted around late 1857); '*Ils me disent, tes yeux*, clairs comme le cristal: / «Pour toi, bizarre amant, quel est donc mon mérite?»' (*Sonnet d'automne*; first published 1859).

added only in 1857, in the first proof for the *Fleurs du Mal* edition of that year. And yet it would be improper to regard the poem as recording merely a confrontation between a voluble poet and his mute mistress. In a much wider sense, on the contrary, I would regard the title as being wholly appropriate — indeed, as I have suggested above, it could well be extended to two others of Baudelaire's poems, as well as to a third of the same period, *Chant d'automne* (though in its second part only). [4] In all four of these poems, within an anecdotal framework, Baudelaire recounts a single, intimate moment in his relationship with a loved one; in each he offers us, throughout, continual reminders of her immediate presence — her physical appearance and demeanour, her implied response to him, her inner character as he divines it[5] — and thereby allows us to infer the very gist and progress of the interchange between them. And thus we may legitimately speak, I feel, of a true genre perhaps inaugurated by Baudelaire, and having something of the impact, on the reader/viewer, of those traditional paintings given the name that I have borrowed: 'Conversation Pieces.'

The poem is launched with a form of tribute which Baudelaire, here again, was one of the first to exploit: a metaphor of the *âme-paysage* type, in which the loved one is figured as an autumn skyscape with its bright yet slightly muted colours, pink rather than red.[6] It is striking that in this highly intimate context he should begin by addressing her, almost formally, in the second person plural: it is as if at this point he sees her (imaginatively if not literally) from a certain distance, almost as an art object. No sooner is the tribute uttered, however, no sooner has he complimented her on her beauty, than he feels obliged, almost compelled, to tell her of the great, overwhelming sadness that he finds sweeping over him. Baudelaire does not immediately explain this unexpected response — introduced by a cautionary 'Mais', which has the

---

4 First published 1859. My belief is that this poem as a whole is a composite of two originally separate pieces, which Baudelaire chose to unite by virtue of their common autumnal mood and setting. See in this connection my monograph on *Les Fleurs du Mal*, in the Cambridge University 'Landmarks of World Literature' series (Cambridge, 1992), p. 23.

5 For specific examples of this procedure, from the other three poems named, cf. *Semper eadem*, lines 1–2, 6–10, 13–14; *Sonnet d'automne*, lines 1–4, 12–14; *Chant d'automne*, lines 17–19, 21–4, 26.

6 The term 'âme-paysage' is here used to distinguish this type of metaphor from its more conventional obverse, the 'paysage d'âme' — so common in Romantic and pre-Romantic writing; see, in this whole connection, my *Baudelaire and Nature* (Manchester: Manchester University Press, 1969), pp. 235–50.

same mood-changing function as the dashes in lines 5 and 11 — preferring for the moment to expand the rather conventional simile of line 2 (we speak commonly of a 'wave' of emotion) into an altogether more personal and innovative metaphor, whereby his sadness, his 'moroseness', is likened to a physical sensation, to a taste in the mouth, to the sharp bile which leaves its 'remembered' imprint on the lip as it flows back into his gullet — just as the sea, flowing back also, may lay down some lingering trace of silt.[7]

The dash at the beginning of the second quatrain signals a further change of register. No longer the 'remote' admirer of the opening line, he has become once more aware of Marie's intimate contact with him, of her hand ('*Ta* main', the hand of his 'amie'), gliding over his breast as he, in turn, 'swoons' in immediate physical response. Yet this response is ambiguous: his mind has become wholly invaded by the astringent and intrusive sadness he has already declared, and which he goes on to explain by the astonishing pair of metaphors, vivid and powerful, that follow in the next five lines. Her caressing gesture he now chooses to interpret as an act of violent predation, likened to so many he has known and suffered in the past: is she not seeking, surely, to pluck out his very heart? If so, too late! That site has been laid waste already by the fierce teeth and claws of ravaging womankind — of all those 'beasts' or 'monsters', as he designates them, which in the past have had their way with him.[8] The metaphor invites, indeed compels biographical speculation: one thinks, above all, of Jeanne Duval, with whom Baudelaire had for so long been locked in an implacable relationship, and to whom specifically, some ten years later and in retrospect, he was to apply the self-same image, in a formulation this time borrowed from the first Epistle of Saint Peter: 'Quaerens quem devoret.'[9]

---

7 For an earlier, even more audacious variant of this metaphor — again associated with past sadness and bitterness, in the context of love — cf. *[Un] Voyage à Cythère* (first text 1851–2), lines 45–8. The sea/sadness metaphor, in its simplified form, recurs of course in the lines (1–2) already quoted from *Semper eadem*.

8 I give 'monsters' here as an alternative to 'beasts', since this was Baudelaire's first choice of image in his earliest, manuscript draft of the poem, in which line 8 as a whole ran thus: 'Mon cœur a disparu. Des monstres l'ont mangé' (Abé, p. 176).

9 See *Iconographie de Charles Baudelaire*, ed. Claude Pichois and François Ruchon (Geneva: Cailler, 1960), reproduction (no. 122) of a pen drawing by Baudelaire of Jeanne (dated by Poulet-Malassis: 27 February 1865), under which the poet had scribbled these words; the relative note in the Pichois-Ruchon

The second of these metaphors (lines 9–10) is still more graphic, though here the imagery is less closely wedded to its starting-point (the vehicle to its tenor, to use I. A. Richards' terminology) than was its predecessor in lines 6–8. The scene evoked: a drunken, squabbling, murderous rabble laying siege to a palace, perhaps had its origin in some imagined or pictured episode from the French Revolution;[10] as to its correspondence to the violation of Baudelaire's heart, this lies in the desolating impression it conveys of endless carnage (which is to say, emotional havoc) wrought by so many hands.

And yet, and yet... Against all expectation, the last line in this tercet (line 11) not only marks a return to the formally voiced admiration of the opening line (the possessive, once again, is 'votre'), but leads on, in the poem's final tercet, to total, unresisting capitulation. As Marie's perfume swirls around her naked breast,[11] the irresistible Beauty she personifies asserts itself again, more intimately still: for all those memories vivid from the past, for all his seeming inhibitions, he now must, come what may, surrender and submit; she must do what she will; it is decreed. And so, in the concluding couplet, Baudelaire returns to and extends his image of the second quatrain: let her eyes, in their full, festive brilliance, con -

---

Iconographie, p. 127, quotes the whole passage from Saint Peter's epistle, in which the phrase borrowed by Baudelaire is applied, rather, to the Devil seeking human prey. For a still more elaborate version of this image (which has obvious associations with the whole vampire mythology of the Romantic era), cf. the episode in a far earlier poem of Baudelaire's, *Bénédiction*, lines 45–52, in which the generic Poet's wife shows her total disdain for him by threatening to tear out his heart with her bare hands and fling it to her favourite pet.

10 Here again, in this image too, Baudelaire may have harked back to an earlier variant; cf. the sonnet *Sisina*, lines 5–8. I say 'earlier' advisedly, since I am convinced that a first version of *Sisina*, which saw publication under this title only in 1859, will have been drafted by him in his youth; see my *Baudelaire: Collected Essays* (Cambridge: Cambridge University Press, 1990), p. 23.

11 In the present context, the word 'gorge' needs certainly to be taken in this euphemistic sense, rather than as denoting Marie's 'throat' (which would hardly need specifying here as being 'naked'). For a nineteenth-century definition, with examples, of *gorge* used in the sense of 'breast' (anticipating our modern term *soutien-gorge*), see É. Littré, *Dictionnaire de la langue française* (Paris: Hachette, 1874), II. 1895. col. 2. It is interesting in this connection to compare Baudelaire's first (manuscript) draft of this line: 'Un parfum nage autour de votre gorge émue' (Abé, p. 176). The adjective in that version, 'émue', is less precise: I take it to refer to the heaving of Marie's breast in the grip of emotion, rather than to any flood of colour to her throat.

sume utterly, burn up, the few shreds of his heart that have survived the depredations of that past![12]

Since the art of reading poetry ought always to include the art of read-ing it aloud (or, at the very least, articulating it sub-vocally), some final attention must be paid to the practical detail of Baudelaire's versification. Not all his alexandrines in this sonnet maintain a strict median cesura: the most adventurous line, in this respect, is the one ending the first tercet (line 11), where the sense requires absolutely that the voice should pause briefly after the fourth (rather than the sixth) syllable — but briefly only, since the elision compels the reader to press on, and merge the one word 'nag[e]' into the next, 'autour'. Sense, again, in lines 1 and 7 (reinforced by punctuation, in the first case) dictates that the main pause should come after the ninth and third syllables, respectively, rather than the sixth. As to line 12, here there is effectively no median break at all: the punctuation (always significant for recitation, as Baudelaire himself reminded his publisher),[13] divides the line into three groups (3: 6: 3) which thereby override the notional half-way cesura.

At the outset of this commentary, I related *Causerie* to three later poems of Baudelaire's *(Semper eadem, Sonnet d'automne,* the second part of *Chant d'automne),* having the same 'conversational' framework and development. But what is equally notable is that all four of these poems share a marked *thematic* continuity; we may see them, indeed, as a linked sequence in which Baudelaire plays out, within a literally or figu-ratively autumnal context, the drama of his failing amorous ardour, his incapacity for (or incapacitation from) all passionate love, his retreat into a consoling if illusory tenderness purged of all violent and destructive elements — a near-death which, for a while, may blunt the fear of death to come.[14] Already, in many previous poems, Baudelaire had pictured

---

[12] Another of Baudelaire's muses, Mme Sabatier (for whom the later *Semper eadem* was shortly to be written) must clearly have been a careful reader of this poem, and especially of its ending; in her letter to him of 13 September 1857, she asks pointedly: 'Comment se comporte *ce qui vous reste de cœur?'* (*Lettres à Baudelaire,* ed. Claude and Vincenette Pichois (Neuchâtel: La Baconnière, 1973), p. 324; my italics).

[13] When writing to Poulet-Malassis, on 18 March 1857, in these terms: '(*Quant à ma ponctuation, rappelez-vous qu'elle sert à noter non seulement le sens, mais* LA DÉCLAMATION.)' (*Correspondance,* ed. Claude Pichois, Bibliothèque de la Pléiade (Paris: Gallimard, 1973), I. 384; the parenthesis and double emphasis are Baudelaire's own).

[14] An anticipation of this final solution — but within the impossible context of the 'marriage' with Jeanne Duval — is to be found in *Le Léthé*, with its prophetic

love as a ferocious battle between the sexes, or as a consented martyrdom in which he or generic Man plays the role of classic victim of the woman or Cupid-child.[15] Now, at this still further stage, as I have suggested elsewhere,[16] we might apply to our whole sequence of four poems the title of a novel by Elizabeth Bowen: 'The Death of the Heart'; even more accurately, perhaps, we might rather speak of 'The *Dying* of the Heart', since in the first of these poems, in *Causerie*, Baudelaire shows himself still capable of summoning up a last, reckless response to Marie's still inviting, challenging Beauty.

line: 'Je veux dormir! dormir plutôt que vivre!'; cf., conversely, *A une passante* (first published 1860), with its fleeting, if wholly fantasised reversion to earlier amorous reflexes.

15 Cf. the final quatrain of *L'Amour et le crâne*, in which the human skull exclaims to its tormentor: 'ce que ta bouche cruelle / Éparpille en l'air, / Monstre assassin, c'est ma cervelle, / Mon sang et ma chair!' The various other poems here recalled include *Hymne à la Beauté, Le Vampire, Les Métamorphoses du vampire, Duellum,* and *La Prière d'un païen,* while in the essay on Wagner of 1861 there is a passing reassertion, in a reference to the *Tannhäuser* Overture, of the essential 'barbarie' of love (*OCP* II. 795).

16 *Baudelaire: Les Fleurs du Mal* (Cambridge: Cambridge University Press, 1992), pp. 21–2.

15

Voices in the Night:
'A une heure du matin'

Sonya Stephens

A UNE HEURE DU MATIN

Enfin! seul! On n'entend plus que le roulement de quelques fiacres attardés et éreintés. Pendant quelques heures, nous posséderons le silence, sinon le repos. Enfin! la tyrannie de la face humaine a disparu, et je ne souffrirai plus que par moi-même.

Enfin! il m'est donc permis de me délasser dans un bain de ténèbres! 5
D'abord, un double tour à la serrure. Il me semble que ce tour de clef augmentera ma solitude et fortifiera les barricades qui me séparent actuellement du monde.

Horrible vie! Horrible ville! Récapitulons la journée: avoir vu plusieurs hommes de lettres, dont l'un m'a demandé si l'on pouvait aller en Russie 10
par voie de terre (il prenait sans doute la Russie pour une île); avoir disputé généreusement contre le directeur d'une revue, qui à chaque objection répondait: « — C'est ici le parti des honnêtes gens», ce qui implique que tous les autres journaux sont rédigés par des coquins; avoir salué une vingtaine de personnes, dont quinze me sont inconnues; avoir 15
distribué des poignées de main dans la même proportion, et cela sans avoir pris la précaution d'acheter des gants; être monté pour tuer le temps, pendant une averse, chez une sauteuse qui m'a prié de lui dessiner un costume de *Vénustre*; avoir fait ma cour à un directeur de théâtre, qui m'a dit en me congédiant: « — Vous feriez peut-être bien de vous adresser à 20
Z....; c'est le plus lourd, le plus sot et le plus célèbre de tous mes auteurs, avec lui vous pourriez peut-être aboutir à quelque chose. Voyez-le et puis nous verrons»; m'être vanté (pourquoi?) de plusieurs vilaines actions que je n'ai jamais commises, et avoir lâchement nié quelques autres méfaits que j'ai accomplis avec joie, délit de fanfaronnade, crime de respect 25
humain; avoir refusé à un ami un service facile, et donné une recommandation écrite à un parfait drôle; ouf! est-ce bien fini?

Mécontent de tous et mécontent de moi, je voudrais bien me racheter et m'enorgueillir un peu dans le silence et la solitude de la nuit. Âmes de ceux que j'ai aimés, âmes de ceux que j'ai chantés, fortifiez-moi, 30
soutenez-moi, éloignez de moi le mensonge et les vapeurs corruptrices du

monde, et vous, Seigneur mon Dieu! accordez-moi la grâce de produire
quelques beaux vers qui me prouvent à moi-même que je ne suis pas le
dernier des hommes, que je ne suis pas inférieur à ceux que je méprise!

(Charles Baudelaire, *Le Spleen de Paris*)

There are few poems which better emphasise the prosaism of *Le Spleen de Paris* than 'A une heure du matin' (1862), cataloguing, as it does, the vicissitudes of an ordinary day in the life of the poet-narrator. Indeed, this is a poem which has been seen as 'wilfully prosaic',[1] and a close reading of it bears witness to such determined prosaism in what is usually, for Baudelaire, poetic space. This is the space of the poetic interior; that of the sister poems in *Les Fleurs du Mal*, 'L'Examen de minuit' and 'La Fin de la journée', where space and time are one in the expansion of the lyric consciousness. Such expansion is also the realm of the *journal intime*, the text of solitude where one can off-load the tensions of inner and outer worlds. The purging of such tensions and similar (superior) relief is also afforded, in solitude and privacy, by prayer — in theory, at least. It is not surprising, then, that in a work as generically experimental as *Le Spleen de Paris*, desperate self-examination should be explored through different modes of discourse relating to the spaces in which such introspection occurs. The exploration of these modes of discourse does not stop here, however, for the voices of the outer world break through the barricades and, quite literally, invade poetic space. The tension between inner and outer worlds is thus staged, not only in the poet-narrator's elaborate mental parade (this is, after all, an interior monologue, in every sense), but in the jostling between different voices (speaking in different idioms) which occurs on the page.

The two poems in *Les Fleurs du Mal* and this prose poem all bear witness, in the exhausted 'Enfin!', to the ambiguous relief that darkness affords. But where they differ is significant. In 'La Fin de la journée', the expletive 'enfin!' occurs at the end of the quatrains; in 'L'Examen de minuit' it announces the final stanza; but here, in 'A une heure du matin', it opens the poem and punctuates it. The prose poem begins, in other words, with the (en)closure of solitude, the relief of a privacy enhanced by the 'double tour à la serrure' (l. 6). But the solitude so prized (because so often repeated) is an illusion. The personal pronouns of the first paragraph suggest the presence of another, as we move through the implied *je* of 'seul', through the impersonal 'on' which hears, with the

---

[1] J. A. Hiddlestone, *Baudelaire and* Le Spleen de Paris (Oxford: Clarendon Press, 1987), p. 58.

poet-narrator, those last carriages, and come to the 'nous' (l. 2) which shares in the solitude, if not the suffering of the final 'je''s inner self (l. 3). These pronouns do not only represent, then, a shift from the impersonal and collective to the private and personal,[2] they also lock us into textual complicity.[3]

This 'Enfin!' of frustration and of exhaustion is thus shared by the reader, its tiredness reflected in the weary clatter of the few remaining carriages, as in the rhythm of their 'roulement' and their epithets 'attardés et éreintés' (l. 2); these are carriages which are, in every way, symbolic of the daily traffic silenced (if not put to rest) by the enclosure of the night. They are the last vestiges of street noise, but for the noise that enters the text in the form of the clamouring voices which will not be silenced. The desired silence yields, in fact, to enumeration, an enumeration which itself gathers such pace that the exhaustion of the day is compounded by its memory (as exhaustive list) and the 'Enfin' is transmuted into the yet more desperate 'ouf! est-ce bien fini?' (l. 27) which, instead of suggesting closure, re-opens the case for further exam- ination.

The day's closing is synonymous with an end to such external pres- sures,[4] and the locking of the door is little more than a symbolic gesture. It is recognised as such in the suggestive use of the term 'barricades' (l. 7), which ironically overturns the ideology of the solidarity of the crowd and makes that crowd the tyranny against which such protection is necessary. There is also, however, recognition that these defences are ineffectual in the already defeated hopes expressed by 'Il me semble que' (l. 6), a half-hearted belief in the myth of fortifications against such tyranny. We are reminded here of the spectres of 'La Chambre double' who hammer on the locked door and enter to disturb the same poetic space. It has been suggested that this withdrawal from the world is a re- curring theme in *Le Spleen de Paris*, where retreat into darkness and solitude is 'a cleansing and soothing antidote to the self-loathing pro-

---

2 This is Jonathan Monroe's interpretation. See *A Poverty of Objects: The Prose Poems and the Politics of Genre* (Ithaca, NY and London: Cornell University Press, 1987), pp. 98–9.

3 Such complicity is not uncommon in the prose poems, but is perhaps most striking in 'Au lecteur', *Œuvres complètes*, texte établi, présenté et annoté par Claude Pichois, Bibliothèque de la Pléiade (Paris: Gallimard, 1975), I. 6. All references to quotations are to this edition which will henceforth be abbreviated as *OC*.

4 In 'La Fin de la journée', as in 'Examen de minuit', night is seen as appeasing, for example: 'la nuit voluptueuse monte / Apaisant tout' (*OC*, I. 128).

duced from daily contact with the life of the city'.[5] The poet-narrator certainly feels that he has earned the reward ('Enfin! il m'est donc permis', l. 5) and the desired antidote is indeed self-immersion to regain spiritual balance, but there is little sense here of this 'bain de ténèbres' being of the requisite kind, that is to say the 'rafraîchissantes ténèbres' of 'La Fin de la journée', or of the prose poem 'Le Crépuscule du soir'. It is an immersion in darkness, solitude, and silence (provoked by its opposite, the 'bain de multitude' of 'Les Foules'), but even in the inner space the multitude still lingers.

The crowd is generalised into the human race which, in its assault upon the poet-narrator, is equated with a tyrant. The terms of the text emphasise the battleground where tyrant is opposed by barricades and fortifications and the night is cease-fire ('nous posséderons le silence sinon le repos', ll. 2–3). As Claude Pichois has pointed out, the idea of the tyrant itself is one borrowed from de Quincey and a return to Baudelaire's 'Un mangeur d'opium' foregrounds the same conflict between crowd and inner sanctuary:

> Mais au bout de quelques années, j'ai payé cruellement toutes ces fantaisies, alors que la face humaine est venue tyranniser mes rêves, et quand mes vagabondages perplexes au sein de l'immense Londres se sont reproduits dans mon sommeil...
>
> (*OC*, I. 470)

> Notre auteur avait trop aimé la foule, s'était trop délicieusement plongé dans les mers de la multitude, pour que la face humaine ne prît pas dans ses rêves une part despotique. Et alors se manifesta ce qu'il a déjà appelé, je crois, la tyrannie de la face humaine.
>
> (*OC*, I. 483)

So, whilst separation from the crowd might be a desire, it is not one readily achieved and 'A une heure du matin' — with its emphasis on locking out the clamouring but with a textual fabric comprising (indeed, encouraging) such intrusions (through deliberate recapitulation) — brings the reality of the conflict and of modern creative life into the space of the text.

It is a reality described as horrible and immediately identified as an acutely urban horror by the balanced repetition of the epithet and the

---

5 See Christopher Prendergast, *Paris and the Nineteenth Century* (Oxford: Blackwell, 1992), p. 148.

subtle but striking shift from 'vie' to 'ville'.[6] The horrors of city life are then enumerated in the recapitulation, which moves back into the impersonal mode, but retaining, therefore, the complicity of the reader (we are, after all, privy to this recapitulation). This is emphasised by the sequence of past infinitives, but these rarely lose sight of the authorial *I*: 'avoir vu' (l. 9), 'avoir disputé' (ll. 11–12), 'avoir distribué' (ll. 15–16) as a formula is, therefore, balanced by personal structures such as 'm'a demandé' (l. 10), 'm'a prié' (l. 18), in which things are required of the poet, and these come together in a more positively self-centred way with 'avoir fait ma cour' (l. 19) and 'm'être vanté' (l. 23). This complicity is further compounded by the parentheses, acting as dramatic asides, which invite us to share the joke and to ask or answer the question.

The list of the day's activities is centred upon contact and contacts. On the one hand, the poet-narrator takes to the streets with the intention of placing his writing (for some return); on the other, he expends time and energy on meaningless encounters where others beg him for favours. He starts out in what we might think good company, that of 'plusieurs hommes de lettres' (ll. 9–10), but these men (and their collective worth) are summarily dismissed by the rejection of one man's question. The pretension of the implied question is equalled only by its idiocy and ignorance; and its heavy irony is determined by the poet-narrator's association of education and stupid question, of Russia and island (distancing the narrator from his interlocutor), and by the veiled apostrophe to the reader (the parenthesis and the 'sans doute' insisting upon the joke, but excluding the butt of it). He then goes to kill time (suggesting at least some entertainment) and ends up wasting it with an illiterate 'sauteuse' (l. 18) whose mispronunciation comes to characterise her.

These encounters are compounded by an argument with another (more powerful) figure from the literary world whose retort to each and every objection, '« — C'est ici le parti des honnêtes gens»', brings into question not only the honesty of his colleagues, but also his own candour and intelligence. The inclusion of direct speech here, as with the

---

6 The urban nature of this phenomenon is already present in the passages quoted from 'Un mangeur d'opium', but Pichois notes another occasion on which Baudelaire uses the appropriated expression, which is when he is planning to join his mother in Honfleur. This is roughly contemporary with the first publication of this prose poem: 'Enfin! Enfin! Je crois que [je] pourrai à la fin du mois fuir l'horreur de la face humaine. Tu ne saurais croire jusqu'à quel point la race parisienne est dégradée', *Correspondance*, texte établi, présenté et annoté par Claude Pichois, Bibliothèque de la Pléiade (Paris: Gallimard, 1975), II. 254.

mispronunciation of 'Vénus', introduces another voice and also a different idiom, and here it expresses a view in a way which is patently at odds with that of our narrator. This dispute draws upon the same techniques of opposition as the earlier exchange, with 'honnêtes gens' — 'coquins' (l. 14) introducing a hierarchy of superiorities. This episode of rejection has been linked to a biographical detail from Asselineau's *Baudelairiana* which recounts that, upon returning a re-jected manuscript, a certain M. Amail (described as a 'saint-simonien' and 'républicain vertueux') said to Baudelaire: 'Nous n'imprimons pas de ces fantaisies-là, nous autres.'[7] By drawing out through opposition and linguistic implication the attitudes inherent in such a statement, the poet-narrator can play upon this notion of 'honnêtes gens' (as equiva-lent to 'nous autres') as heavily ironic.[8] His superiority is revealed by a dismissive attitude disclosed by the choice and position of the adverb 'généreusement' (l. 12), which draws attention to itself by breaking the rhythm of the sentence, slowing it down to insist upon the quality of the narrator's contribution and upon the derisive mocking of his interlocu-tor. The range of potential meanings calls into question the narrator's stance. Does 'généreusement' here mean 'nobly', or 'at length', or does it mean 'without sympathy or prejudice for the interlocutor's position'?[9] Retrospectively, the generosity of the narrator's spirit attracts all magnanimous acts (handshakes, letters of recommendation) and shows each such act to be counterfeit.

This same dynamic can also be seen to operate in the exchange with the theatre director, to whom the poet-narrator pays court in the hope that such an investment will pay off. The return is less than he bargains for, as he is dismissed (*congédier* (l. 20) having the somewhat am-biguous undertones both of the courteous 'to be given leave' and the rather more discourteous 'to be sent packing') with advice which amounts to selling his soul (to Z.... — the initial indicating greater uni-versality than a name — a man who is living proof that merit has no currency). There is no situation more prosaic than the need to keep body and soul together, and this list of the day's activities becomes a balance sheet on which all transactions are recorded and where outlay and profit

---

[7] See *Petits poëmes en prose*, edited by Henri Lemaître (Paris: Garnier, 1962).

[8] This is a commonplace which Baudelaire enjoys exploiting; cf. *Fusées* XI: 'Ceux qui m'ont aimé étaient des gens méprisés, je dirais même méprisables, si je tenais à flatter *les honnêtes gens*' (*OC*, I. 660).

[9] The Dictionnaire É. Littré defines *généreusement* in the following terms: 'D'une manière généreuse, avec un grand cœur; d'une main libérale; courageusement; se montrer magnanime; d'un naturel noble' (Paris, 1885).

are examined. The rejections (by 'directeurs' — 'de revue et de théâtre', ll. 12, 19) connect the stupidity of the successful with that of the press (for it is here that reputations are made),[10] and emphasise how little purchasing power the true artist really has.

What is worse, however, is that the exchange mechanisms of our poet-narrator do not succeed in maintaining face value either, for he brags of actions not accomplished and denies successes; he refuses simple favours to friends and writes recommendations for those for whom he has no respect or time. In other words, he is as corrupted by the transactional system as the next man. He waves to folks he does not know and exchanges handshakes hypocritically (the gloves are the vestimentary equivalent of the locked door),[11] ever fearful of contracting some form of contagion which is as much spiritual as physical. Each and every exchange into which he enters is, in other words, as meaningless and dishonest as the next, whether it is a question of giving or receiving. The currency is counterfeit, the power-holders corrupt, and all exchange dysfunctional.[12] There is a progressive devaluation of mood and language, as the clamour of the day overwhelms the space reserved for poetic expansion and as it becomes apparent that the darkness of this particular night will not bring the 'repos' required to compose the 'beaux vers' (l. 33) so badly needed. The devaluation of art and of self which occurs in the day's transactions, the question of artistic merit, and the attendant frustrations and disappointments all come together in the climactic prayer. Even here, there is question of a return on earlier investment, almost as if the poet-narrator in addressing the intercessors ('Âmes de ceux que j'ai aimés, âmes de ceux que j'ai chantés', ll. 29–30) is recalling a debt. The capital once regained can be put back to

---

10 This is reminiscent of 'Les Tentations' where the third temptress, Fame, represents some kind of gain for favours. Here the courtesan which is the Press arrives blowing the trumpet of wordly renown, and is resisted by the poet only because the seductive virago is recognised as a woman who keeps the company of men with whom he would not wish to be associated. The poet overcomes the temptation here, but with the same form of twisted morality and worship as is present in the litany of 'A une heure du matin'.

11 This is a *reprise* of a locution in Baudelaire's own *Journaux intimes* in a section where there is a high concentration of ideas occurring in the prose poems in note form: 'Beaucoup d'amis, beaucoup de gants, — de peur de la gale' (*Fusées* XI, *OC*, I. 660).

12 For an analysis of failed communication in the prose poems, see Rosemary Lloyd's article 'Dwelling in Possibility: Encounters with the Other in Baudelaire's *Le Spleen de Paris*', *Australian Journal of French Studies*, XXIX, no. 1 (1992), 68–77.

work with the purpose of redemption ('je voudrais bien me *racheter*, l. 28).

The ending of the poem is highly significant, for it returns to the desires of the opening paragraphs to frame the central vicissitudes which militate against the fulfilment of these desires. The prayer of the final paragraph is itself framed by a statement of the poet's discontent ('Mécontent de tous et mécontent de moi', l. 28, balancing with 'que je ne suis pas le dernier des hommes, que je ne suis pas inférieur à ceux que je méprise!', ll. 33–4), a framework which operates like a *mise-en-abyme* of the whole textual dynamic of multitude and solitude.

The prayer also introduces another idiom into the text, one which breaks with all that has preceded and seems to move into a more lyrical voice. Like the locking of the door, there is in prayer a certain anticipation of relief and release. Apart from the strengthening effects, and it should be noted that *fortifier* occurs in reference to both the barricades and the prayer (ll. 7 and 30), this discourse of litany changes the dynamic of the text by its very rhetoric. The listing of the banal develops into an entirely different dynamic, with the accumulation of requests in the prayer lifting the text into the realm of the lyrical.

There is in this prayer both the desire for redemption (implying penitence) and for recognition (or flattery of his sinful vanity). These two desires are clearly incompatible, since to obtain forgiveness all sins must be disavowed. There is already a hint of these conflicting values in the narrator's bragging about crimes never committed and his disavowing of others accomplished with delight. This is, in part, an alternative view of what impresses, but the *délits* committed are here also marked by the guilt which attends any Catholic sensibility. The narrator cannot disavow claims to intellectual superiority when faced with the fatuousness of his entourage, and there is in this poem an implicit reference to the self-congratulatory Pharisee ('Mon Dieu, je vous rends grâces de ce que je ne suis point comme le reste des hommes').[13] There is also, however, the formulaic rhetoric of another kind of prayer, the night prayer which seeks protection during the hours of sleep, and offers a form of closure. This formula is recognisable not only by the apostrophe (both to God and intercessors), but also by the accumulation of imperatives and the nature of the requests: 'fortifiez-moi, soutenez-moi, éloignez de moi le mensonge…accordez-moi la grâce' (ll. 30–2). These are formulaic in the discourse of prayer, and elsewhere appear as such.

---

[13] This is discussed by J. A. Hiddleston, op. cit., pp. 56–7.

In the *Journaux intimes* there is an entry relating to precisely this relationship between artistic creation and divine intervention:

> Faire tous les matins ma *prière à Dieu, réservoir de toute force et de toute justice, à mon père, à Mariette et à Poe*, comme intercesseurs; les prier de me communiquer *la force nécessaire* pour accomplir tous mes devoirs...; faire tous les soirs une nouvelle prière....
>
> (*OC*, I. 673)

The italics of the entry suggest formula, and the choice of intercessors raises a smile, alerting us to the dangers of taking too seriously something written tongue-in-cheek. Indeed, in *Mon cœur mis à nu*, Baudelaire is clear about the paradoxical nature of prayer:

> Dieu et sa profondeur.
> On ne peut manquer d'esprit et chercher dans Dieu le complice et l'ami qui manque toujours. Dieu est l'éternel confident dans cette tragédie dont chacun est le héros. Il y a peut-être des usuriers et des assassins qui disent à Dieu «Faites que ma propre opération réussisse!». Mais la prière de ces vilaines gens ne gâte pas l'honneur et le plaisir de la mienne.
>
> (*OC*, I. 705)

Baudelaire's enterprise is not murder or usury; it is nothing more than 'quelques beaux vers' which, in the poet's mind at least, serve to raise him above other mortals. The narrator is not, however, the self-congratulatory Pharisee who believes in the righteousness of his prayer. The poet-narrator recognises that the values of this prayer are, in a conventional sense, misplaced. These are handled with ironic disregard for convention, therefore subverting the frame of reference which equates the act of praying with a fixed conception of Christian morality. The subversion is accomplished in 'A une heure du matin' with irreverent and irreligious delight in what is a parody of prayer. Baudelaire here borrows the self-deprecating rhetoric of the petitionary prayer where humility precedes a request and which usually asks for others to be granted divine favours as well as oneself, only to overturn this with a clear statement of pride which rejects the earlier humility and militates against any suggestion that this could ever be a real petitionary prayer (on behalf of others).

The ludic nature of Baudelaire's use of formulaic discourse also alerts us to his awareness of language as a dynamic force. He clearly equates the rhetoric of prayer with the act of writing through the idea of magic and sorcery:

De la langue et de l'écriture, prises comme opérations magiques, sorcellerie évocatoire.

Il y a dans la prière une opération magique. La prière est une des grandes forces de la dynamique intellectuelle. Il y a là comme une récurrence électrique.

(OC, I. 658 and 659).

The terms of the comparison are enlightening. Language and writing, as well as prayer, are seen as magical operations which are highly evocative. That prayer, so subject to standard repetitions,[14] should have a powerful intellectual dynamic should serve to remind us of its infinite individuality despite the recognisable forms of its discourse. The interest of such discourse lies, of course, precisely in the original expressive depths which become obscured by familiarity with the formula; as Baudelaire says in *Fusées*, there is a 'profondeur immense de pensée dans les locutions vulgaires, trous creusés par des générations de fourmis' (*OC*, I. 650). This accounts not only for his interest in clichés, commonplaces, and maxims,[15] but could also be applied to other formulas dependent on recognition and usage. It can be argued that, in the use of the formulas of prayer, the same linguistic and ideological pleasures are to be gained as in the reinvention of commonplaces; with the difference that the one form tends strongly towards prosaism, the other towards a transcendent lyricism.

The prayer at the end of the prose poem is, in its conscious use of discursive models and its subversion of more than linguistic convention, a microcosm of the question at the very heart of this text. It is not a simple question of whether or not the poet believes in the power of prayer, nor of his ironising of the Church (and its hypocritical adherents), but rather the power of art to redeem. The prayer is more than formula. Its

---

[14] Indeed, the standard nature of prayer occurs in the very next entry in *Fusées*: 'Le chapelet est un médium, un véhicule; c'est la prière mise à la portée de tous' (*OC*, I. 659).

[15] It has been convincingly argued that this use of commonplaces is 'proof of Baudelaire's desire to mingle the genres and to create a new art form by adding to the *ondulations de la rêverie* the *soubresaut* of the most uncompromising prose', and that 'their concision, suggestiveness, irony and paradoxicality, together with the number of ideas and rêveries they arouse in the mind of the reader bear witness to the fulfilment of this desire to be *toujours poète, même en prose*'. See J. A. Hiddleston, 'Fusée, Maxim and Commonplace in Baudelaire', *Modern Language Review*, XL (1985), p. 570.

formal qualities distinguish it from the entry in *Mon cœur mis à nu*; this prayer redeems through the power of its poetic expression.[16]

The different voices in indirect and direct speech, the parentheses which introduce asides, the italicised inclusion of another's mispronunciation, the intertextual voice of de Quincey and the rhetoric of prayer all contribute to the clamour of this text and are woven into the discursive and poetic fabric. The poem's prosaism is finally overthrown by lyricism and the ending transports us into an entirely different realm, the realm of prayer where the clamour of other voices is silenced. It is significant that the poem ends with a prayer. This, Jérôme Thélot suggests, is because 'la prière et la fin de la poésie [sont] en Baudelaire réclamées l'une par l'autre, et la poésie, dont la fin réclame la prière autant que celle-ci en réclame la fin, [est] pourtant ce qui rend la prière possible'.[17] Thélot is right to insist upon the close relationship between prayer and the ending of poems, especially when this reflects an exhaustion not unlike that of the carriages in the opening lines of 'A une heure du matin'. But incantation can bring relief and success, because the poet's liturgy represents the triumph of his voice in silencing all others, including God's, who (although here apostrophised) is not believed in sufficiently for there to be any sort of dialogue. Formulaic discourse of all kinds yields fruit. The frustrations of the day, with its clichéd exchanges, tests the poet to his limits and offers prose; in the anxiety of creative impotence, he utters a prayer which makes the poetry come. Prayer does, therefore, bring redemption in a value system which has no real belief in, or need for, God and this paradox (as well as the prose-poetry one) is thus internally resolved. Only, in Baudelaire, for this creative cycle to begin again in the morning.

---

16 This has been persuasively argued by Jérôme Thélot. See 'La Prière selon Baudelaire', in Jean Delabroy and Yves Charnet, eds, *Baudelaire: nouveaux chantiers* (Lille: Presses Universitaires du Septentrion, 1995), pp. 86–8.

17 Ibid., p. 89.

16

'Effet de soir', Ephraïm Mikhaël

Rosemary Lloyd

Cette nuit, au-dessus des quais silencieux,
Plane un calme lugubre et glacial d'automne.
Nul vent. Les becs de gaz en file monotone
Luisent au fond de leur halo, comme des yeux. 4

Et dans l'air ouaté de brume, nos voix sourdes
Ont le sens des échos qui se meurent, tandis
Que nous allons rêveusement, tout engourdis,
Dans l'horreur du soir froid plein de tristesses lourdes. 8

Comme un flux de métal épais, le fleuve noir
Fait sous le ciel sans lune un clapotis de vagues.
Et maintentant, empli de somnolences vagues,
Je sombre dans un grand et morne nonchaloir. 12

Avec le souvenir des heures paresseuses
Je sens en moi la peur des lendemains pareils,
Et mon âme voudrait boire les longs sommeils
Et l'oubli léthargique en des eaux guérisseuses. 16

Mes yeux vont demi-clos des becs de gaz trembleurs
Au fleuve où leur lueur fantastique s'immerge,
Et je songe en voyant fuir le long de la berge
Tous ces reflets tombés dans l'eau, comme des pleurs, 20

Que, dans un coin lointain des cieux mélancoliques,
Peut-être quelque Dieu des temps anciens, hanté
Par l'implacable ennui de son Éternité,
Pleure ces larmes d'or dans les eaux métalliques. 24

('Effet de soir', Ephraïm Mikhaël[1])

---

[1] 'Effet de soir' was published in Mikhaël's *Œuvres* (Paris: Lemerre, 1890). It has been anthologised in Bernard Delvaille's *La Poésie symboliste* (Paris: Seghers, 1971), p. 308.

On 19 December 1889, a young poet wrote to thank Mallarmé for the latter's role in awarding him a prize for his poem, 'Florimond', apologising that an illness brought on by the season's fogs prevented him coming in person.[2] A year before, Ephraïm Mikhaël had seen his *féerie*, 'Cor fleuri', performed at Antoine's Théâtre-Libre. The promising career that seemed to be shaping up for him was brought to an abrupt end when Mikhaël died suddenly on 5 May 1890, not yet 24 years old. 'Effet de soir' is certainly a young man's poem, but it raises timeless questions that gain a particular poignancy when set in the particular historical context I have just outlined. How could one write poetry at the end of the nineteenth century, overshadowed as one must have been by the great figures of Romanticism, by Baudelaire and Leconte de Lisle, Gautier and Heredia, not to mention Mallarmé, whose shadow was no less deep for not yet being long? For Ephraïm Mikhaël, preparing his poetic and prose-poetic works for a volume Lemerre was to publish a few months after the poet's death, the question of finding a personal voice in the echoing chamber of contemporary poetry was both daunting and vital. His solution, at least in this poem, seems to have been to make the whole question of citation, allusion, and pastiche the subject of the poem's central reflection, which thus becomes a meditation on poetic creativity in a world irrevocably changed by the collapse of Romanticism, by the transformation of the rural into the urban landscape, and by the simultaneous heroism and banality of modern life.

The very title of Mikhaël's poem plays wittily if wistfully on the implications of such a problem: reminiscent of the great Impressionist paintings whose ostensible subject is always merely a pretext for an exploration of light and vision, 'Effet de soir' is also redolent of Baudelaire's 'Coucher du soleil romantique', of Delacroix's emotive evening scenes, of Romanticism's manipulation of the relationship linking autumn, evening, and death.[3] Yet this is a poem which also turns firmly away from French Romanticism's already nostalgic focus on the individual and the countryside, shifting attention resolutely to Baudelaire's image of the heroism of modern urban life and Mallarmé's stress on universal rather than personal experience. No blazing suns dipping into a wild sea here, just the gas lights weeping in the sluggish water of a canalised inland river. Nature is mediated and controlled, as human existence is regu-

---

2   See Mallarmé, *Correspondance*, ed. L. J. Austin, III (Paris: Gallimard, 1969), p. 368.

3   For Mikhaël's earlier treatment of the theme, see Yves-Alain Favre, 'Ephraïm Mikhaël et le thème de l'automne en 1886', *Littératures*, XXIV (1991), 71–81.

lated and impersonalised by urban existence, and as a poet's ability to find a personal voice is limited by the countless reflections of other poets that the intellectual landscape inescapably imposes.

The very choice of stanzaic form, the six quatrains with their *rimes embrassées*, while it might seem a deliberate rejection of the late nineteenth century's preferred poetic form, the sonnet, nevertheless conveys a sense less of design than of purposeless circularity, the final rhyme of each quatrain harking back to, reflecting, the first, and the stanzas themselves presenting a continuous progression that goes nowhere, reproducing instead that implacable boredom of eternity evoked in the penultimate line. No detectable turning point appears in this flux of lines, where the fact that there is an even number of stanzas allows for random couplings, proposes different possible orders, until the last two quatrains, with their interstrophal enjambment, suggest a conclusion that offers not so much a closure, despite the conceit of the bored god, as a return to the beginning to discover that what presides over this urban landscape is not, after all, a divine presence but merely a 'calme lugubre'.

The deliberately jarring shift between the title's reference to evening and the opening line's allusion to night serves to focus attention more sharply on the *entrée en matière*, a quotation which would have been more obvious to contemporary eyes: Mallarmé's sonnet, now known as 'Quand l'ombre menaça', was originally entitled 'Cette nuit', a title it continued to carry even as late as the 1887 publication in *Écrits pour l'art*.[4] The urban nature of the experience is established from the opening line, where the river is metonymically evoked through the reference to the *quais*: bound in by the artificial nature of the city, the river can reflect only the man-made: not the stars, but the gas lights. Moreover, as the metonymy suggests, there can be no complete apprehension of external phenomena, no awareness of the totality of the river, just a fragmented vision of an aspect of that river, an aspect, moreover, that thrusts into prominence not its own essence but that to which human intervention has reduced it, as the poet himself, through his insertion into a specific historical moment, finds himself reduced and controlled by that historical reality. No longer a potent symbol of freedom, movement, and inspiration, the river can be named only through what constrains it: where romantic poetry could still negotiate its own choice of names, symbolist poetry is forced either to mirror the growing state control of names and identities, or to sidestep it by allusion and suggestion.

---

4 Mallarmé, *Œuvres*, ed. Yves-Alain Favre (Paris: Classiques Garnier, 1985), p. 604.

Moreover, where Lamartine can depict the poet's soul as a river which has failed, through a fault inherent in the poet, to reflect 'les clartés d'un beau jour', [5] the poet here seems alienated even from this urbanised element of nature, unable to offer the easy transference of metaphor. If the *quais* are silent, it is because the city, unlike Baudelaire's 'nature' in 'Correspondances', does not offer even so much as 'confuses paroles' to its citizens. Mikhaël insists on this eery silence not merely by putting 'silencieux' at the end of the line, but by liberating within that word the syllable 'cieux': just as Impressionism tended to place its horizons higher than had Romanticism, to suggest the absence of a divine presence, so here the night sky, dominated as it is by artificial light rather than by stars, is silent and empty, the only gods it can suggest being those of a long-distant past. Not even a breath of wind, then, to suggest a divine or external source of inspiration for the watcher on these river banks, whose rivalry with the poets of the past can count on no muse *ex machina* for assistance.

The word 'plane' transforms the noun 'calme' into a bird soaring above the river, recalling Hugo's affection for this verb, especially in *Les Châtiments,* but it also evokes, through its unusual intensity, Baudelaire's use of the word in 'La Mort des artistes', where the artists hope that 'la Mort, planant comme un soleil nouveau, / Fera s'épanouir les fleurs de leur cerveau'. [6] Mikhaël, moreover, builds on these associations to intensify the suggestion of the bird of prey and to liberate what had already become a frozen image, that of the 'becs de gaz': the juxtaposition of verb and noun here allows the metaphor to regain its initial energy. This growing suggestion of hostility in the ambient universe ushers in the element of the fantastic, the eyes floating along the quays, reflected both in the diegetic river and in the repeated *o* of 'monotone' and 'halo'; but it is typical of the world-weariness of the fin-de-siècle that the fantastic here is instantly stripped of its power through the deliberate banality, not only of the simile itself, but of the very choice of this rhetorical trope rather than that of metaphor.

While the first stanza concentrated on sight, the second turns to sound, a natural shift in a world where mists and fogs limit vision. The impersonality of the first strophe also gives way to the ambiguous introduction of the first person plural: with the expression 'nos voix sourdes / Ont le

---

5 Lamartine, *Méditations poétiques*, ed. Marius-François Guyard (Paris: Gallimard, 1981), p. 42.

6 Baudelaire, *Les Fleurs du Mal*, ed. Jacques Dupont (Paris: Garnier-Flammarion, 1991), p. 180.

sens des échos que se meurent' the poem not only achieves a perceiving consciousness, but simultaneously begins to emphasise its questioning of personal voice. The dying echoes here are not merely those of friends strolling on a chill autumn evening; they are also and more centrally the constantly competing voices of past poets. Moreover, this sense of countless predecessors is echoed by the assonantal patterns introduced by such pairings as 'meurent', 'horreur', 'soir', 'froid', and, reinforcing the rhyme 'sourdes / lourdes', 'engourdis'. 'Échos' itself picks up the 'halo' of the previous verse, an understated piece of wordplay that highlights the idea of reflection as both visual and aural phenomenon.

The third stanza begins with a further deliberate calling of attention to the rhetorical trope of the image. Here the triteness of the technique is further thrust into evidence by the banality of the lines: 'Comme un flux de métal épais, le fleuve noir / Fait sous le ciel sans lune un clapotis de vagues.' As a result, the onomatopoeia that results from both rhythm and alliteration is seen less as a virtuoso effect than as a mechanical gesture, and the subject of the lines shifts further from the natural world to the poetic medium itself. Like the river, the poem moves not with the ease of liquid, but with the awkwardness of metal, the sound patterns are reduced to a meaningless 'clapotis', and the word 'vagues', used at the rhyme as both noun and adjective, transparently evokes the poet's or, perhaps more accurately, contemporary poetry's inability to be other than diffuse, inexact, imprecise.

With the appearance of the first-person singular, moreover, the strophe slips further into parody, signalled by the presence of the space-filling words 'Et maintenant'. The image of the 'je', 'empli de somnolences vagues', falling into 'un grand et morne nonchaloir' recalls both Baudelaire's depiction of the hookah-smoking *ennui* who dominates human vice, and Verlaine's pastiche, 'Langueur':

> Je suis l'Empire à la fin de la décadence,
> Qui regarde passer les grands Barbares blancs
> En composant des acrostiches indolents
> D'un style d'or où la langueur du soleil danse.[7]

Just as 'nonchaloir' recalls frequent uses of the word in Charles Cros's *Le Coffret de Santal* of 1873, Sully Prudhomme's *Les Vaines Ten-*

---

[7] Verlaine, *Œuvres poétiques complètes*, ed. Y. G. Le Dantec and J. Borel, (Paris: Gallimard, 1962), p. 370. 'Langueur' is in the collection entitled *Jadis et naguère*, published in 1885.

dresses of 1875, and Jean Moréas's *Premières Poésies* of 1886, 'morne' appears in countless lines of Gautier's *Émaux et camées*, Banville's *Odes funambulesques* and *Les Exilés*, Verlaine's *Poèmes saturniens*, and Léon Dierx's *Premières Poésies,* and becomes almost a linguistic tic in Leconte de Lisle and Hugo. However parodic of Parnassianism these lines may appear, it is less the kind of parody that invites laughter than that which suggests the impossibility of escaping from that metallic flux of all that has previously been written and read. Moreover, it is at this point in the poem, the nadir, that the possibility of inspiration from other sources begins to arise. Somnolent and uncaring, no longer seeking the divine afflation or the sudden illumination, in a moonless and windless cityscape, the narrator is now open not to the literary memories that oppress but to the personal memories that alone may be able to terrify him into creativity.

Part of that creativity stems from the fact that by drawing so strongly on cliché and unquestioned modes of thinking, Mikhaël is able to embed in his lines expected formulations which are not in fact what is said. In evoking memory at the beginning of his fourth strophe, for example, and by including the trigger word 'heures', he is able to suggest both a happy past and one whose recollection brings pleasure. Yet the hours remembered are not 'heureuses' but 'paresseuses': time has not just been lost but wasted, frittered away, reduced to the same undifferentiated flux as that of the river. Hardly surprising, then, that the juxtaposition of sounds in 'heures paresseuses' releases both the sense and the sound of the word 'peur' and that the related image of the flow of time suggests the ineluctable nature of future 'lendemains pareils'. How can time be made to reveal the uniqueness of individual experience, and how can literature capture that uniqueness, given the multiplicity of past experiences, and the throng of all who have attempted to use literature to give value to the fleeting moment? Mikhaël's formulation of what is in itself a trite problem, and had already become an almost complacent expectation of Decadent writers, nevertheless finds an element of originality in its symbiosis with the urban landscape and a touch of pathos for those of us reading it with the knowledge that he had so few tomorrows in which either to capitulate to or escape from the oppression of repetition.

Where Baudelaire's poetic persona in 'Sed non satiata' sought to assuage boredom by drinking in the sensuous delights of erotic love, Mikhaël's seeks 'longs sommeils' and 'l'oubli léthargique'. The river now becomes that of Hades, whose water brings an oblivion that heals because it offers escape from those memories that enchain rather than enrich. The adjective 'guérisseuses', thrust into prominence not only through its length and its position at the rhyme but also by the richness of that rhyme and the opposition with its partner 'paresseuses', further suggests by its very unexpectedness that some degree of healing has taken place, that the poet has found a way to break free from the cliché-bound flow of language in which he has hitherto been trapped. The sound patterning in this stanza is especially rich: the harshness of the repeated *p*s and *b*s is balanced by the softer *l*s and prepares while it does not predict the *g* of the final rhyme.

With the beginning of healing comes an intimation of how fresh inspiration may be received, both in terms of how the familiar world can be perceived in ways that will present its *unheimlich* qualities, and in those of how the multiple reflections of the past can be drawn on and yet extended and revitalised. 'Mes yeux vont demi-clos', affirms the poet, with the choice of verb at last suggesting a more conscious movement that may bring change. No longer moving 'rêveusement' as in the second stanza, the narrating perception takes control, as any rhetorical technique must, determining what will be seen and how it will be seen, linking the world above the river with its reflection in the river, the world of phenomena with their transformation into literature. The suggestion here evokes Rimbaud's exploration of *voyance*, with the specifics of which Mikhaël was unlikely to be familiar but which was part of a much broader pattern of thought and experimentation that would have been accessible to him. The half glance, the sideways look, the stolen glimpse through half-closed eyes, like Baudelaire's emphasis on the limited frame of perspective, the vision of illumination rather than realism, enables the escape from the predictable that the image begins to suggest and that is more powerfully conveyed in the choice of verb, 's'immerge'. Here the poet not only refuses the expected 'plonge' but playfully echoes that word in the 'songe' and 'long' of the following line. The choice of 'berge', furthermore, seems to imply a turning away from the city as source of inspiration, or more precisely, a liberating of the river from the artificial quays that had bound it, in a gesture that ushers in the final conceit.

Both thematically and phonetically, 'Tous ces reflets tombés dans l'eau, comme des pleurs' reflects the last line of the first strophe: 'Luisent au fond de leur halo, comme des yeux.' The nasal *o* of 'tombé' and 'fond', the *o* of 'eau' and 'halo', the repetition of 'comme des' all reinforce the suggestion that the eyes we had seen gleaming in the halo of the gas lights have now fallen into the water as tears. Though Baudelaire's lighthouses, the great artists who have guided mankind through history, have been metamorphosed into mere gas lights, their reflections, Mikhaël suggests, continue to evoke the suffering and grief of human experience.

That suffering is transposed in the final stanza into a conceit that seems to sum up much of the atmosphere and mood of Parnassian disdain for all that the modern world had to offer. In Mikhaël's image, the tears are shed by some, no doubt minor, god, lost in a far-off corner of the after world. It is hard not to think of Sainte-Beuve's notorious suggestion that Baudelaire would find a form of literary eternity in a kiosk in some remote outpost in Kamchatka. If the god weeps, it is because he is overwhelmed by the 'implacable ennui' of eternity. 'Implacable' is frequently encountered in Parnassian poetry, from the 'implacable blancheur' of Gautier's 'Symphonie en blanc majeur',[8] and Leconte de Lisle's 'implacable fardeau de l'immense univers',[9] to Baudelaire's line in 'La Chambre double': 'Je suis la Vie, l'insupportable, l'implacable Vie',[10] and the unforgettable formulation of Charles Cros which refers to time as an 'implacable alchimiste'.[11] Nevertheless, the phrase 'implacable ennui' seems to be Mikhaël's own creation, a bravura instance of the poet bringing together two well-worn terms to forge something novel. Equally innovative is the intricate sound patterning in this final stanza, where the nasal *an* at the end of the first and second lines in 'mélancoliques', 'anciens', 'hanté' create a form of alternate rhyme, reinforced by the enjambment between the stanza's second and third lines. That enjambment in itself ties thematics and techniques together here, offering its own version of endless continuity. A similar form of echoing repetition occurs in the last line, where the *-té* rhyme of the stanza's second and third lines is taken up assonantally in the last line's final word, 'métalliques'. Fortuitously or not, Mikhaël's initials recur on no fewer than four occasions in this last stanza, in 'mélancoliques', 'temps', 'larmes', and 'eaux métalliques', as if to confirm the presence of the individual voice among all these echoes and allusions to the multitude of poetic voices.

In a poem that opposes the modernity of the city and the timelessness of boredom, the desire for uniqueness and the sense of eternal repetition, the poet appears as a wastrel, lazily frittering away precious time or prodigally scattering the abundance of his poetic legacy. Yet what arises from this meditation on the simultaneous need for, and impossibility of,

---

8 Gautier, *Émaux et camées*, ed. J. Pommier (Geneva: Droz, 1947), p. 23.

9 Leconte de Lisle, *Poèmes antiques* (Paris: M. Ducloux, 1852), p. 195. This collection contains several other instances of *implacable*.

10 Baudelaire, *Œuvres complètes*, ed. C. Pichois (Paris: Pléiade, 1975), I. 282.

11 Charles Cros, *Œuvres complètes* (Paris: J. J. Pauvert, 1964), p. 126.

uniqueness is a sense that Mikhaël, despite that almost parodically Parnassian final conceit, has been able to transform the banal matter of a common cityscape into something verging on the fantastic, something that is potentially quite powerful. There is always a temptation with a poet who dies very young, as Mikhaël did, to project future greatness denied by the harsh hand of fate. The destiny of many symbolists warns against such easy fables. Nevertheless, the poem does take up a central problem, that of originality, and explores it with charm and wit, using the very temptation that faced him, that of echoing and quoting his predecessors, as his means of attaining at least some degree of originality.

17

Reading, Elucidating, Creating

Leighton Hodson

Mes promenades de cet automne-là furent d'autant plus agréables que je les faisais après de longues heures passées sur un livre. Quand j'étais fatigué d'avoir lu toute la matinée dans la salle, jetant mon plaid sur mes épaules, je sortais: mon corps obligé depuis longtemps de garder l'immobilité, mais qui s'était chargé sur place d'animation et de vitesse accumulées, avait 5 besoin ensuite, comme une toupie qu'on lâche, de les dépenser dans toutes les directions. Les murs des maisons, la haie de Tansonville, les arbres du bois de Roussainville, les buissons auxquels s'adosse Montjouvain, recevaient des coups de parapluie ou de canne, entendaient des cris joyeux, qui n'étaient, les uns et les autres, que des idées confuses qui m'exaltaient et 10 qui n'ont pas atteint le repos dans la lumière, pour avoir préféré à un lent et difficile éclaircissement, le plaisir d'une dérivation plus aisée vers une issue immédiate. La plupart des prétendues traductions de ce que nous avons ressenti ne font ainsi que nous en débarrasser en le faisant sortir de nous sous une forme indistincte qui ne nous apprend pas à le connaître. Quand 15 j'essaye de faire le compte de ce que je dois au côté de Méséglise, des humbles découvertes dont il fut le cadre fortuit ou le nécessaire inspirateur, je me rappelle que c'est, cet automne-là, dans une de ces promenades, près du talus broussailleux qui protège Montjouvain, que je fus frappé pour la première fois de ce désaccord entre nos impressions et leur expression 20 habituelle. Après une heure de pluie et de vent contre lesquels j'avais lutté avec allégresse, comme j'arrivais au bord de la mare de Montjouvain, devant une petite cahute recouverte en tuiles où le jardinier de M. Vinteuil serrait ses instruments de jardinage, le soleil venait de reparaître, et ses dorures lavées par l'averse reluisaient à neuf dans le ciel, sur les arbres, sur 25 le mur de la cahute, sur son toit de tuile encore mouillé, à la crête duquel se promenait une poule. Le vent qui soufflait tirait horizontalement les herbes folles qui avaient poussé dans la paroi du mur, et les plumes de duvet de la poule, qui, les unes et les autres se laissaient filer au gré de son souffle jusqu'à l'extrémité de leur longueur, avec l'abandon de choses inertes et 30 légères. Le toit de tuile faisait dans la mare, que le soleil rendait de nouveau réfléchissante, une marbrure rose, à laquelle je n'avais encore jamais fait attention. Et voyant sur l'eau et à la face du mur un pâle sourire répondre au sourire du ciel, je m'écriai dans mon enthousiasme en brandissant mon pa-

rapluie refermé: «Zut, zut, zut, zut.» Mais en même temps je sentis que   35
mon devoir eût été de ne pas m'en tenir à ces mots opaques et de tâcher de
voir plus clair dans mon ravissement.

(Proust, *A la recherche du temps perdu*)[1]

To speak in metaphor — something Proust and his narrator would surely
favour — the complex body of *La Recherche* is a series of interrelating
systems corresponding to the setting up and the elaboration of themes. In
Combray, from which this passage is taken, we encounter sleep, dreams,
memory, time, oblivion and, not least, the urge to justify existence by encapsulating contingent experiences in words, the biggest theme in *La
Recherche* being the narrator's sense of finding at the end of a long quest
his literary vocation. To pursue the metaphor — what use are systems in
the economy of any organism without the connective tissue that supports
them and allows them to function together? That tissue seems secondary,
but there is no heart without a pericardium, and so on in every vital case,
to each its own 'membrane séreuse'. Without the connective tissue there
would be no strength, no co-ordination of parts, no life, no spirit. This
particular extract shows Proust handling precisely that interactive element
in the complex living mechanism of his novel. Here in *Combray* he presents that special moment when awareness of both pleasure and duty
strike the young narrator for the first time and bring him to the point of
understanding that the urge to spiritual progress, and especially the realising of it in words, must be made through the working out of a technique.
The acceptance of a method and the prestige that is to be attached to it
over and above the visceral sense experience is the acknowledgement of
that connective tissue that interlinks systems and allows individual organs
to be more than the sum of their parts. It is important that the discovery
of this fundamental tool of the trade should be made evident here early in
the proceedings, for without the urge to understand and explain what
happens beyond the lyrical moment of experience, the writer's message
would remain locked for ever in a self-referring world that could not then
be shared. The beginning of that invisible vocation, which the narrator in
Le Temps retrouvé realises has been his aim all along, is embedded in the
discovery of an aesthetic and ethical duty to elucidate the narrator's sense
of joy. The passage pinpoints the very moment when the technique is acquired which sets in motion the accumulating synergy that gives *La
Recherche* the semblance of a drama.

---

[1] *A la recherche du temps perdu*, ed. Jean-Yves Tadié, Bibliothèque de la Pléiade
(Paris: Gallimard, 1987–), pp. 152–3.

The description of his intention is the narrator's literary equivalent of acknowledging the dependence of the separate elements of *La Recherche* on seemingly incidental moments. These become with hindsight nodal points concentrating the energy of his spiritual quest. It is the very moment of finding the spark that through his green fuse drives the flower of his potential creativity. The overall title of *La Recherche* reminds us of the striving element in a scheme that involves not only time lost but, by a play on 'perdu', time wasted. The driving force is therefore the desire not for nostalgic indulgence but for retrieval combined with justification. The extract fits very well, no doubt, into that part of *Combray* that has come magically out of his cup of tea, but the crucial point within it is the dissatisfaction with remembering yet again a moment of sweet pleasure and perhaps seeing it yet again disappear. Here for the first time is expressed the determination to confront the duty of seeing how it may be evaluated; a kind of morality for the artist sits astride the pleasure principle, and not to dominate, but rather to enrich it further.

While the burden of the passage is the arriving at a method for evaluation, in that lies also the turning point in the development of the narrator's aesthetic adventure. He finds joy in a relentless ratiocination leading to the analysis of what to any one else would have appeared fleeting, imprecise, and amorphous. As so often in *La Recherche* Proust sets up in proleptic fashion an example that spontaneously exhibits the full command of the technique he discovers here. The shift in time sequences allows us — after the event — to see how the narrator actually arrived at it. So here the message of this passage — 'tâcher de voir plus clair dans mon ravissement' (ll. 36–7) — has already been fully and memorably enjoyed by the reader in that star moment of the *madeleine* dipped in the cup of tea. In that passage the narrator shows, by insisting on watching himself retrace its very energy step by step until the mechanism is understood precisely, how he will not let the elusive power of the experience escape until he can establish 'un éclaircissement décisif'. Here in this extract, with the force of what Proust is alluding to well established in our minds, we see the young narrator at the very stage of becoming, actually moving with the visceral tropism of that connective tissue towards his future. *La Recherche* is read to some extent for its picture of a period but above all for the sense of evolving — for the evolution in time of the characters and above all for the evolution of the narrator's spiritual progress. The sheer energy of that aesthetic search in *La Recherche* is not possible without the strength given by the connective tissue we see created here. How many in the gymnast's powerful grace forget the ligaments? Not Proust; he is watchful and appreciative of what prepares for the narrator's development and in this less than charismatic moment — it has none of the glamour of the *madeleine*, and many a reader may pass over it as the routine passage work it at first appears to be — he displays an element of that strategic foresight he always claimed for his novel when it was criticised for its formlessness. What he gives evidence of is sinewy writerly skills that contrast with the ineffable and elusive qualities that are the very stuff of the narrator's sensibility. He prepares in a tough and uncompromising Cartesian spirit for the transmission of a moment of bliss, aligning the duty of intellectual rigour with the urge for poetic effusion, so that the firmness of the one may prevent the dissipation of the other and give the apparently incommunicable the clarity of a local habitation and a name. Naming, the narrator learns, is the fundamental problem for the writer; he who can name, can create. The technique for capturing an observation, giving it a value and especially a name — all quintessential procedures of *La Recherche*, whether concerning people, places, or feelings — starts here in the narrator's first steps in establishing an aesthetic theory and practice.

The passage links the theme of reading to the narrator's first attempt to go beyond the literary pleasures either reading or being read to afford, for in the closing pages of *Combray* he will create for himself a verbal equivalent corresponding to the urge to balance feelings with literary expression. The passage is the transfer-point of two attitudes to the power of words: words read and words written. The earliest expression of that power appears in the introductory part of *Combray* where the narrator's mother reveals the power of words to pacify, words as escapism, words as a balm. What she exemplifies above all is the particular attraction to the narrator of literature as a consolation and therefore as something to be prized above all since in that is the justification — as he later understands it — for the inadequacy of existence. She is obliged to pacify his nervous exacerbation at the absence of her goodnight kiss by opening ahead of time the parcel of books he has been given as a birthday present. While this reading has the power of retaining his mother in his room and resolving in a pleasurable way the unpleasant conflict of a family scene, it has also the dimension of the consolation provided by the imaginative distraction of words either as narrative or in description. The book chosen, George Sand's idyllic recreation of childhood and adolescence in rural Berry, *François le Champi*, is discreetly edited by his mother — 'elle passait toutes les scènes d'amour' — but the important thing is that she reads it in a way that lulls him like the administration of a spell. The story is less important than its atmosphere and the encouragement he finds in it to let his mind wander from the effort of comprehension to day-dreaming: 'L'action s'engagea; elle me parut d'autant plus obscure que dans ce temps-là, quand je lisais, je rêvassais souvent, pendant des pages entières à tout autre chose.' Reading, it is already hinted, becomes something that allows the reader to take on board its subliminal qualities and feel an expansion of the soul as a result. The mother's voice is as important as the words, taking the willing listener deeper into himself, into that deeper awareness that is the purpose of the 'recherche' of the title and nearer the desire and eventually the ability to create such magic himself: 'elle insufflait à cette prose si commune une sorte de vie senti-mentale et continue.'

When it comes to reading alone, during his idle summer days in the garden of Combray under the chestnut tree, the emphasis is again on that further dimension beyond reading that opens up the reader to the experience of a fuller sense of personality by association. The detail of the content is not specified at all, let alone itemised; the emphasis is on what extra challenge reading may offer, and especially introspective discovery. Reading is the path to deeper spiritual progression where the real is less important than the potential that always lies elsewhere; fact is less important than the search, and the search is always for the unspoken, the undiscovered: 'Un être réel, si profondément que nous sympathisions avec lui, pour une grande part est perçu par nos sens, c'est-à-dire nous reste opaque, offre un poids mort que notre sensibilité ne peut soulever...La trouvaille du romancier a été d'avoir l'idée de remplacer ces parties impénétrables à l'âme par une quantité égale de parties immatérielles, c'est-à-dire que notre âme peut s'assimiler.'

This connecting passage, lying between the mother's performance, the narrator reading in the garden, and the narrator's little essay on the Martinville steeples, picks up the spiritual force that has been accorded to reading and replaces it with action, the need to get something done. A kind of spiritual impatience demands more than the passivity that reading can provide. The narrator's mind has been primed by hours of reading, by which we must understand that he is in that exalted state of wanting more than reading can give. He describes himself as wound up like a top ready to be set spinning (l. 6); his actions are abrupt as he breaks out of his reading trance, driven by an urge (as yet only vaguely understood) to resolve that unsatisfactory feeling of the promise of what the personality can offer and that is always thwarted. The passage draws the places and scenes of the locality — Tansonville, Roussainville, Montjouvain (ll. 7 – 8) — into the narrator's spiritual state, expressed literally in the mimetic action of aimless thrashing movements with umbrella or cane that are the only realisable counterparts to the surges of as yet unclarified feeling.

Even to attempt to translate them provides a relief which is unsatisfactory, because it remains merely at the level of emotional energy, totally lacking any characteristic of intellectual understanding. He arrives at a relief which is only 'une forme indistincte qui ne nous apprend pas à le connaître' (l. 15). This first half of the passage is rich with the edgy temper of exacerbated feelings demanding cool resolution in thought. The 'connaître' that clinches this section is also the preparation for the clear formula of the end and its triumphalism in the determination to seek lucid resolutions. The passage throughout derives its stylistic impetus from the paralleling of vague emotional effusions and hard Cartesian instructions. In this first half 'immobilité', 'animation', 'vitesse' (ll. 4–5), 'cris joyeux' (l. 9), 'idées confuses', 'le repos dans la lumière' (ll. 10–11), 'forme indistincte' (l. 15) balance 'lent et difficile éclaircissement' (ll. 11–12), 'toupie qu'on lâche' (l. 6), 'coups de parapluie ou de canne' (l. 9) which culminate in the direct use of *apprendre* and *connaître*.

This pattern of alternating feeling and intellectual resolution is repeated more elaborately and persuasively in the second half. This part begins more anecdotally, setting up a typical scene in which this emotional/ intellectual puzzle will be fully confronted. Again place names are invoked and this time the narrator's development is emotionally associated with them to almost mystical effect. He is no longer, as in the first half, simply referring to places so as to state where he happened to be; he is here expressing something entirely new, namely his debt to the 'côté de Méséglise' (l. 16). Fortuitous location though it may well be, it is also the essential turning point, 'le nécessaire inspirateur' (l. 17), in a species of self-realisation that carries him beyond the 'rêvasseries' previously associated with the passivity of reading. We are presented with one of those moments that Proust engineers to show the actual move forward in the narrator's development. We are on the point of observing an actual transition, with the narrator not so much nostalgically recalling as being carried along existentially into a new phase of thinking. The problem is categorically stated and we share the narrator's awareness of the gap that exists between sense impressions and the normal, automatic, and hence inadequate, verbal reaction that passes for a realisation of them in language. That gap having been posited, the only further interest must be in its closure. An automatic expletive can be no more than that, a filling in and not an extension into a full-blown and exploratory linguistic adventure. The setting up of the moment which will be crucial follows in the now detailed and colourful part of the description — garden hut, sunshine glinting on wet surfaces (sky, trees, roof-tiles). The banality of the situation is in itself powerfully important. The narrator's greatest shifts in understanding — almost geological landslips in their value to him — are based on ordinary things, though always linked to the urge to question and elucidate, such as the *madeleine*, the changing position of the church steeples and, most impressively, the whole series of involuntary memories in *Le Temps retrouvé*: the uneven paving stones, the clink of the spoon on the plate, the starched napkin. It is there, on the point of realising he is to embark on his act of creation, that the narrator reasserts the driving force of his need and duty to make the intermediate step of elucidation: 'je m'efforçais de tâcher de voir clair le plus vite possible dans la nature de ces plaisirs identiques que je venais par trois fois en quelques minutes de ressentir, et ensuite de dégager l'enseignement que je devais en tirer.' The importance is not in the material worth of the event so much as in the associative power attached to it, what the narrator in the next adolescent stage in *A l'ombre des jeunes filles en fleurs* will call the 'pouvoir réfléchissant'. Here the sheer homeliness of the incident adds to its charm and underlines more strongly therefore the point of change; the narrator makes an adjustment that seems small and insignificant but leads unfailingly to a fundamental switch of attitude. There is a playful humour as well as charm in describing the hen's downy feathers and the waving grass which, without heaviness, symbolise the contingent elements of the scene (ll. 27–9). The 'abandon de choses inertes et légères' (ll. 30–1) parallels the concrete detail in a way that echoes the technique of the first half. With delicate touch but with strong effect, the 'marbrure rose' (l. 32) and the linking of water, wall, and sky (ll. 33–4) are used to prime a normal, low-powered, and inadequate expression of delight. The little drama ends with a firm resolve to move to a new form of action that encapsulates the idea of the inadequacy of the language of expostulation and the paradox that delight or enjoyment demand a language of elucidation or must be forever locked in the comic abruptness of an imagination-thwarting 'Zut!'. The whole passage has a self-contained quality that moves from an imprecise wondering to a precise formula which, while satisfying the narrator, challenges the reader also who is left thinking how it may be applied and with what revelation of a new departure in aesthetic development. The precision of 'tâcher de voir plus clair dans mon ravissement' (ll. 36–7) has already been demonstrated in the *madeleine* episode, where words are proven to be far from opaque. What Proust goes on to do in order to complete the literary theme of *Combray* is to show the young narrator, having started from the point of passive meditation on reading, applying his new-found determination to wrestle with language and make it fit an experience in his juvenile composition on the Martinville steeples. It is the direct application of the formula the narrator has arrived at, and it is the intellectual satisfaction — his decision to resort to words echoes a sense of aesthetic duty: 'pour soulager ma conscience et obéir à mon enthousiasme' — that provides the energy to convert feeling into literature. The outing of the secret that lies behind the changing positions of the steeples of Martinville and Vieuxvicq as seen from Dr Percepied's carriage moves into the realm of elucidation before finding its literary solution: 'ce qui était caché derrière les clochers de Martinville devait être quelque chose d'analogue à une jolie phrase.' It is the bonding strength of the apparently insignificant piece of connective tissue in this extract that allows the narrator — and the reader of Proust's text — to appreciate the value to be put on a change of direction in literary discourse, from perceived feeling to realisation in a pleasing form of words, words that can be left living when the feeling that occasioned them has long evaporated.

18

Céline and the Anarchical Text: Bardamu Recounts his First Glimpse of New York

Michael Tilby

> To a teacher of languages there comes a time
> when the world is but a place of many words
> and man appears a mere talking animal not
> much more wonderful than a parrot.
>
> (J. Conrad, *Under Western Eyes*)

Pour une surprise, c'en fut une. A travers la brume, c'était tellement étonnant ce qu'on découvrait soudain que nous nous refusâmes d'abord à y croire et puis tout de même quand nous fûmes en plein devant les choses, tout galérien qu'on était on s'est mis à bien rigoler, en voyant ça, droit devant nous... 5

Figurez-vous qu'elle était debout leur ville, absolument droite. New York c'est une ville debout. On en avait déjà vu nous des villes bien sûr, et des belles encore, et des ports et des fameux même. Mais chez nous, n'est-ce pas, elles sont couchées les villes, au bord de la mer ou sur les fleuves, elles s'allongent sur le paysage, elles attendent le voyageur, tandis que celle- 10 là l'Américaine, elle ne se pâmait pas, non, elle se tenait bien raide, là, pas baisante du tout, raide à faire peur.

On en a donc rigolé comme des cornichons. Ça fait drôle forcément, une ville bâtie en raideur. Mais on n'en pouvait rigoler nous, du spectacle qu'à partir du cou, à cause du froid qui venait du large pendant ce temps-là à 15 travers une grosse brume grise et rose, et rapide et piquante à l'assaut de nos pantalons et des crevasses de cette muraille, les rues de la ville, où les nuages s'engouffraient aussi à la charge du vent. Notre galère tenait son mince sillon juste au ras des jetées, là où venait finir une eau caca, toute barbotante d'une kyrielle de petits bachots et remorqueurs avides et 20 cornards.

Pour un miteux, il n'est jamais bien commode de débarquer nulle part mais pour un galérien c'est encore bien pire, surtout que les gens d'Amérique n'aiment pas du tout les galériens qui viennent d'Europe. «C'est tous des anarchistes» qu'ils disent. Ils ne veulent recevoir chez eux 25 en somme que les curieux qui leur apportent du pognon, parce que tous les argents d'Europe, c'est des fils à Dollar.

J'aurais peut-être pu essayer comme d'autres l'avaient déjà réussi, de
traverser le port à la nage et puis une fois au quai de me mettre à crier:
«Vive Dollar! Vive Dollar!» C'est un truc. Y a bien des gens qui sont   30
débarqués de cette façon-là et qui après ça ont fait des fortunes. C'est pas
sûr, ça se raconte seulement. Il en arrive dans les rêves des bien pires
encore. Moi, j'avais une autre combinaison en tête en même temps que la
fièvre.

A bord de la galère ayant appris à bien compter les puces (pas seulement   35
à les attraper, mais à en faire des additions, et des soustractions, en somme
des statistiques), métier délicat qui n'a l'air de rien, mais qui constitue bel et
bien une technique, je voulais m'en servir. Les Américains on peut en dire
ce qu'on voudra, mais en fait de technique, c'est des connaisseurs. Ils
aimeraient ma manière de compter les puces jusqu'à la folie, j'en étais   40
certain d'avance. Ça ne devait pas rater selon moi.

(Céline, *Voyage au bout de la nuit*)[1]

When the narrator-hero of *Voyage au bout de la nuit* arrives off the coast
of New York on a ship he would have us believe is a slave-galley, his
initial reaction is purportedly one of amazement: 'Pour une surprise c'en
fut une.' This reaction not only replicates the effect each new experience
had produced on him at earlier stages in his journey, but engenders a narrative discourse that produces a parallel effect on the reader, even if by
this stage the constants of this unorthodox discourse are firmly established in our minds. Both in this first sentence and in the rest of the passage, Bardamu's narration, as elsewhere in Céline's novel, is suffused
with an orality that is immediately perceived as a provocative break with
literary convention, challenging (though the break is less radical than it
may at first seem) the assumption, rooted in the tradition of the bourgeois
novel, that the very concept of narrative is predicated on the logic inherent
in the syntactical forms of the written language. The result is a text which
imitates New York's scandalous break with the assumption that cities are
articulated according to a horizontal 'syntax'. Just as the city is immediately experienced by Bardamu in its aspect as transgressor, so Céline's
text establishes itself from the outset as an act of transgression.

The provocative nature of the orality that pervades Céline's text is reinforced by the text's specific identification with popular discourse. The
range of examples of popular linguistic usage in this passage, which may
be considered representative of the novel as a whole, is immediately
identifiable and encompasses both the pleonastic or redundant (e.g. the
'proleptic' use of pronouns, subject and object) and the elliptical ('y a' or

---

[1] Céline, *Romans*, Bibliothèque de la Pléiade (Paris: Gallimard, 1981), I. 184–5.

the omission of *ne*). Given Céline's obvious fascination with popular speech patterns and their difference, it might be supposed, initially, that his primary concern is with a post-Naturalist or populist form of representation, and that Bardamu's linguistic usage is the means by which he can be 'placed' and assessed. It will be seen, however, that Céline's ultimate purpose is, in fact, to move beyond the representational. To that end, Bardamu is conceived as a narrative voice rather than as a literary character to be analysed in terms of his relation to Society or his psychological make-up. The activity required of the reader, when faced with this unorthodox figure, is thus diametrically opposed to that employed in the novel itself by such entities as the Army medical board or the American Immigration Service.

The conscious reproduction of examples of popular usage plays on the conventional assumption that they imply some form of inadequacy on the part of the speaker or writer. They are knowingly wielded by Céline as the accepted markers of a 'lack' that may be said to relate, variously, to education, politeness, class and even, at the most basic level of all, logic. Céline ironically ensures that the fundamental assumption (or prejudice) relating to popular speech is further fed when he makes Bardamu's utterances the vehicle of a certain vulgarity that displays itself most evidently through his predilection for allusions to sexual activity in its most basic form. It will be seen, however, that the self-consciousness with which the popular idioms are reproduced invites the reader to participate in a radical redefinition of their implications.

Implicit in this self-conscious imitation of popular speech is an appreciation of the way the latter constitutes a different (rather than deficient) representation of the individual's experience of the world. The predominantly staccato effect of Bardamu's narration in this passage is the product of an overriding recourse to juxtaposition rather than to the varied range of conjunctions normally to be found in 'literary' narratives and which denote a sustained reflection on the relationship and implications of the various thoughts and emotions recorded. It is a narration which takes the form of a monologue punctuated by occasional rhetorical addresses to the inevitably silent reader, and this may give the initial impression (though, like all other impressions of a lack of control exercised by Céline over his hero's narration, it is misleading) of a flow of spontaneous observations unchecked by the restraints imposed by the more complex sentence structures of 'literary' prose. Yet the relative absence of slang terms or even of a consistently popular lexis is indicative of the fact that what interests Céline is not the mere transcription of typical features of oral usage, but the relationship between experience and its communication. It is here that we can begin to see Céline highlighting what he knows to constitute a lack from a conventional point of view, in order that he may proceed with his attempt to re-evaluate the supposedly deficient discourse in positive terms. In this case, it is the accepted hierarchical relationship in literary narrative between an immediate emotional reaction and the subsequent explicit or implicit reflection upon it that is overturned. Conventionally, the value of a retrospective narrative resides in its capacity to use the formal structures of the written language to order and make sense of emotional, physical, and sensory experience. For Céline, priority is to be given to capturing, at least on the surface of his text, the fullness of such experience at a moment preceding definition.

Céline's exploitation of popular usage for the purpose of a redefinition of conventional assumptions may appropriately be explored through analysis of the widespread use of the indeterminate pronoun 'ça' in introductory locutions, a device of unparalleled importance throughout the novel, in that it opens with the seemingly uninformative utterance 'Ça a débuté comme ça'. The opening lines of the present extract might seem to connote a failure to communicate, in that the subject is concealed from the reader throughout. The 'ça' that replaces the as yet unstated subject is only revealed to be New York in the following paragraph. This may legitimately be thought of as being, on one level, a means of creating suspense in the reader, and thus an example of Bardamu delighting in his power over us, but, more significantly, Céline may also be seen as exploiting popular speech in order to convey the immediacy and primacy of emotional or physical reactions. (It will be noted that the passage is very largely concerned with physical experience.) For the corollary of the noncommunication contained in the series of 'ça' constructions is the conveying of a sense of the experience being a highly intimate part of the experiencing self. It is only with a degree of detachment that the experience can be expressed in a way that permits communication or the sharing of the experience. With that detachment comes, as will be seen, a loss of the sense of its uniqueness to the experiencing self. Certain laborious stages are rehearsed here before the naming can take place, before, that is, contrary to the accepted norms of grammar, the pronoun can be replaced by the noun. Thus Céline's starting point in this description, as in so many others, is his conviction that the world perpetually defies language. Implicit in this viewpoint is a sense of the way any linguistic utterance represents a movement away from the original experience. Céline's ambition, in adopting an idiom rooted in popular speech, is to restrict this slippage to a minimum. Paradoxically, 'ça', with all its lack of definition, remains true to the original experience, for, by excluding nothing, it encompasses the totality of that experience. And to the extent that Bardamu's monologue is addressed to himself as well as to an imaginary listener or reader, the act of communication is not the fundamental issue. The passage is, thus, in general terms, a reflection upon the relationship between language and experience, an authentic, self-conscious representation of the struggle for expression.

Céline's delayed revelation of the subject of his description, while being a perverse refusal of the conventional economics of description, derives considerable additional resonance from the relationship the passage entertains with the thematic underpinning of the composition as a whole. Thus the emergence of the New York skyline from the fog is a further example of the archetypal attempt in Bardamu's narrative to effect a progression from the state of darkness to one of at least partial illumination. This multi-layered nature of Céline's text is, as will be seen, the means by which the surface act of representation is subordinated to a much more complex discourse that is designed to destabilise consistently those assumptions which Céline perceives, uncontroversially, as conventional.

At this point it is necessary to observe that Bardamu's narration is not composed uniquely of the examples of popular usage that are, initially, its most striking features. For the latter are interwoven with elements that, paradoxically, constitute recognisable markers of the status of his narrative as writing. At the most basic level the narrative betrays its literariness, through Bardamu's prominent use, at the outset at least, of the past historic, though this tense gives way fairly soon to the other past tenses. The status of the narrative as writing is, furthermore, emphasised quasi-parodically through the recourse, in the third paragraph, to descriptive adjectives in pairs ('grise et rose', 'rapide et piquante' (l. 16), 'avides et cornards' (ll. 20–1)), and, more generally, through the mounting lyricism of the description at this point, which both exemplifies Céline's readiness to compare his writing to music and, in a manner reminiscent of Rimbaud, creates a provocative contrast with his deliberately lugubrious and unalluring referent.

It would, nevertheless, be wrong to imply that the passage merely juxtaposes written and oral forms. For all its use of the characteristics of popular speech, Bardamu's narrative draws attention to its writerly status throughout. The oral devices produce their effect by operating as part of a written text. Their self-conscious display confers upon them an essentially poetic function that exists at a considerable remove from a set of oral utterances with a purely naturalistic function. Yet insofar as both the oral and the 'literary' elements retain their original labels within the text, the composite, synthetic idiom that Céline creates exhibits a constant ambiguity, varied only by the shifts in emphasis.

There can be no doubt that Bardamu's narrative is placed under the sign of language itself, Céline's novel being quite straightforwardly the product of a compulsion to speak (and indeed to speak out). Significantly, the novel ends with the representation of silence and the pre-Beckettian sense of there being nothing more to say. ('Il appelait vers lui toutes les péniches du fleuve toutes, et la ville entière, et le ciel et la campagne, et nous, tout qu'il emmenait, la Seine aussi, tout, qu'on n'en parle plus.') Until that point, as can be seen very well from the present passage, the unchecked flow of words is to be understood as a defence against the threatening nature of the physical world.

The general linguistic self-consciousness that is the hallmark of the passage (constituting, in Jakobsonian terms, its 'poetic' nature) is enhanced by a number of specific instances. The referential function of language is continually repressed by the way the text highlights its own medium. Thus in the description of the small boats, the collective noun selected ('kyrielle', l. 20) comes from the lexis of language itself. It is also the self-generative nature of the composition that is responsible for the pre-eminence at certain moments of the *signifiants*. Thus 'une grosse brume grise et rose' (l. 16) betrays, through its use of alliteration and assonance, its largely internal origins as much as it communicates the sense of a referential function determined by a reality external to the text. In Céline's writing as a whole, the sense of artifice is more often highlighted than concealed. This same third paragraph, in which, as has been seen, the quasi-parodic descriptive function is subtly present throughout, parades its artificial construction through the structural echo, from one end of the paragraph to the other, of 'cornichons' (l. 13) and 'cornards' (l. 21), the parodic potential being increased by the ignoble nature of the terms and their specific associations, and, in the case of 'cornards', by its status, when applied to boats, as a comic invention. That the entire passage appears first and foremost a composition of words is further ensured by such blatant examples of wordplay as 'New York c'est une ville debout' (ll. 6–7), which the recurring image of mud in *Voyage* leads us to read simultaneously as 'une ville de boue'. Such a reading is reinforced by the introduction subsequently of the phrase 'eau caca' (l. 19) (the conjunction of such phenomenological opposites may be seen as part of Céline's pervasive exploitation of contradiction as a means of undermining the received point of view, a strategy to which it will be necessary to return below), which may even be felt to set up a scatological relationship, not just with other instances of latrine imagery in the novel, but also, through a visual analogy, with the opening words of the novel, 'Ça a débuté comme ça.'

As has been seen, it is only in the second paragraph that the cause of Bardamu's amazement is at last revealed. French requires cities to be feminine, but here this fact is given an abnormal degree of emphasis. Although the description begins with a strikingly direct visual image that owes its graphic quality to its unconventional starkness, it does not develop in visual terms, but as a cumulative evocation of the feminine that leads ultimately to a highly specific evocation of female sexuality. So overpowering is the metaphor that it comes close to losing its original function in order to assume the status of referent itself. Thus the towns of Europe could be said to be portrayed here as 'grandes horizontales': they are 'belles' and 'couchées'. The expected femininity continues with the triple nominal and pronominal conglomeration of 'celle-là l'Américaine, elle...' (ll. 10–11). But no sooner has the city been introduced in her sexual role, with the attendant expectation of her availability to all men ('les miteux' and 'les galériens' included), than there is a switch in mid-sentence to a phallic image ('elle se tenait bien raide', l. 11) that erases her female sexuality ('pas baisante du tout', ll. 11–12). Yet rather than offering a straightforward avowal of an initial misconception of gender, the text goes on to create an almost tangible sense of the androgynous, or, to speak with the specificity that the text requires, a nightmarish vision in keeping with the rest of this misogynistic fiction, in which the female turns into a castratory being ('raide à faire peur', l. 12) depriving the male observer of his virility (and reproductive capacity). This is duly acknowledged at one of the more secret levels of the text, with the appearance in the very next line of a simile through which Bardamu, self-mockingly, compares his companions and himself to 'cornichons'.

The doubtless unconscious recognition of the castratory effect of the monstrous vision of virility presented by the vertical city is continued through two further details the specificity of which is perfectly eccentric at the naturalistic level: the laughter of the 'galériens' is possible only from the neck up, while the paralysing effect of the biting wind is described as being 'à l'assaut de nos pantalons' (ll. 16–17), which itself is reminiscent of the process by which the ship on which Bardamu earlier experiences such paranoia is called the *Amiral Bragueton*, a name which appears to allude to *la braguette*, just as the alleged slave-galley bears a name which, to a French ear, possesses obscenely androgynous associations: the *Infanta Combitta*.

In addition to this complex exploration of the non-referential possibilities of writing, Céline incorporates in this passage a level of significant self-reflexivity. The statements concerned — 'ça se raconte seulement' (l. 32) and 'on peut en dire ce qu'on voudra' (ll. 38–9)— belong to the clichéed language of everyday storytelling. Yet if it is accepted that they have a self-reflexive function, they serve to provoke further under-standing of the status of the writing of which they are part. When relieved of its banal primary significance, the statement 'on peut en dire ce qu'on voudra' stands as a reflection of the way Céline's composition proceeds free of referential constraints, and develops its own internal logic through the associative principles that ensure that there are levels at which every detail can be recuperated within the whole. Even the ostensibly in-significant 'ce qu'on voudra' invites re-interpretation in relation to the impulses within the writing self that dictate the nature of the associations that come into play. Such instances of re-interpretation are by no means of purely local significance in that they illustrate the extent to which this is a composition that invites a reading against itself. In similar fashion, the seemingly deprecatory formula 'ça se raconte seulement' reveals the extent to which *Voyage* is a multiple composition of stories about stories, with the attendant feature of an infinitely delayed referent. As in so many other instances in Céline's text, the dismissive or self-deprecating observation is discovered to have a wholly contrasting valorisation when we follow the pointers it contains to another level of significance.

But these two phrases also raise the question of truth and falsehood in relation to fiction. And it is in this respect that they serve as pointers to perhaps the most striking feature of Céline's writing. For alongside the text's assertiveness, its willingness to indulge in generalisations and even to display a propensity for the (albeit unhoned) aphorism, the text is seen to undermine radically its own authority. The tendency towards exag-geration and caricature is apparent throughout and descends into absur-dity in the proud claims that Bardamu makes for his flea-counting prowess as well as in his confident prediction that this prodigious activity will win him adulation in America (ll. 35–41). A similar ironic naïvety may be seen in his expression of admiration for the Americans ('Les Américains on peut en dire ce qu'on voudra, mais en fait de technique, c'est des connaisseurs') and in his view of the talismanic value of the cry 'Vive Dollar!' (l. 30). Yet the reader has no difficulty in recuperating the real that in broad terms is perceived as lying behind the exaggeration and apparent absurdity, precisely because the reference points are obvious clichés relating to the dreams and aspirations of the would-be immigrant and the known severity of the Ellis Island authorities, and to the image of America as a country obsessed with both money and technological ad-vance. Thus the fictional text is of uncertain status, oscillating between the real and the fantastic, between the ludicrous and apt cultural commentary. The text, in other words, obeys throughout a logic that is forever refining a strategy of surprise.

The sense of the ambiguous status of Bardamu's referent is heightened by the ambiguous identity of Bardamu himself, as his curious name suggests. He remains an elusive and unreliable figure. The reader has earlier realised that his claim to be a *galérien* is a fabrication. In this passage, the suggestions of fever and madness point towards the conclusion that his account is coloured by a hallucinatory tendency. Yet this undermining of the authority of the narrative is not the end of the process but a strategy that clears the way for a redefinition of the significance of the vision. The role Bardamu adopts as a naïve traveller is thrown into question by the signs of his being in fact a much more focused and knowing observer than his surface idiom would suggest. The demythologisation of the various societies to which he travels requires the vision of an individual who comes to each new experience without any preconceived notions, so that he may register maximum surprise. But this in turn is subversive of our widespread tendency to accept as natural that which is by no means so.

Bardamu thus functions as a composite figure who has no existence outside his embodiment of the contradictions required by Céline's subversive strategy. The passage reveals a number of further examples. Bardamu's account of his experience incorporates an oscillation (*nous/on/je*) between a sense of belonging to a group and being a unique individual. He combines a feeling of superiority with the conviction that he is a victim, and, thereby, appears to believe simultaneously in his ability to exploit or defeat the American system and in his inevitable subordination to it. He portrays himself instinctively as both aggressive and the object of aggression, just as he combines a simultaneous sense of freedom and imprisonment that can vary the emphasis at will. His ambiguous response to his situation is apparent in the emphasis he gives to laughter. Laughter is a manifestation of a freedom of the spirit that has not been entirely crushed ('tout galérien qu'on était on s'est mis à bien rigoler', l. 4). But the positive effect of the laughter is restricted by the subsequent avowal that they were only able to laugh 'à partir du cou' (ll. 14–15), while the description of the scene that provoked the laughter itself communicates the fact that the laughter is a defence mechanism competing with fear. Throughout the passage, Bardamu's assertiveness succeeds in communicating a sense of vulnerability as much as one of superiority. The discourse is designed to make his self-confidence seem both admirable and hollow.

The contradictory logic present in Bardamu's confessional narrative may be felt to invite an analysis in psychoanalytic terms. Symptoms of classifiable states doubtless abound, but to engage in such an analysis is to ignore the fact that Bardamu stops short of being a conventional literary character. To analyse him as such is to make the dubious assumption that he is a knowable individual rather than a literary device imbued with certain consistent, if contradictory, characteristics. The text seeks not to resolve the contradictions at the level of Bardamu as an individual but to exploit their subversive potential on a much wider plane.

The narrative discourse that Céline attributes to Bardamu explodes the notion of purely individual or personal beliefs and characteristics. It is an anarchical discourse or, rather, a highly generalised discourse of anarchy that undermines all fixed points. And rather than a defining feature of Bardamu the individual, the discourse is the product of a perverse adoption of the role to which the alien American society wishes him to conform. ('«C'est tous des anarchistes» qu'ils disent', l. 25.) It is, thus, a discourse of which he remains in control. In this way the 'wise fool' succeeds in undermining the very world (or society) that makes of him an outsider, re-enacting his outsider's status on his own terms, without there being, needless to say, any possibility of that status being overcome. The flea-counting may be an ironic *reductio ad absurdum,* but it is not open to Bardamu to change the rules of the game.

Thus the very assumption by Céline's narrator-hero of an anarchical driving principle ultimately encounters the limitations of that principle's efficiency. But prior to the reaching of that point, its subversive and satirical power is considerable. Prevailing norms are thrown into question. The location of madness shifts from the individual to the world that is believed to be the cause of the latter's state of mind and which dictates not only his function but ultimately his discourse as narrator. It becomes clear that the apparent confessional nature of his narrative is not what it seems. Rather, the discourse is designed to disturb the norms it justifiably assumes will be those informing the reader's own life. Yet if the reader is left with a powerful sense of unease and uncertainty, such a feeling is eclipsed by our awareness of having proceeded beyond a self-conscious dismantling of the conventional distinction between writing and speech to an exhilarating encounter with the forces of creative renewal inherent in a narrative discourse that has taken the literary text still further into the realm of that which cannot be said.

19

'La Fin approche':
A Reading of the Last Prose Poem of
Queneau's *Morale élémentaire*

Carol Sanders

A onze heures cinquante-neuf minutes comme à vingt-trois heures
cinquante-neuf minutes, la fin approche. L'aiguille marche avec précaution
vers les ultimes secondes; à chaque fois, elle fait les mêmes gestes.
L'instrument ne comporte pourtant aucun carillon et tout s'effectuera dans
le silence. Glissant avec fermeté sur la patinoire gelée du temps, la plus   5
grande atteint son but. Elle ne s'arrête point là et continue sa course, si et
seulement si l'animateur a bien remonté le système. On peut alors regarder
avec satisfaction le parcours accompli. Pour en arriver là, il aura fallu
remuer ciel et terre.

(Raymond Queneau, 'A onze heures cinquante-neuf minutes')

This text is the last prose poem of the third part of *Morale élémentaire*,
written and published shortly before the author's death. The first part of
the volume consists of highly evocative, occasionally autobiographical,
but always deeply spiritual poems, which reflect the crisis that Queneau
went through after the death of his wife as well as his renewed interest in
Eastern philosophies and religions. Their form is innovative, with
Queneau inventing a new poetic 'genre', the 'lipolepse', consisting of
three columns of 'binômes' (usually noun plus adjective). The poems are
characterised by a strong patterning of rhymes, repetitions, and allusions,
which weave a dense web of associations, forcing the reader to weigh
each cluster of words and challenging notions of linear reading.

   In contrast, sections 2 and 3, while highly poetic, are set out as a series
of prose passages. There is a certain underlying unity of theme and tone
to the volume as a whole, and to each section. In particular, the coherence
of the third part derives from the way in which it reflects the sixty-four
koua of the *I Ching*, following notes made by Queneau as a young man.
In the title *I Ching*, commonly translated as the 'Book of Change', the

first character in fact refers to both change and changelessness. According to Waley, its reference shifted from the outer order (of the elements, the cosmos) to the inner order and would be better translated as the 'Book of Morality' (Waley, 1934). Each poem is illuminated by its place in the cycle, although it is also apparent that each prose poem functions as an autonomous text.

The definition of the prose poem is notoriously difficult. The fact that much of Queneau's prose, in *Morale élémentaire* and elsewhere, is highly poetic according to Jakobsonian definitions of *poéticité* is not in doubt, and is frequently alluded to by critics. In her article on Rabelais and Queneau, Dorothy Gabe Coleman (1987) defined 'poetic prose' thus:

> imagination, judgement, sensitivity, word-consciousness and the interlocking of rhythm and imagery…A dense, ambivalent texture which can only be grasped if we read it as poetry with the willingness for a phrase to be obscure in itself but expecting that the context around it will eventually make clear the meaning.

The prose poem is often seen, despite its prose form, as quintessentially poetic (des Esseintes's 'l'osmazôme de la littérature'), 'mysterious' (e.g. by Aragon). Beyond this, there are a number of features that recur in discussions of the prose poem.

There is agreement that prose poems show great variety, and are frequently experimental in nature. A commonly mentioned characteristic of the prose poem (cf. Bernard, 1959) is its textual autonomy and its brevity, with a corresponding 'totalité de l'effet'. Because the prose poem combines the rich network of meanings found in much poetry with some of the typological and stylistic features of prose, it is often said to elicit a feeling of *dépaysement*. The oxymoronic nature of the name *poème en prose* points to the genre as an 'association de contraires', the text being long enough to evoke tensions but not to solve them. Thus Johnson (1979) writes of a 'conflit de codes', and Todorov (1987) of duality in Baudelaire's prose poems. The brevity of the prose poem conflicts with our normal expectations of a prose genre; in much the same way as some painters draw our attention to the edge of the canvas, so the prose poem makes us conscious of the space and silence beyond its boundaries. While the archetypal prose text is perhaps the *récit chronologique*, Todorov points out that the prose poem often functions in a 'présent perpétuel'. Let us see if these characteristics are shared by, or serve to illuminate, Queneau's text.

It is immediately apparent that a major theme of this last prose poem is the passage of time. The dominant image is that of the clock: the representation on a limited circular surface of the movement of the sun, moon, and earth in space. Underlying the poem there is creative tension between temporality, mobility, predictability, and their opposites. Throughout, there is also an interplay between temporal and spatial referents, with the balance tilting from the former to the latter as we move through the poem.

First of all, the description of the timepiece, with its hands sliding ineluctably forward behind a glass face, leads to the secondary image of the ice-rink. The French word *aiguille* acts as an *embrayeur* from the temporal to the spatial, as it means both hand (on a clock) and needle (on a compass). The 'slipperiness' of time is a familiar and evocative concept: on the 'patinoire gelée du temps' (l. 5), there is forward but circular movement against a frozen background, recalling the Augustinian 'image mobile de l'immobilité éternelle'. The advancing hand allows a backward glance at 'le parcours accompli' (l. 8), which refers to distance covered in a certain time, and implies a combination of intentionality and perfectivity. The small, round timekeeper turns into an expanse of frozen space, which by the end of the poem has opened out further into 'ciel et terre'.

The interplay between temporality and spatiality is reinforced by the salient use of *à* and *là*. While both can have either temporal or spatial reference, *à* tends to be more commonly used with temporal associations and *là* with spatial ones. *A* dominates the early part of the poem: it is used at the very beginning with a precise temporal reference and occurs three times in the first two sentences. There is a shift through *là*, meaning 'at the moment' ('Elle ne s'arrête point là', l. 6) to *là* indicating a distant place or final goal: 'Pour en arriver là' (l. 8).

The forward movement of time is associated with elements of intentionality and accomplishment. The first sentence consists of a long initial temporal phrase, with a string of monosyllabic and disyllabic words, and a postponed verb, all of which force the reader to mark time. A number of expressions suggest gradual but inevitable progression ('marche avec précaution', l. 2, 'Glissant avec fermeté', l. 5); in this movement there is both finality ('fin', l. 2, 'ultimes secondes', l. 3) and achievement ('atteint son but', l. 6, 'Pour en arriver là', l. 8). Accompanying the image of instrumental precision is that of the clockmaker, the word chosen here being not *horlogier* but one containing the Latin *anima*. With this hint at a cosmic order of things, this poem is linked to the previous one in the cycle. In the sixty-third poem, 'Le Capitaine fait le point', the sailor is making detailed calculations for his departure 'vers le large', in much the same way as Cidrolin — his past and present, his ego and alter-ego, reconciled — did at the end of *Les Fleurs bleues:*

> Le navire avance avec ponctualité, traçant son village. Demain peut-être on cassera l'erre.

From the penultimate to the ultimate poem, the overt human presence has gone, the 'instruments de bord' have become a clock, and the sea and gentle rain have turned to ice. Thus, despite those expressions which ex press a forward movement, there are others which imply that progress towards a final goal may be fraught with doubt and possible deviation. In a text such as this, where every word is given weight, the reader cannot help but reinvest the *locution figée* with its original significance. In the first sentence, it is less a question of the hands of the clock moving slowly forward, as of the future moving back towards a near-frozen present ('la fin approche').

This challenging of the conventional order of chronology is strikingly apparent in the tense usage which patterns the text as a whole. Throughout *Morale élémentaire*, the overwhelming majority of verbs used is in the present, which contributes to the impression of a world frozen outside time. The third part is no exception to this, the tentative future of the penultimate poem ('Demain peut-être on cassera l'erre') being one of the few non-present tense forms. Within the last poem of the collection, the slow forward march of time is at first expressed in the present, culminating in a firm prediction about the clockwork regularity of the system ('tout s'effectuera', l. 4), which is followed by an ambiguous present. Two notable features of the French verb system are, firstly, the multivalent nature of the present tense, and, secondly, the subtle and fleeting intersections that occur between temporal and aspectual systems (see Fleischman, 1985). Here this multivalency is exploited to the full in the uneasy use of the present with 'atteint son but' (is reaching? will reach? has reached?). This ambiguity, and the uncertainty as to whether or not the hands of the clock have stopped, are reinforced by the negative and concessive nature of the subsequent phrases which refer to this movement. ('Elle ne s'arrête point là et continue sa course, si et seulement si l'animateur a bien remonté le système', ll. 6–7). The connector 'alors' (as an indicator of sequentiality, or of causality, or simply as semantically empty *mot-charnière*?) marks the transition to the next sentence, in which the combination of three verb forms not strongly marked for tense (modal auxiliary, infinitive, past participle used adjecti vally: 'peut' 'regarder' 'accompli') leaves the reader in a temporal no-man's-land. The poem then ends in a combination of futurity and perfectivity, whether predicted or realised is not clear, with 'il aura fallu remuer'. This text thus ends on the only future perfect tense to occur in the whole collection.

Ironically, it is only at the end of *Morale élémentaire* that the 'figure de l'auteur', otherwise largely absent from the collection in contrast to the frequent, tantalising, and often jocular appearances of the author in his earlier works, perhaps puts in a shadowy appearance in the two impersonal expressions 'on peut' and 'il faut'. Earlier in the poem, there has been a hint at personification in the movement of the hand ('elle fait les mêmes gestes', l. 3), implying the idea of hands joined (in peace? in prayer? in death?). If there is ambiguity and doubt, there is also what appears to be a quiet satisfaction at the reconciliation of opposites. Past and future are united as the hands came together at midday/midnight, which represents both the zenith and the nadir, the end of the old hour and the beginning of the new. The goal striven for coincides with the greater order of things; intentionality is not necessarily incompatible with 'l'harmonie pré-établie'. The poem that has begun with a precise reference to present time opens out at the end to a future perfect and the whole of 'ciel et terre'.

In his use of tense, and his manipulation of spatial and temporal imagery, Queneau has created a text which escapes and challenges Western causal, linear thought. Writing about the *I Ching*, Jung (an important influence on Queneau for example in *Les Fleurs bleues*) refers to this 'synchronistic principle', the realisation that causality cannot explain a number of phenomena, whether of the workings of the universe or of the human mind, both of which are put in parallel throughout the *I Ching*. This principle, according to Jung, has been absent from western thought since Heraclitus, to whom there are frequent references in Queneau.

Although there are many points of contact between this last volume and Queneau's earlier work, the reader wonders what to make of the fact that the author's own brand of *français parlé*, which had almost become his hallmark, is absent save for a few traces. The prose poems link Queneau to certain contemporary poets as much as to his own earlier poetry. With Philippe Jaccottet, Queneau often shares a *style dépouillé* and a preoccupation with the silent pulse of the universe and the elements. Both *Morale élémentaire* and Jaccottet's *Paysages avec figures absentes*, for example, contain prose poems which recall the haiku, attempting as they do to capture for an instant the ephemeral and unsayable essence of being. Treharne's description of Jaccottet's volume as a 'paradoxical formulation of absence and presence' recalls Bonnefoy's preoccupation with a question that is crucial to Queneau: 'Suis-je présent dans le livre que je publie?' Because of his close involvement with French Phenomenology and with Heideggerian thought, Queneau's use of *français parlé* was never (as I have demonstrated elsewhere — Sanders, 1994) merely a stylistic device, or delight, but an expression of certain philosophical beliefs about the relationship between authentic language, consciousness, and being. This 'speaking' to the reader in a poetic form of 'ordinary language', as well as the author's playful appearances in his work, all contrive to achieve what Bonnefoy calls an 'effet de présence'. Bonnefoy (p. 509) continues:

> Quel faux-semblant, de ce point de vue, qu'un livre! Tout semble y être impliqué, directement ou par allusion, mais de chaque chose qui fut présente, et d'aussi près que ce soit, à qui l'écrivit, il n'y reste pourtant que la dépouille que des besoins divers, les uns de l'inconscient de l'auteur les autres de l'infrastructure sociale ou errants au sein de language, laissent après…leur sommeil enfin côte à côte dans un étrange paysage, qui est du monde mental plus que de la terre.

Treharne shows how for Jaccottet a poem 'creates its own sense of time…a "suspense" of common language', as opposed to prose which is 'related to a more contingent sense of duration, a state of language of a more ordinary kind'. The last prose poem of *Morale élémentaire* throws into stark relief the dual nature of being: contingent and at once outside chronological time. It is sometimes said that the end of a literary work is invested with a particular significance; a good deal has also been written recently about the poetics of punctuation (e.g. Laufer, 1978). After the open, multi-directional poems of the first part of the volume, with their highly individual form, part 2 appears to bring the volume to a more traditional close, on a note of detached tranquillity and (at least partial) reconciliation of opposites. In comparison with Queneau's earlier work, the 'voice' of the author is conspicuously absent. While relations between words and images in the prose poem open up new horizons, the form is sober and appears to revert to tradition in matters of layout and typography. Indeed, some minor aspects of punctuation are unusual for Queneau. In most of his previous poems, for example, full stops are sparingly used, but within *Morale élémentaire* the prose poems of parts 2 and 3 end in a *point final*.

Bibliography

Bernard, S., *Le Poème en prose de Baudelaire jusqu'à nos jours* (Paris: Nizet, 1959)

Bonnefoy, Y., *La Vérité de parole et autres essais* (Paris: Folio, 1995)

Fleischmann, S., 'Discourse Functions of Tense-Aspect Oppositions in Narrative: Towards a Theory of Grounding', *Linguistics*, XXIII (1985), 851–82

Gabe Coleman, D., 'Polyphonic Poets: Rabelais and Queneau', in D. Gabe Coleman and G. Jondorf, eds, *Words of Power* (Glasgow: Glasgow University Press, 1987)

Treharne, M. and D. Constantine, eds, Philippe Jaccottet, *Under Clouded Skies and Beauregard*, (Translation and Commentary) (Bloodaxe Books, 1994)

Jaccottet, P., *Paysages avec figures absentes*, (Paris: Gallimard, 1970)

Johnson, B., *Défigurations du language poétique* (Paris: Flammarion, 1979)

Jung, C. G., *Commentary on the Secret of the Golden Flower: A Chinese Book of Life*, trans. R. Wilhelm (London: Kegan Paul, 1932)

Laufer, R., 'Texte et typographie', *Littérature*, XXXI (Oct. 1978)

Queneau, R., *Les Fleurs bleues*, (Paris: Gallimard, 1965)

—, *Morale élémentaire* (Paris: Gallimard, 1975)

Sanders, C., *Raymond Queneau* (Paris: Eds Rodopi, 1994)

Todorov, T., *La Notion de littérature* (Paris: Seuil, 1987)

Waley, A., *The Way and its Power* (London: George Allen and Unwin, 1934)

20

Display and Disguise:
Textual Activity in a Passage from
Claude Simon's *Les Géorgiques*

Celia Britton

On retirait les housses, on battait les tapis pendus à cheval sur le balcon de
la véranda et d'où s'échappait comme un subtil et faible parfum de choses
fanées (les bouquets de roses pâlies, les guirlandes décolorées mêlées aux
fades volutes décoratives) tandis que les pendeloques du lustre soudain
dérangées, agitées par les courants d'air, s'entre-choquaient dans une   5
cascade de tintements légers, cristallins, semblables à ces musiques
aigrelettes au son desquelles se meuvent, tournent sur eux-mêmes et
s'inclinent des automates costumés en marquis et en bergères comme ceux
que l'on pouvait voir, gracieux et mélancoliques, sous la forme de
porcelaines de Saxe ou peints à l'aquarelle au milieu d'arabesques dorées   10
sur les éventails aux branches d'ivoire déployés dans les vitrines emplies de
ces menus et précieux objets (les pistolets aux crosses de nacre, les bourses
brodées de perles, les poignards florentins et les flacons de sels) dont la
réunion sur les rayons tendus de brocard semblait comme l'inventaire, la
panoplie de symboles miniaturisés, élégants et coûteux, d'actes élémentaires   15
et brutaux comme le meurtre, le troc ou le coït, incongrus, inconvenants
presque, tenus sous clef, mis pour ainsi dire hors d'état de nuire, conservés
là comme par une sorte de superstition, de craintif respect, comme ces
objets familiers ou précieux, ces armes, ces bijoux, ces coupes chargées de
tenir compagnie dans l'au-delà à quelque potentat défunt, le monumental   20
ancêtre toujours présent, sculpté dans deux cents kilos de marbre, amené
cent ans plus tôt par charroi du lointain château et installé (déporté),
étranger, au cœur de l'ambitieuse et trop grande maison où, l'énorme
cadavre à peine refroidi, avait émigré le fils renégat qu'une miniature
décorant le couvercle d'une tabatière d'écaille représentait, boudeur et   25
joufflu sous la touffe de cheveux blonds hérités sans doute de la
Hollandaise et coiffés en caniche, fuyant après l'avoir bradé le vieux tas de
pierres ancestral en même temps qu'il dépouillait, jetait aux orties, sa
tunique d'enseigne, inaugurant cette opulente et oisive déchéance sur
laquelle le buste du formidable et sourcilleux géniteur semblait avoir veillé 30
avec une maligne patience, cette espèce de léthargique désastre à l'image
d'un siècle sorti épuisé d'un sanglant accouchement, avide de respectabilité

et de profit, trébuchant dans des révolutions avortées, menant de rapaces
conquêtes coloniales et laissant derrière lui en témoignage officiel, achetée
année après année par le faux pasteur baptiste (le fils du renégat, le père de   35
la vieille dame), la collection complète de cette revue des Salons dont le
nom (L'ARTISTE) se lisait en lettres dorées au dos des reliures de cuir rouge
réunissant les livraisons rangées par millésimes sur l'un des rayons de la
grande bibliothèque d'ébène aux vantaux vitrés où elle (la vieille dame) les
conservait dans le même esprit de cornélienne piété filiale comme d'intou-   40
chables reliques, elles aussi sous clef, moins sans doute par peur des
voleurs que pour cacher aux yeux des enfants (ils les découvrirent plus tard
au moment de l'inventaire, du partage) les pâles nudités d'Andromèdes ou
d'odalisques aux vulves épilées, pâmées, dodues et uniformément glabres,
comme de blêmes tentatrices peuplant d'orientalistes et libidineux empy-   45
rées, apparaissant sournoisement au tournant d'une page entre «L'Assassinat du duc de Guise», quelque chlorotique allégorie ou de crépusculaires
retours de troupeaux.

(Claude Simon, Les Géorgiques)[1]

This passage from *Les Géorgiques* is part of a section in which the narrator remembers his childhood; he had lived with his grandmother, uncle,
and cousins in a large, dilapidated house which had been in the family for
three generations. Once a month they invited other members of the family to dinner, and this involved opening up the salon, which was normally
kept locked, and doing a lot of cleaning. The narrator is the grandson of
'la vieille dame' (l. 39), who is the daughter of 'le faux pasteur baptiste'
(l. 35), who is the son of 'le fils renégat' (l. 24), who is the son of 'la
Hollandaise' (ll. 26–7) and 'l'ancêtre' (l. 21). This 'ancestor' plays a
large role throughout the novel; he was one of Napoleon's generals and
he had voted for the death of the king. As such, he is a very potently ambiguous figure, being at the same time the most glorious ancestor that the
family, now fallen on hard times, can boast, but also a revolutionary and
regicide, and, as we later discover, a man betrayed and disowned by his
second wife and their son.

Thus the theme of family history is a prominent strand of this text. So
too, obviously, is that of pictorial or plastic representation, illustrated by
the references to china figurines, sculpture, paintings, etc. Both of these
are typically Simonian topics; what is striking in this particular text, however, is the way that these disparate 'series' are woven together. A third,

---

[1] Paris: Éditions de minuit, 1981, pp. 173–5.

much less obvious theme — but again one that recurs in his novels — is that of commercial exchange.

Les Géorgiques, appearing in 1981, seemed to mark the end of the experimentation with anti-representational, so-called 'formalist' novels that had characterised Simon's work in the 1970s. It was greeted by critics as a 'return to realism', and to the narrative and thematic concerns of his earlier and more popular novels. And the passage that I have chosen to analyse does indeed seem to fit into very familiar realist terrain. In the first place, it is taken from the most apparently autobiographical of the three narratives that interweave throughout the whole novel. It also belongs to the recognised genre of the family novel; and finally, both of these are realised though the familiar discourse of childhood memories — indeed, as elsewhere in Simon's fiction, there is a perceptible Proustian intertext in the sensuous descriptions, the sustained and elaborate sentence construction (taken here to almost caricatural lengths, since the whole passage consists of a single sentence), the Genettian 'iterativity' of the imperfect tenses, and so on.

It also, however, exhibits two other features associated with realist discourse, and it is these that I intend to develop in more detail. Rather than attempting an exhaustive analysis of the passage, I shall try to show how even within the apparently solid realist conventions on which the text is based, a level of generative textual activity takes over from time to time.

The first of these two features is a technique common in the narrative structure of the realist novel (particularly those of Balzac, for instance), which the passage deploys on a much smaller scale: a contrast between reality and appearances, between what is *shown* and what is *hidden*. This springs from the immediate context of the passage: in the preparations for receiving their infrequent visitors, the family are in effect putting the house on display — which at the same time means disguising all its imperfections. Thus the subject matter of the passage is articulated around this opposition between concealing and revealing. Moreover, it is repeated on an even smaller scale within the structure of the passage, in which the story of the acquisition of the house by the 'fils renégat' is briefly told in between two longer descriptive sequences concerning two sets of objects both on 'rayons' behind glass. But whereas those in lines 8–18 are on display ('que l'on pouvait voir', 'éventails...déployés dans les vitrines', 'la panoplie de symboles'), those in lines 37 to 48, the numbers of the review *L'Artiste*, are in contrast kept under lock and key to prevent the children looking at the pictures of nudes *inside* them — which are discovered only when they are released ('apparaissant sournoisement') by the death of the old lady. This inaugurates a kind of *censorship* which, I shall argue, ultimately moves beyond a purely realist frame of reference to mobilise the resources of ambiguity in the language of the text.

The second feature concerns the enormous number of references to pictorial and plastic representations in the passage — from the above-mentioned reproductions of paintings to the rose pattern on the carpet to the Dresden china figurines, the water-colours on the fans, the marble bust, the portrait on the lid of the snuff-box, etc. This, according to Philippe Hamon, is again a common feature of realist writing; he says: 'Très souvent le lisible s'articule sur le visible, et le visible inversement peut s'identifier au lisible, au racontable.' [2] As an example of this he in fact gives 'la photographie ou la carte postale dans le Nouveau Roman' (ibid.), presumably thinking of Simon's work in particular.

However, most of the criticism which has been written on the Nouveau Roman has seen the use it makes of pictorial representation as far more anti-representational. Jean Ricardou, for instance, analyses it in terms of narrative reflexivity, as 'mises en abyme', [3] or else, more radi-cally, in terms of the 'récit transmuté', as he calls it, where pictures come to life and vice versa. [4] In this particular case, clearly, the textual use to which visual representations are put is in no way as definitely anti-realist as the 'récit transmuté': nothing actually contradicts, or blocks, the estab-lishment of a diegetic reality. Nor does the subject matter of the pictures 'mirror' the narrative as 'mise en abyme'. Nevertheless, I want to sug-gest that the objects which in this passage act as supports for various pictorial representations are presented in a way which undermines rather than reinforces the reality effect. In the first place, their description con-tains typical examples of Simonian word-play: even simple echoes like 'décolorées'—'décoratives' in lines 3–4, and 'la réunion sur les rayons' (ll. 13–14), repeated in line 38: 'réunissant...sur l'un des rayons' — suggest that the choice of words is governed as much by the alliterative qualities of the signifier as by fictional referents.

More significantly, several of them are 'produced' through the purely textual operation of figurative language — usually of simile. For instance, in lines 4–12, the sounds made by the chandelier are 'semblables à' the music of, presumably, a music box which would have on it 'automates'

2 Philippe Hamon, 'Un discours contraint', in *Littérature et réalité*, edited by G. Genette and T. Todorov (Paris: Éditions du Seuil, 1982), p. 139.

3 Jean Ricardou, *Le Nouveau Roman* (Paris: Seuil, Collections Points, 1990), pp. 60–85.

4 Ibid., pp. 121–34.

dressed as 'marquis et bergères', which *in turn* are like the Dresden china figurines and the figures painted on the fans. It is thus a double comparison; and of the three terms, the first and last (the chandelier and 'ceux que l'on pouvait voir...sous la forme de porcelaines de Saxe ou peints...sur les éventails') are clearly present in the diegesis — but the middle one, the music box, is not. This same ternary structure is then immediately repeated: the china figures and the fans (i.e., the third term of the first double simile) form part of a collection of objects displayed in the glass cabinet; and this as a whole is then compared with collections of objects found in the tombs of great kings of past civilisations ('comme ces objets...ces coupes chargées de tenir compagnie dans l'au-delà à quelque potentat défunt' (18–20)). But then the hypothetical 'potentat défunt' himself is compared, implicitly, with the family's ancestor who is diegetically present in the form of yet another visual representation, the marble bust — and whose presence is, indeed, stressed by the text: 'le monumental ancêtre toujours présent' (ll. 20–1). Here again we thus have three terms, of which only the middle one is non-diegetic.

Finally, in a third instance of this same procedure, lines 31–2 puts the 'fils renégat' in relation with post-Revolutionary France: 'à l'image d'un siècle....' This is followed by five verbal or adjectival phrases describing the nineteenth century. The first four — 'sorti de...', 'avide de...', 'trébuchant...', 'menant...' — characterise it in general and fairly predictable ways (revolution, capitalism, colonialism, etc.). The fifth — 'laissant derrière lui...' — is both far more specific and slightly odd (in what sense does the review *L'Artiste* constitute an 'official testimony' of the nineteenth century in general?); its function seems to be primarily to lead us back, once again, into the particular fictional reality of this family and this house: *L'Artiste* has been 'achetée année après année par le faux pasteur baptiste' (ll. 34–5). It is as though the text is setting up, on the basis of all these occurrences of 'comme', etc., a kind of *shuttling* movement in and out of the diegesis, and this has the effect of blurring its edges.

The other opposition I referred to earlier, between showing and concealing (or display and disguise), is also elaborated in a way which destabilises the realist problematic that originally defines it. It can be located figuratively in one category of the 'pictorial' objects: the fans (l. 11), which in the first place exemplify the very idea of display, in that they are 'déployés dans les vitrines'. These fans are of course lying immobile, opened out on the shelves of the glass case. But they could in principle be closed — in which case whatever is painted on them would be hidden. And on a figurative level, they seem to set off a fan-like textual alternation between opening and closure, expansion and concentration. An expansive, displaying movement, traceable through 'arabesques' (l. 10), which itself links back to 'volutes décoratives' (l. 4), 'déployés' (l. 11), 'tendus' (l. 14), 'panoplie de symboles' (l. 15) — is interwoven with an opposite movement of contraction and concentration: 'emplies' (l. 11), 'menus' (l. 12), 'réunion' (l. 14), 'miniaturisés' (l. 15). Even on the pho-netic/graphic level, the phrase 'éventails [aux branches d']ivoire' (l. 11) is later *condensed* into 'inventaire' (l. 14), which itself in turn *expands* to combine with 'élégants' (l. 15) and generate 'élémentaires' (l. 15).

The fan, then, offers a visual representation that oscillates between display and concealment: the closed fan hides what is painted on it. On a more general level, the display of objects in the glass cases also turns out to invoke the idea of concealment in the form of *censorship*. The objects, which include pistols and daggers, are dangerous, so that they have to be 'tenus sous clef, mis pour ainsi dire hors d'état de nuire' (l. 17); just as the issues of the review are 'comme d' *intouchables* reliques, elles aussi sous clef' (ll. 40–1); and these latter are of course dangerous specifically *to look at*: 'moins par peur des voleurs que pour cacher aux yeux des enfants…les pâles nudités d'Andromèdes.'

This thematic idea that what is apparently apparent, so to speak, can contain a hidden, secret dimension is linked to a textual process which exploits the potential ambiguity of language in order to produce a mean-ing which remains more or less implicit — an almost subterranean 'trail' of associations through the text — and which could be seen in psycho-analytic terms as a strategy for getting round censorship. This more purely textual activity is, however, at least initially less clearly motivated. But one notices, for instance, that the two sequences describing objects displayed behind glass — i.e. those in the glass-fronted cabinet (ll. 8–18), and the magazines in the book-case (36–48), use a lot of the same or similar vocabulary. Some of these repetitions are not very remarkable insofar as they are more or less required by the subject-matter — e.g. 'conservés' (l. 17) and 'conservait' (l. 40), 'sous clef' — (ll. 17 and 41). But others are less obviously explicable: 'arabesques dorées' (l. 10) and 'lettres dorées' (l. 37); 'vitrines' (l. 11) and 'vantaux vitrés' (l. 39); 'la réunion sur les rayons' (ll. 13–14) and 'réunissant…sur l'un des rayons' (l. 38); 'l'inventaire' (ll. 14 and 43).

These coincidences in themselves merely suggest that the level of tex-tual activity is particularly high in this section of the text. But it also turns out that some of the repeated words, and others used in one or other of the descriptions, are ambiguous. In the first sequence (ll. 8–18), 'vitrine' can also mean a shop-window; 'rayon' can also mean a department of a store; and 'inventaire' can also mean stock-taking. None of these are on the face of it appropriate to the actual context; but they are supported by the entirely straightforward references to commercial value ('précieux' (l. 12), 'coûteux' (l. 15)) and commercial activity ('bourses' (l. 12), 'troc' (l. 16)). Also, it is possible to see the phrase 'tendus de brocard' (l. 14) as a transformation of *brocante*, which would give an additional item of commercial activity which the implicit context again supports. The three ambiguous terms ('rayon', 'vitrine', and 'inventaire') reappear in the second sequence in question, lines 34–48, which also contains the equally ambiguous 'livraisons' (l. 38) — on the face of it, the 'issues' of the magazine, but also possessing the sense of (commercial) delivery.

Thus a pair of descriptions of objects in an apparently purely domestic and familial context — heirlooms, invoking questions of descendance, inheritance, etc. — both contain an insistent undercurrent of ambiguous references to the business of buying and selling — to commercial, as opposed to sentimental, value. It is as though the text were surreptitiously posing the question of what, in the family inheritance, can or should be cashed in.

In between these two descriptive sequences, moreoever, we find an account of what the ancestor's son did: as soon as his father died he sold the family château and bought another house. This seemingly fairly innocuous action is treated by the text with obvious disapproval — 'fuyant après l'avoir bradé' (l. 27) — as is the son's subsequent behaviour: like the times he lives in, he is only interested in making money — 'avide de respectabilité et de profit' (ll. 32–3), 'menant de rapaces conquêtes' (ll. 33–4). And it is this that provides an explanation for the disguised allusions to commercial exchange in the two descriptions that frame the son in the text — he has 'sold out' on the family, and thus betrayed his father. From the 'bourses *brodées*' of lines 12–13 we arrive at the château 'bradé'. So although the son's betrayal — selling the family château — is narrated only very briefly and as it were incidentally (lines 22–31) compared with the lengthy detail of the two descriptive sequences, it turns out to be the central issue of the whole passage, insofar as it is this action by the son that motivates, and is orchestrated by, the system of double meanings analysed above.

What remains unexplained, however, is the need for disguise. Why should the idea that the son betrayed his inheritance be so unacceptable that it has to be censored and can only be expressed indirectly, by drawing on these resources of lexical ambiguity? We are led to wonder whether there is not perhaps another meaning underlying this one; and, returning to the detail of the two descriptive sequences in the text, we can

indeed find traces of something more sinister. A further equivalence between them is that each one refers to a crime: murder in the first case ('le
meurtre, le troc ou le coït', l. 16) and theft in the second: 'par peur des
voleurs' (ll. 41–2). The text thus perhaps invites us to equate murder and
theft, or to substitute one for the other, or at least to consider the relation
between them, and whether either of them has a precise referent in the
novel. We can see that the son has in effect 'stolen' the château by selling
it whereas it should have been kept in the family: so sale — or 'troc' —
equals theft. Theft itself is simultaneously proposed and negated by the
text: '*moins* sans doute par peur des voleurs' (ll. 41–2) — and negated in
favour of a prohibition placed on seeing — 'que pour cacher aux yeux
des enfants' — which applies first of all to sexual material — 'les pâles
nudités d'Andromèdes ou d'odalisques aux vulves épilées' (ll. 43–4) —
thus referring back to the 'coït' of the first sequence — but which extends
also to murder, since among the titles of paintings quoted we find also
the 'Assassinat du duc de Guise' (ll. 46–7). In this way the text
juxtaposes three crimes: murder, theft/'troc', and the sexual act. On an
explicit level, only the third of these is censored (i.e., hidden from the
children). But other indications suggest that in fact it is murder that is in
question here, and specifically that the censorship takes the form of sub-
stituting theft for murder. That is: the (metaphorical) theft of the château
by the son can perhaps be interpreted as the (equally metaphorical?)
murder of the *father* by the son.

The evidence for this is that the father appears in this passage in only
two forms: a corpse ('l'énorme cadavre', ll. 23–4) and a marble bust
(l. 21, 30). In other words, he is dead, and he is made of stone. As far as
this second attribute is concerned, it allows the text to construct, again
purely on the level of its figurative vocabulary, an equivalence between
the château and the ancestor himself. On the one hand, he is 'le monumental *ancêtre* toujours présent, sculpté dans deux cents kilos de *marbre*' (ll. 20–1); and on the other, with noticeable symmetry, the château is
referred to as 'le vieux tas de *pierres ancestral*' (ll. 27–8) — a
description which could almost apply to the ancestor himself. By thus
superimposing the ancestor and the château, or the 'père' and the
'pierres', the text seems to suggest that the object of the son's actions is
his father's person, rather than his father's property. From this point of
view his flight from 'l'énorme cadavre à peine refroidi' (ll. 23–4) appears
as more sinister than the text can overtly acknowledge; although in the
novel as a whole the ancestor's death is certainly surrounded by much
deception and malpractice to do with the inheritance, there is no explicit
indication that he was murdered by his son.

The point is not to solve this particular mystery, however. Rather, I have tried to demonstrate how in this instance the realist topos of disguise and the 'hidden truth' coexists with a much less representational kind of textually disguised, or censored, meaning. More generally, I hope to have shown that this passage from *Les Géorgiques* is a good illustration of some of the ways in which, through its *play* with language as alliteration, figure, polysemy, and ambiguity, Simon's writing activates a covert level of meaning which sometimes underpins, sometimes exceeds, and sometimes even runs counter to the diegesis.

QMW LIBRARY
(MILE END)